7/-

gaty
KN '37  bH '38
KN '39

# The LETTERS
## OF
# JONATHAN SWIFT
## TO
# CHARLES FORD

# THE LETTERS OF JONATHAN SWIFT TO CHARLES FORD

Edited by

## DAVID NICHOL SMITH

*Merton Professor of English Literature in the University of Oxford*

AC. OX.

*OXFORD*

AT THE CLARENDON PRESS

MCMXXXV

OXFORD
UNIVERSITY PRESS
AMEN HOUSE, E.C. 4
London   Edinburgh   Glasgow
New York Toronto Melbourne
Capetown   Bombay   Calcutta
Madras Shanghai
HUMPHREY MILFORD
Publisher to the
University

# THE
# CONTENTS

# INTRODUCTION

THIS volume presents what survives of the correspondence of Jonathan Swift with Charles Ford, for many years his most trusted friend. Their intimacy has always been known, but how intimate they were is only now revealed by a series of fifty-one letters by Swift, the existence of which none of his editors or biographers would seem to have suspected. On Ford's death these letters passed, with other papers, into the possession of Sir John Hynde Cotton, his executor, and thereafter were lost to view among the papers of the Cotton family at Madingley Hall, Cambridge. Cotton's great granddaughter, Miss Philadelphia Letitia Cotton, has the credit of uncovering them and recognizing their importance, but she had no inducements to make them known beyond the circle of her friends. From her they passed to Mrs. Rowley Smith, of Shortgrove, and in time to younger members of the family who are responsible for the publication of this volume.

We have no reason to think that the collection as Ford left it was in any way broken till 1896, when ten of the fifty-one letters were chosen at random and dispersed by auction. But as nine of these ten letters have been available through the facilities offered by their new owners—most of them are now in the Pierpont Morgan Library—and as the one letter that has not been traced is described in the sale catalogue, the collection as presented in this volume has suffered little from the dispersal. Of all the fifty-one letters only one was included in full in the great edition of Swift's Correspondence which we owe to the unflagging zeal of the late Dr. Frank Elrington Ball. It is the last letter that Swift wrote to Ford, and it had been secured in 1896 for the British Museum.

We have only eighteen letters from Ford, and all were printed in the eighteenth century by Swift's first editors. For historical purposes Swift had put aside the eleven letters which he received during the political crisis of July and August 1714. Nine of these, together with the only letter of 1716, were used by Hawkesworth and presented to the British Museum. Deane Swift printed eight—the two of 1714 which Hawkesworth had somehow missed, and the six of latest date, from 1732 to 1737. How he disposed of them is not known, and his edition remains our sole authority for them. Altogether sixty of the letters of Swift and Ford are now printed in this volume from the originals.

There are no letters from Ford between 1716 and 1732—the years to which most of Swift's letters belong—and we may assume that Swift had not kept any. Ford was not in a position at that time to give such information on public matters as was worth preserving, and the loss is chiefly to be regretted for the light which they would have thrown on what Swift wrote in reply. When an intimate and sometimes a gossipy correspondence is carried on irregularly for thirty years, with immediate answers at one time and long silences at another, by two friends who have often no occasion to write because they meet or one is the other's guest, we hardly expect them to take care of every letter which they receive. Swift and Ford must have written to each other well over a hundred letters, and of these we have sixty-nine. That is not a small portion. It is ample to exhibit the character of their friendship; and it is made up of the letters which they themselves thought best worth keeping.

The correspondence as we have it begins in November 1708 when Swift, at the age of forty-one, was steadily rising to power in the political and social circles of London, and when Addison was finding him 'the most agreeable companion, the truest friend, and the greatest genius of his age'.[1] Ford, who was then a young man of twenty-six, had seen much of Swift during a visit in the autumn of that year, and on going home to Dublin had sent a letter about the glorious life which he had enjoyed in London; and Swift, to judge from the tone of his reply, was pleased to receive it. As in their correspondence, so in their acquaintanceship, Ford must have made the first advances. 'Dr. Swift, upon the score of his merit and extraordinary qualities, doth claim the sole and undoubted right, that all persons whatsoever shall make such advances to him as he pleases to demand, any law, claim, custom, privilege of sex, beauty, fortune or quality to the contrary notwithstanding'[2]— so it was written even in these early years. But it is clear that from the beginning he liked the free and easy ways of Ford, whom Gay was to describe as 'joyous',[3] and who was a good scholar as well. They came to know each other during the three years which Swift divided mostly between Dublin and Laracor, and probably in 1707 not long before he left for London.[4] Woodpark, the small estate to which Ford had recently succeeded, was half way on the road to

---

[1] The inscription in the presentation copy of Addison's *Remarks on Several Parts of Italy*, 1705. It is reproduced in Forster's *Life of Swift*, 1875, p. 160. Dr. Elrington Ball has shown in *Swift's Verse*, 1929, p. 63, that it should be dated 1707–9.

[2] 'A Decree for concluding the treaty between Dr. Swift and Mrs. Long', printed in *Letters, Poems and Tales, Amorous, Satyrical and Gallant*, Curll, 1718; cf.

Swift's letter to Miss Hoadly of 4 June 1734, *Correspondence*, ed. Elrington Ball, v. 70. It appears to belong to December 1707 or January 1708, *id.*, iii. 457.

[3] Gay, *Mr. Pope's Welcome from Greece*, l. 131. He is also called 'sprightly', *Correspondence*, i. 161.

[4] A sentence in one of Swift's letters suggests that he knew Ford's father, who died in 1705: see Letter XLVII, p. 114.

Laracor. Their friendship was to continue without a break, and to decline only with long absence and failing health.

Charles Ford was born in Dublin on Tuesday 31 January 1681/2, and was baptized on 11 February in the church of St. Michan. His father, Edward Ford, or Forth, was at that time a captain in the King's Foot Guards in Ireland, and was afterwards member for Monaghan Borough in the Parliament of 1692–3 and for Ratoath Borough from 1703 till his death in 1705. His grandfather was Sir Robert Forth, of County Cavan, who was knighted in 1628, and was himself the son of Sir Ambrose Forth, a Judge of the Prerogative Court and Master of Chancery in the time of Elizabeth.[1]

Edward Ford married in 1676 Letitia, the widow of Phineas Preston of Ardsallagh, and the daughter of Robert Hamond of Chertsey. They had eleven children, of whom four lived beyond childhood—Elizabeth (1678–1698), Penelope (1680–1763), Charles, and Richard (1686–1731).[2] Swift's references to Letitia Ford, and her one extant letter, written to the widow of her only child by her first marriage, suggest that she was a woman of strong character. Little is known of Edward Ford beyond what is learned from army and parliamentary records. He is responsible for the definite adoption of 'Ford', instead of 'Forth', as the family name; it is common from about 1680, and regular by 1690.

The English birth of Charles Ford's mother may

[1] For this information about Ford's grandfather and great-grandfather, correcting what has hitherto been stated, the editor is indebted to Mr. T. U. Sadleir, Deputy Ulster King of Arms.

[2] Ford left a list with the names of the eleven children and their birthdays. The entry for himself is 'Charles Jan: 31. 1681 at 7 in the Eve: Tue:'—i.e. 1681/2.

have had some bearing on his being sent to England to be educated at Eton; but the Eton records are defective at this time, and the only evidence for his having been there is found in the entry of his admission to Trinity College, Dublin.[1] He was admitted on 31 July 1695, at the age of thirteen, as a fellow commoner, and in due course, in the spring of 1699, he received his Bachelor's degree. That his time had been well spent is suggested by his later proficiency in Latin verse, and by the conferment of the Master's degree, *honoris causa*, in 1707.[2]

The great event of his undergraduate days was the purchase by his father in 1698 of the estate of Woodpark.[3] On his father's death in 1705 he succeeded to all estates in fee, his mother being left the 'use of Woodpark, house, orchards, woods, and gardens, together with a hundred acres of land contiguous to the house'.[4] She chose to remain in her Dublin house in

---

[1] See *Alumni Dublinenses*, ed. Burtchaell and Sadleir. A certificate of admission is among the Ford papers: 'Carolus Ford Sociorum Commensalis, examinatione habita, admissus est in Artes, die Julij tricesimo primo anno Domini millesimo sexcentesimo nonagesimo quinto. Geo: Browne Præp^{tus} Joh: Hall Præl. Prim.'

[2] The editor is indebted to the Provost of Trinity for the following extract from the Board's Minutes for 15 July 1707:— 'Matthew Ford and Charles Ford, Members of the House of Commons, had the grace of the House for an honorary degree of Mr. in Arts.' Matthew Ford was a Member, but Charles Ford

is not known ever to have stood for election. Swift, however, expected him to stand in 1709: see Letter II, p. 5.

[3] The town and lands of Woodpark, 'alias Beggstown', were purchased from Nicholas Barnwell in October 1698, and the town and lands of Vessingstown and of Killmartin and lands at Castleknock from Henry Earl of Romney in November. Charles Ford purchased Bennetstown from Henry Luttrell in October 1707.

[4] This extract from the will of Edward Ford, now destroyed, was supplied by Dr. Elrington Ball. Should Mrs. Ford have decided to live in Woodpark, she was to pay her son a rent of £40.

Dawson Street, and henceforth Swift, and readers of Swift's verse, were to know Woodpark as the residence of Charles Ford.

In 1708 he was on the point of marrying Dorothy Naper, elder daughter of James Naper of Loughcrew and Drewstown. In the agreement for the marriage settlement his estate was valued at about £700 per annum, and his mother gave up her right to the use of Woodpark.[1] The agreement was signed on 16 August, but the marriage did not take place. Ford went to London, cultivated the acquaintance of Swift, thoroughly enjoyed himself, and remained a bachelor for the rest of his life.

He was back in Dublin by November, while Swift remained occupied with politics in London, and all that we know of him during the next two years is derived from Swift's two letters to him. There are no letters during the fourteen months which Swift spent in Ireland in 1709 and 1710. But when Swift returned to London in September 1710 to be more deeply involved in politics, Ford, as if by arrangement, appeared there about the same time, and was to remain there till June 1711. Again there was no occasion for letters, as they met regularly, but in their place we have the *Journal to Stella*, which shows what Ford meant to the older man and how their friendship steadily strengthened :

'To-day I presented Mr. Ford to the Duke of Ormond' (12 Sept. 1710)—'I was weary of the Coffee-house, and Ford desired me to sit with him at next door; which I did, like a fool, chatting till twelve' (28 Oct.)—'Ford and I went to see the tombs at Westminster' (25 Nov.)—'I dined to-day with [Erasmus] Lewis and Ford, whom I have brought acquainted' (15 Dec.)—'I called at Mr. Ford's, and desired him to lend

---

[1] A copy of the agreement is among the Ford papers. James Naper is described in it as 'of Druistown'.

me a shaving' (5 Jan. 1711)—'To-day Ford and I set apart
to go into the City to buy books' (9 Jan.)—'I dined with Ford
because it was his Opera-day and snowed, so I did not care to
stir farther' (20 Jan.)—'Ford is as sober as I please; I use
him to walk with me as an easy companion, always ready for
what I please, when I am weary of business and Ministers'
(7 March).

While Ford was spending that summer in Ireland he
received a letter—the third in the collection—which is
full of political news and testifies to increased confidence. But he was back in London by December,
again to see Swift regularly and to be mentioned as
frequently to Stella:

'Ford has been sitting with me till peeast tweeleve a clock'
(2 Jan. 1712)—'I have made Ford copy out a small pamphlet,
and sent it to the press, that I might not be known for author;
'tis A Letter to the October Club' (18 Jan.).

The opportunity came for official recognition when
William King, who showed greater aptitude as an ir-
responsible wit than as director of a government organ,
laid down the editorship of *The London Gazette*. Swift
appears to have had less difficulty in persuading the
Earl of Dartmouth, then Secretary of State for the
Southern Department, to offer the editorship to Ford
than in persuading Ford to accept it:

'I have made Ford Gazetteer, and got two hundred pounds
a year settled on the employment by the Secretary of State,
beside the perquisites. It is the prettiest employment in
England of its bigness; yet the puppy does not seem satisfied
with it. I think people keep some follies to themselves, till
they have occasion to produce them. He thinks it not genteel
enough, and makes twenty difficulties. 'Tis impossible to make
any man easy. His salary is paid him every week, if he pleases,
without taxes or abatements. He has little to do for it. He
has a pretty office, with coals, candles, papers, etc.; can frank
what letters he will; and his perquisites, if he takes care, may
be worth one hundred pounds more.'

Ford was installed Gazetteer on 1 July 1712 and held office till the political upheaval which came with the death of Queen Anne. It was now his turn to give Swift much political information. He wrote eight letters—all of which are lost—in 1713, when Swift had retired to Dublin as Dean of St. Patrick's; and in the critical months of 1714, when Swift had been recalled to London to strengthen the crumbling government, but had stolen away to Letcombe on the Berkshire Downs in disgust at delays and divided counsels, Ford sent regular reports of what was happening, or not happening. They told what Swift wanted to know. 'Your letters will make good Memoirs', he wrote; ' I have put up your last among my Papers.'[1] Previously he had destroyed Ford's letters, but in July and August 1714 they were docketed and preserved.

Ford was competent rather than energetic as Gazetteer, but he appears to have satisfied the government and to have done as well as Swift had expected. He was not himself satisfied with what he had written on the death of Queen Anne, and confessed to be ashamed to have it seen; as he had nobody to consult with he had chosen to err on the side of saying too little. But Swift thought better of it:

'Your Gazette is perfectly right, and what is said of the Queen very decent and proper: had there been more it might have been better; and indeed I know no body has a better Style for Letters or Business than you: which considering your Lazyness, you may be said to have acquired in spight of your Teeth.'[2]

He was Gazetteer throughout the doubtful weeks which followed the death of the Queen, and expected for some time to retain his post. But when Bolingbroke was dismissed with purposed indignities, Swift saw what the new government intended. ' I expect', he

[1] p. 24.    [2] p. 50.

wrote from Dublin, 'the worst they can compass, and that they will be able to compass it', but he advised Ford not to resign.[1] Even before he wrote this warning, Ford had ceased to be Gazetteer. His removal followed as a consequence on Stanhope's appointment as Secretary of State in succession to Bromley on 22 September. The change was thorough and extended even to the printer of the *Gazette*. The number for 21 to 25 September and all the numbers since Ford's appointment were 'Printed by Benj. Tooke at the Temple-Gate, and John Barber on Lambeth-hill'; the number for 25 to 28 September is 'Printed by J. Tonson in the Strand', and is described in a manuscript note on a copy in the British Museum as 'first Gazette by Mr. Buckley'.[2] Ford had been editor from No. 5025 to No. 5262.[3] During the period they cover, from 1 July 1712 to 25 September 1714, his residence in London had been continuous.

Thereafter for six months we lose sight of him, but

[1] pp. 62, 3.

[2] The Whig *Flying-Post* announced in the issue for 25–28 September that 'Mr. John Barber is remov'd from being Printer of the Gazette', but said nothing about the editor.

[3] Of the many letters and papers which he must have received as Gazetteer he appears to have kept only two. One is a letter (dated 'Sunday night') which the Duke of Shrewsbury as Lord Chamberlain addressed to Bolingbroke about Peter the Great: 'Her Majesty having read in the Extract of News your Lordship sent her, an Article about the Czar and a miller, was apprehensive it might by in-

advertence be put into the Gazzette, and tho I told her I believed there was no danger, yet she commanded me to write to your Lordship to this effect.' The other is the signed statement which Colonel John Hamilton, the Duke of Hamilton's second in the famous duel which *Esmond* has made familiar to modern readers, sent for insertion in the *Gazette* as an advertisement. The covering letter is dated 12 February 1712/13 and addressed 'To Erasmus Lewis Esqr Secretary To The Rt Honoble The Earle of Dartmouth'. The advertisement appeared in the *Gazette* for 10–14 February.

we should expect him to have remained in London with his old political leaders. As Gazetteer he had been in closer touch with Bolingbroke than with any other member of the government, and when we next hear of him he is with Bolingbroke in France. Bolingbroke had fled at the end of March 1715, and Ford is known to have been in France before the end of April; in June, Swift wrote to a friend that 'Charles Ford is with Lord Bolingbroke in Dauphiné within a league of Lyons'.[1] It is an easy assumption that he was therefore implicated in Bolingbroke's designs, but Bolingbroke may have been no more confidential then than he had been a year previously, in pursuance of his usual policy of using his associates as much as he could and telling them as little as he needed. When Ford crossed to England later that summer he was arrested, possibly about the time when his other political leader, the Earl of Oxford, was committed to the Tower. Official evidence of his arrest has not been discovered, and our knowledge of it is derived from a sentence in a letter which Swift wrote some years later to the second Earl,—'The person is Mr. Ford, whom you may remember to have been employed as writer of the *Gazette*, a very worthy gentleman of a considerable fortune here, and long in confinement upon his first return from France'.[2]

[1] *Correspondence*, ii. 285.

[2] *Id.*, iii. 262. His confinement is implied in a letter written to him by the Duc de la Force on 2 February 1716: 'J'ay receu Monsieur avec le plus sensible plaisir, il y a deux ou trois jours, votre lettre du 3ᵐᵉ du mois passé . . . Votre silence par consequent me donnoit la plus grande inquietude, et ne voyant arriver aucune de vos lettres je comtois que vous n'estiez pas en estat d'en ecrire. Comme je connois très bien le mauvais naturel et l'esprit chicaneur de Gruby, je ne suis pas surpris des vexations qu'il vous suscite. S'il avoit en mains surquoy fonder un proces, vous n'en seriez pas quitte à bon marché. Je vous souhaitte de tout mon cœur tiré de cette facheuse affaire.' There are three letters from La Force among the Ford papers.

He was free by the end of the year, and remained in London till the following June, when he crossed to Dublin and had his first meeting with Swift since May 1714. It was only a brief visit, for he had planned to return to the Continent. This time he was to make the Grand Tour, with little thought of politics, though he was to meet Bolingbroke and correspond with him. He was in Paris about the middle of October, and on 12 November was granted a passport 'valable seulement pour huit jours' from Paris to Lyons. He travelled by Turin and Venice to Rome, where he stayed from February till April, and probably much longer. In October he was at Siena, where he had an adventure with sharpers which he thought worth recording in sixteen quarto pages—'An Account of an Adventure that happened to Mr. Wight and me at Sienna, Oct. 12. 1717'.[1] Legal proceedings, in which he was successful, sent him back to Rome, and he was still there in January. 'We took Florence in our way home,' he writes, 'on purpose to thank the Great Duke, who seemed extremely pleased with our compliment, and rejoiced at the success we had met at Rome.' He came home by easy stages, passing through Parma in May, Lyons in June, and Lille in July, and spending four weeks on the way in Paris.[2] On 20 August 1718 he was back in Dublin, after an absence of exactly two years. It was his last visit to the Continent. Henceforward Dublin was to remain, if we may believe Swift, contemptible in his esteem. By December he was again in London, to reside there

---

[1] The 'Account' describes fully how he was cheated at ombre. He had to give up his repeating watch, which bore the name of Daniel Quare, its inventor, and had cost him seventy pounds; but he recovered it at Rome.

[2] These details of his tour are collected from his 'Account', two French passports, the addresses of letters, and the *Stuart Papers*, iii. 173, 260, v. 351, vi. 527.

till the summer of 1720. London was becoming
definitely his home; but he was usually to return to
Ireland for a month or two in the summer or autumn
during the lifetime of his mother.

He made an exceptionally long stay in 1723, and
he must have made it by arrangement with Swift.
That was the year in which Vanessa died, and in which
Swift, for reasons that have not been adequately explained, took his long southern journey. This obscure
period in Swift's life has not been made clearer by
gossip and surmise, but his relations with Ford at this
time leave no room for doubt. Ford had been in
Dublin in the previous July, and a sentence in Swift's
last letter to Vanessa suggests that he was still there
in August. If he returned to London before the end
of the year he was not there for long. On 8 January
1723 Swift wrote to Gay that 'we keep him here as
long as we can'.[1] Evidently it was his presence in
Dublin or Woodpark which suggested the remarkable
birthday greeting of 31 January which can be read
both as an invitation to remain and as an expression
of satisfaction that he was likely to remain.

> If you have London still at heart
> We'll make a small one here by Art :
> The Diff'rence is not much between
> St. James's Park and Stephen's Green.
>
>   .    .    .    .    .    .
>
> Then, for a middle-aged Charmer,
> Stella may vye with your Mountharmar :
> She's Now as handsom ev'ry bit,
> And has a thousand times her Wit.
>
>   .    .    .    .    .    .
>
> You see, my Arguments are Strong ;
> I wonder you held out so long.

If it be fanciful to detect in the tone of this poem a

----

[1] *Correspondence*, iii. 151.

feeling of expectant gratitude, it is at least significant that the only birthday verses which Swift is known to have addressed to Ford should belong to this year. The poem is printed in this volume from the very copy that Ford received, and of all Swift's manuscripts there is none more fair and handsome.

Ford fell in with Swift's wishes, and remained. More than that, he invited Stella and Mrs. Dingley to be his guests at Woodpark, and they stayed with him for no less than six months, from April to 3 October. Their visit is celebrated in another poem :

> Don Carlos in a merry Spight
> Did Stella to his House invite,
> He entertain'd her half a year
> With richest Wines and costly Cheer.

This poem, and the other poem on the 'fatal day' when she had to return to Dublin—two separate poems which have hitherto been wrongly combined—are to be read as Swift's humorous testimony of gratitude for the care which had been taken of Stella during his long absence from Dublin ; and it is none the less sincere because, as the manuscript shows, Ford had some part in its composition.[1] He was, in Delany's words, ' a cheerful, generous, good-natured friend of the Dean's, whom she also much loved and honoured'.[2] Vanessa he knew well too ; she called him 'Glassheel', as Stella called him 'Don Carlos'. She died on 2 June while Stella was at Woodpark. Ford could have solved for us problems that have baffled all Swift's biographers. What we do know is that Swift trusted Ford, and chose him of all his friends to ease the awkwardness of circumstances which we do not fully understand.

When Swift next wrote to Ford he said, ' it is an

[1] See pp. 197–202.
[2] *Observations upon Orrery's Remarks,* 1754, p. 57.

infamous case indeed to be neglected in Dublin when a man may converse with the best company in London. This misfortune you are able to fly from, but I am condemned to it for my life.'[1] Ford had fled not long after Stella's visit was over, and, fortunately for us, Swift was given occasion to write. He sent twelve letters from January 1724 to August 1725, most of them containing references to *Gulliver's Travels* or to *The Drapier's Letters*; and they are the most important group of letters in their correspondence.

Then comes a long gap, which is partly explained by Swift's two visits to England for six months in 1726 and 1727. Among the Ford papers we have only two Latin poems by Ford to fill it.[2] The verses for Stella's birthday in 1726 appear to have been dashed off to take the place of Swift's regular greeting when he was starting for England.[3] The longer and more serious poem for Swift's own birthday in 1727, the only poem that Ford is known to have addressed to Swift, supplies good evidence for his reputation as a Latin scholar, and anticipates the invocation in *The Dunciad*.[4] Both pieces are now printed for the first time.

There is more, though surmise must take the place of documentary proof. They did not need to write to each other at that time ; we have grounds for thinking that their association was never closer. When Swift crossed to England in March 1726 he took with him *Gulliver's Travels*, and when he left on 15 August it was in the hands of the printer. Pope has told us how it got there. The publisher, Benjamin Motte, he says,

---

[1] p. 99.
[2] There is also the letter which Ford wrote to Motte from Dublin on 3 January 1727, *Correspondence*, iii. 373 and *Gulliver's Travels*, ed. Harold Williams, 1926, xxxiv. Ford had arrived in Dublin shortly after Swift in October, *Correspondence*, iii. 350.
[3] See pp. 212–13.
[4] See pp. 213–15.

'received the copy, he tells me, he knew not from whence, nor from whom, dropped at his house in the dark, from a hackney coach '.[1]  Who dropped it, or caused it to be dropped?  Sir Walter Scott says Ford.[2] We do not know what evidence Scott had, but if he had less than we have, we should say that he guessed shrewdly.  He mentions the part that Ford had played in conveying to the printer *Some Free Thoughts upon the Present State of Affairs* in 1714; but he did not know, as we now do, what instructions Ford had then received from Swift :

'Here it is, read it, and send it to B— by an unknown hand . . . Do not send it by the Penny post, nor your Man, but by a Porter when you are not at your Lodgings. Get some Friend to copy out the little Paper, and send it inclosed with the rest, and let the same Hand direct it, and seal it with an unknown Seal.' [3]

Nor did Scott know that Swift had drafted a letter to be addressed to the printer of *Free Thoughts*, and to be printed before the pamphlet.[4]  It is the same technique. We cannot bring conclusive proof, but, as we shall see, Ford was in the secret of *Gulliver* at every stage.

More and more Ford came to 'think nothing tolerable five miles from London '.[5]  In Thomas Prior's *List of the Absentees of Ireland*, published at Dublin in 1729, his name is in the class 'who live constantly abroad, and are seldom or never seen in Ireland'. He must have protested, as one of the few alterations in the second edition which appeared in the same year is the transference of his name to the class 'who live generally in Ireland, but were occasionally absent in May, June and July 1729, for health, pleasure, or business'.  No doubt could have arisen after the death of his mother in 1730.  In September 1731 Ford let

---

[1] *Correspondence*, iii. 364.  [3] p. 17.
[2] *Works of Swift*, 1814, i. 326.  [4] p. 38.  [5] p. 127.

Woodpark, and never lived in it again ; and in March 1732 the house in Dawson Street was advertised in *The Dublin Gazette* as 'to be set for a term of years or the interest to be sold '.[1] He had been in Dublin early that year, on the last visit of which we have record.

It was probably during this visit, and certainly not before 1730, that Swift had the supper party which Lætitia Pilkington has described in her *Memoirs* :

'There now came in, to sup with the Dean, one of the oddest little Mortals I ever met with : He formerly wrote the *Gazetteer* ; and upon the Strength of being an Author, and of having travelled, took upon him not only to dictate to the Company, but to contradict whatever any other Person advanced, Right or Wrong, till he had entirely silenced them all: And then having the whole Talk to himself, (for, to my great Surprize the Dean neither interrupted nor shewed any Dislike of him) he told us a whole string of Improbabilities, such as, " That each Pillar of St. *Peter*'s at *Rome* took up more Ground than a Convent which was near it, wherein were twelve Monks, with their Chapel, Garden, and Infirmary." By this Account, every Pillar must take up, at least, half an Acre, and, considering the Number of them, we must conclude the Edifice to be some Miles in Circumference. No one present had ever been at *Rome*, except himself, so that he might tell us just what he thought proper.

I took notice, that before this dogmatical Gentleman the Dean was most remarkably complaisant to Mr. *P——n* and me.'[2]

There is some value in this as a picture and as a character sketch. For one thing, it supplies the best

---

[1] Information supplied by Dr. Elrington Ball. The editor is indebted for a transcript of the advertisement to Mr. Edward Phelps of the library of Trinity College, Dublin.

[2] *Memoirs of Mrs. Lætitia Pilkington*, London, 1748, i, pp. 65–6.

comment on four lines in Swift's birthday poem to Ford :

> When to your Friends you would enhance
> The Praise of Italy or France
> For Grandeur, Elegance and Wit,
> We gladly hear you, and submit.

For another, it suggests how Swift enjoyed the easy, continuous flow of Ford's conversation. And it also shows how Swift concealed from the casual observer, as indeed from every one, the degree of confidence which he reposed in Ford.

After this visit they were not to meet again. They corresponded regularly till the end of 1733. Ford asks Swift's help, and gets it, in business difficulties with the tenant of Woodpark ; and Swift consults Ford about the Dublin edition of his works. Their health has become a more regular and plentiful topic, for though Swift had long complained of his giddiness and deafness he has been made uneasy about Ford by what he has heard from others. 'You are a stranger to sickness,'[1] he had once said; but Ford had been seriously ill, and would not take proper care of himself :

'A Person who came not long since from London told me you abated nothing in your plentifull way of eating, and that you drink as much wine as ever, upon which he said, all your friends were concerned. I do not think life is of much value, but health is worth every thing, and Nature acts right in making that method which prolongs life absolutely necessary to preserve health, which makes a short life and a merry, a very foolish Proverb. For my own part I labor for daily health as often and almost as many hours as a workman does for daily bread, and like a common laborer can but just earn enough to keep life and Soul together. . .

I beg you will force your nature as much as possible upon

[1] p. 105.

temperance and exercise, I mean temperance in a physicall sense, and not a moral, for many a moral and pious man's health is ruined by intemperance.'[1]

Swift always held that 'health is worth preserving, though life is not';[2] but the solicitude which he here shows for the health of Ford may come as a surprise to those who have derived their impression of him from some of his critics. This is Swift in the inner circle of his friends. The passage shows a tenderness which he did not allow himself in print, and to students of his character it may prove one of the most interesting in this volume. A little later he says that he wants 'tender people' about him.[3]

Swift loses no chance of recommending what he himself practised, temperance and exercise, and walking in particular. Walking was his lifelong panacea; he is one of the great walkers of English literature. Almost to his seventieth year he would walk six or seven miles a day.[4] Ford on the other hand recommends him to take less exercise: 'I have often wished that you would be more moderate in your walks.'[5]

Thereafter their correspondence ceases to be regular. Ford has to complain that in two and a half years he has written six letters without getting an answer. Swift had no knowledge of having received any of them but the last, and in answering it he says he has not enjoyed a day of health for twenty months. He speaks again about what he has heard of Ford's health, and again recommends exercise, and again says that he himself endeavours to make life tolerable by temperance. Then he speaks about politics and politicians in the old

[1] pp. 143, 145.
[2] So he wrote as early as 18 December 1711, in a letter to Miss Anne Long, printed in *Vanessa and her Correspondence*
*with Swift*, ed. A. Martin Freeman, 1921, p. 67. Cf. p. 140.
[3] p. 163.
[4] p. 169.
[5] p. 150.

manner, and about their friends. He had made up
his mind that they were never to meet again in this
world, 'for', he says, 'I am in no state of health to go
to England, nor will you ever be in a state of mind
to visit Ireland.' But his feelings had not changed.
'As to your self, I have never lessened a grain of that
true love and esteem I ever bore you.' That was his
last letter to Ford.

Neglect of health had not begun to affect Ford as
a correspondent. He replied at once; and a year later
he remembered Swift's birthday.

Swift still heard about him from others. 'Charles
Ford's mistress is his bottle, to which he is so entirely
given up, that he and I converse but little, though he
is a man of honour, and as such to be respected'—
so wrote Erasmus Lewis, whom Ford, as his last letters
show, had come to find dull and uncommunicative.
'Mr. Ford, I am told,' wrote John Barber the printer
and Lord Mayor, 'is the most regular man living; for
from his lodgings to the Mall, to the Cocoa, to the
tavern, to bed, is his constant course'; and again, 'Our
friend Ford lives in the same way, as constant as the
sun, from the Cocoa-tree to the Park, to the tavern, to
bed, etc.' And Swift replied, 'I wonder Mr. Ford is
alive; perhaps walking preserves him'.[1]

When Ford drew up his will in May 1740 he
appointed Swift an executor, leaving to him 'my repeating Watch, my Pictures in Miniature, as also the
Sum of one hundred pounds in Money to buy a
Mourning Ring'. But Swift was passing beyond a
responsible part, and his name was omitted from the
new will which was signed on 26 June 1742 and
proved on 6 May 1743. Nothing appears to be discoverable about Ford's last years. We are left to
picture him as a bachelor of sixty living by himself

[1] *Correspondence,* vi. 42, 72, 89, 92.

in Little Cleveland Court near the foot of St. James's Street with a man servant and a maid servant,[1] calling at fixed hours at the Cocoa-tree—then in Pall Mall and conveniently near, and venturing, always at a slow pace, into the Mall and St. James's Park. Among the friends whom he met at the Cocoa-tree, the haunt of the extreme Tories, probably one was his chief executor, Sir John Hynde Cotton, the Jacobite.

For the day and the circumstances of his death we rely on the brief notice in *The Daily Post* of Friday 29 April, 1743:

'Last Tuesday as the Hon. Charles Ford, Esq., a near Relation to the Right Hon. the Lord Hobart, was at Dinner with several Persons of Distinction, at his House in St. James's Place, he was suddenly taken ill, and expir'd on Wednesday Evening, about Seven o'Clock.'

The notice in *The Daily Advertiser* of the same date (repeated in *The General Evening Post* of the next day) contains gossip; it is wrong in his name, but may be true in part:

'On Tuesday Night Richard Ford, Esq., of St. James's Place, had the Misfortune to fall down Stairs after he had been taking Leave of some Company that supp'd with him, and Yesterday Morning he died of the Bruises he receiv'd by the Fall.'

*The Daily Post* gives the day of his death as Wednesday 27 April. The burial was on Saturday 30 April, in St. James's, Piccadilly.

We get a very pleasing impression of Ford from this correspondence, and perhaps a more striking impression from Swift's letters to him than from his own. He is always to be trusted, always held in love and esteem. There is no change in the tenor of their letters once their friendship is fully established, and those of

[1] They are named in his will—Gotthard Leeders and Catherine Herbert.

early date which Swift purposely kept and those of later
date which he happened to keep have nothing to distinguish them but the assurance that comes with age.
Arbuthnot's prediction in 1714 was justified—'I really
value your judgement extremely in choosing your
friends. I think worthy Mr. Ford is an instance of it,
being an honest, sensible, firm, friendly man, *et qualis
ab inceptu processerat, etc.*' [1]

But the importance of these letters lies in the new
light which they throw upon Swift. Of all his many
friends there was none to whom he habitually wrote
at once so easily, even so carelessly, and on terms so
equal. When he writes to Oxford and Bolingbroke
he weighs his words; when to Pope, he is conscious
of Pope's great gifts; when to Stella, he is her master
—a loving master, but a master none the less. Others
invite a jest, as others some appearance of ceremony,
but he may be no less reticent in his playfulness
than in his courtesies. When he writes to Ford he
is under no constraint. He puts down what he has to
say in the first words that come, and in any order.
He does not trouble to read over what he has written;
sometimes he omits a word, or changes the structure
of a sentence midway. Trivialities and serious matters
follow in turn. He asks Ford to get a good beaver
hat for his 'tolerable large head'; doubtless the
hat was one of the three mentioned in his will. He
reports that Ford's mother has a great cold, and that
he has seen her being rooked at ombre. He acknow-
ledges razors which 'will be a great treasure', and
adds that 'for want of good ones I pass one hour in
eight and forty very miserably'—from which we
gather that he shaved himself every second day. He
sends Stella's snuff-box to be mended; it had a single
fly studded on the bottom. He says that Stella wants

[1] *Correspondence*, ii. 254.

to know if the weather has been as foul in England as it has been in Ireland. More seriously he speaks of Stella's health; she eats about two ounces a week, and then a little later—presumably in accordance with the panacea—she walks three or four Irish miles a day over bogs and mountain. His own ill health he describes with painful regularity. Gossip is mixed up with business, and politics with observations on fools and scoundrels. 'Three fools have lately died and made wise wills'[1]—wise because their money was left whole or in part in charity. All has the freedom of conversation in which nothing that is said will be misunderstood. No letter of all the fifty-one seems quite to stand out as a great letter. To see Swift at his best in this kind of writing we may still turn to the *Journal to Stella*, or to the letters which he penned with deliberation at a crisis, such as those to Oxford and Bolingbroke after their fall. He wrote more amusing and finished letters to his more famous friends. Our enjoyment of these letters to Ford suffers at times from their careless intimacy; they contain —as the editor well knows—much that has to be explained. But their distinction is that, better than any series of letters to any other friend, they give us Swift in undress. We know him the better for seeing him in undress. From beginning to end there is not one word which even the most squeamish editor would wish to omit.

These unguarded letters reveal new details in Swift's life as politician and author. Ford's account of the crisis of 1714 gains by the recovery of the other side of the correspondence. As was to be expected, Ford wrote more letters at this time than he received, for his editorship of the *Gazette* kept him in the thick of

[1] p. 108.

events in London, and Swift had retired to a remote vicarage in Berkshire; but there was no one else to whom Swift wrote so many letters at this time, and brief as some of these letters are, there are none that tell us better what he was then thinking and doing.

'Did I steal away without telling you? No I remember I told you where to direct to me. I am at a Parsons House 52 miles from You, putting some Papers in order. And you may be as mad as you all please for me . . . I drink nothing but ale, and read and write and walk all day. I reckon I shall get the Spleen, but that is nothing. I long till your Session is over, but what have I to do with Politicks.'[1]

A few days later he again writes:

'I hear you grow madder and madder; that I can know at the distance I am. I would ensure a Pitcher for a year that a child carryes nine times a day to a Well, sooner than your Ministry.'[2]

He had seen too much of the conflict of personal ambitions in the previous winter, and, as he said in more measured terms to another correspondent, he cared not to live in storms when he could no longer do service to the ship and was able to get out of it.[3] But the Ministry did not forget him now, any more than they had forgotten him when, a year previously, he had been installed Dean of St. Patrick's. Then he had been told that Oxford desired him to 'make all possible haste over, for we want you extremely',[4] and he had obeyed the summons reluctantly, in the hope of bringing cohesion to a crumbling party. Now it was Bolingbroke who felt the need of him when Oxford had fallen and the Queen was dying. 'Barber was order'd by my Lord Bolingbroke to go down and endeavour to bring you to town. . . I really believe he is

[1] p. 15.
[2] p. 16.
[3] *Correspondence*, ii. 147.
[4] *Id.*, ii. 57.

very sincere in what I hear he has profess'd of you. Barber I suppose will tell you all''¹: so Ford wrote in a passage which he obliterated and Swift could not read; and Barber, the government printer, never went on this errand in these critical days when events moved too rapidly for Bolingbroke's schemes.

Swift might have been persuaded. 'As to my coming to town, I have no thoughts of it, unless they send for me, as I am sure they will not', he had written before the crisis reached its final stages; and Ford had replied, 'it would be imprudence in them to send for you, but I hope you will come'.² Swift had no reason to return. He had gone to the Berkshire Downs to be away from the dissensions of ministers, and he was walking, and putting some papers in order. In this way he might do more service to a government which appeared to him to be intent on its own destruction. He completed the pamphlet called *Some Free Thoughts on the Present State of Affairs* of which he had spoken to Ford before he left London, and, as we have seen, sent it to Ford with instructions how to convey it to Barber without arousing suspicion. Barber at once showed it to Bolingbroke, who characteristically proceeded to make alterations. But the days passed and no pamphlet appeared. 'As for service it will do, a fiddlestick. It will vex them, and that's enough,' said Swift. 'Who would ever do any thing for them when they are so negligent of their own interest?' said Ford.³ Within a few weeks Bolingbroke was out of office and was soon to be out of the country, and Swift was in Ireland, and the pamphlet was not to be printed till 1741.

'Upon second thoughts,' Swift writes, 'how comical a thing was it to shew that Pamphlet to Lord Bolingbroke of all men living.'⁴ He was ready to have one

¹ See p. 42, note 1.            ³ pp. 24, 31.
² pp. 29, 32.                    ⁴ p. 31.

particular softened that seemed hard on Bolingbroke; but he would not have anything harder said on Oxford than he had written.

Swift admits that an inducement to his return would be his appointment as Historiographer. He had hoped for that office since the death of Thomas Rymer at the end of the previous year, but in this crowded July it had already been given to Thomas Madox, another great medievalist who was in the true succession. No one can question the wisdom of the appointment; but Swift, with his eyes fixed on his own day, saw in Madox only 'a worthless rogue that nobody knows',[1] and could have said with cousin Dryden, whom he was not given to quoting, that 'Tom the second reigns like Tom the first'. His object had been to transform the functions of the office by making the Historiographer the official historian of his own times. In his Memorial to the Queen containing his application for the post, he had stated it to be 'necessary, for the honour of the Queen, and in justice to her servants, that some able hand should be immediately employed to write the history of her majesty's reign'; and two years earlier, during Rymer's lifetime, he had said in his *Proposal for Correcting the English Tongue* that he took it to be Oxford's 'duty, as prime minister, to give order for inspecting our language, and rendering it fit to record the history of so great and good a princess'. Even in the days of his friendship with Addison he had been thinking of this history;[2] and he found the need of it the greater when he had experience of the inner workings of government under Oxford and Bolingbroke. His pamphlets and all his writings as a politician—if we interpret the evidence aright—was of small importance in his eyes compared with the record which he hoped to leave to posterity of the

[1] *Correspondence*, ii. 210.    [2] *Id.*, i. 190.

greatness of the reign of Anne. As he foresaw his career while his party was still in power, this History was to be his great work.

This ambition underlies his remark that Ford's letters 'will make good Memoirs', and explains Ford's reply that 'the history we were formerly talking of would swell to a prodigious size, if it was carried on'.[1] His *Four Last Years of the Queen*—which has a misleading title, for it ends with the Peace of Utrecht— may be regarded as a slight sketch for a portion of his great scheme; but with the rout of the Tory party in 1714 he had to abandon the design of a work on a large scale. All that he was to write henceforward as an historian was fragmentary. When he returned to Dublin to become an Irishman for life, the first work he wrote was his *Memoirs relating to that Change which happened in the Queen's Ministry in 1710*. It is dated as early as October 1714. He wrote it quickly, putting on record what he knew at first hand, and giving particulars of the part which he himself had played. A year later he was stirred by the imprisonment of Oxford to a somewhat longer and more important account of the later stages of the ministry. On writing privately to Oxford in July 1715 he had said 'I shall take the liberty of thinking and calling you the ablest and faithfulest minister, and truest lover of your country, that this age hath produced. And I have already taken care that you shall be so represented to posterity, in spite of all the rage and malice of your enemies'.[2] The allusion here is to his *Enquiry into the Behaviour of the Queen's last Ministry*, which is dated June 1715. But only the first part belongs to that time. What has not been known hitherto is that it occupied his thoughts as late as 1721. He had discussed it with Ford, possibly in the summer of 1720, and had been stimulated to

---

[1] pp. 24, 26.          [2] *Correspondence*, ii. 294.

complete it by a second part dealing with the alleged design of bringing in the Pretender. There was more in the mind of both Oxford and Bolingbroke than either communicated to Swift, but this part supplies conclusive evidence, corroborating what we learn from other sources, that Swift was never given reason to suspect this design, even as a possible alternative to the more obvious course; and it likewise shows that on reviewing the whole situation dispassionately seven years later, he did not think that such a design could have been seriously entertained. 'I have finished that Tract you saw, where you said I was mistaken about some persons,' he wrote to Ford on 19 June 1721, 'and I have some thoughts of sending that and the other thing which was sent to you before the Queen died, and have them both printed in a volume by some Whig bookseller.'[1] It was not to be printed till 1765.

Every student of the reign of Anne must regret that Swift did not write his History. It would have been authoritative on many points. Making every allowance for the secrecy of Oxford and Bolingbroke, and for Swift's ignorance of much that has since been revealed, we cannot forget that, in his own words, he was for the space of almost four years very nearly and per- petually conversant with them in their times of leisure as well as of business, and that they had hardly another common friend. Of their relations with each other, and of the stages by which their relations affected the political situation, no one was better qualified to speak. But would he have been a great historian? We cannot easily say why he should not. With the example of Clarendon and Burnet before us, we need not suggest that his feelings were too deeply engaged, and any temperamental disqualification we can think of is nega- tived by his perfect self-command when in the public

[1] p. 93.

eye. His character-sketches and his observations on motives, scathing as they might be in talk or casual jottings, would have been adjusted to the requirements of the printed page. All his life he had been a keen student of history. The catalogue of his library shows a very large proportion of historical works, both ancient and modern. The specimens which he has left us in this kind of writing make us wish that they were more numerous; and they deserve more attention than they seem to receive.[1]

The death of Charles XII of Sweden in 1718 made him revert to a project which he had entertained as early as about 1703,—a brief and simple history of England from Rufus to Elizabeth for the use of 'foreigners and gentlemen of our own country'. The fragment that remains is the least significant of his historical writings, and its interest for us now is centred in the draft of the autobiographical dedication which in November 1719 he addressed to Count Gyllenborg, the Swedish ambassador who had been implicated in a Jacobite plot in 1717. After explaining that he had intended to dedicate the book to Charles, Swift puts it on record that he had had the honour of an invitation to Charles's court, and continues in these words —'which I heartily repent that I did not accept; whereby, as you can be my witness, I might have avoided some years' uneasiness and vexation, during the last four years of our late excellent Queen, as well as a long melancholy prospect since, in a most obscure disagreeable country, and among a most profligate and abandoned people'.[2] But even more interesting is what he says more frankly to Ford:

[1] Part of what is here said about Swift as an historian is taken from a lecture delivered by the editor in the University of Liverpool in 1930, and privately printed.

[2] *Prose Works*, ed. Temple Scott, x. 195.

'I am personally concerned for the Death of the K of Sweden, because I intended to have beggd my Bread at His Court, whenever our good Friends in Power thought fit to put me and my Brethren under the necessity of begging. Besides I intended him an honor and a Compliment, which I never yet thought a Crownd head worth, I mean, dedicating a Book to him. Pray can you let me know how I could write to the Count of Gillenburg.'[1]

In the rout of 1714, when he had warned Ford to expect the worst that the new government could compass, he had seriously thought that he might have to leave the country. He had asked Ford to procure for him 'a Licence of Absence in general, without specifying England', adding cryptically, 'because, who knows, &c.'[2]

Swift had returned to Dublin in 1714 as broken in spirit as the party which he had served so well. 'What do you talk of writing in this country, I can as easily fly',[3] he said in answer to Ford. He was to write little during the coming five or six years. He set himself as well as he could, to 'mend the public'—a favourite phrase of his—in the little sphere of St. Patrick's, and he was spoken of as 'a smart Dean';[4] but life had become for him 'a long melancholy prospect'. The political situation was taking the heart out of his party. 'Every body now', he writes in 1718, 'is as desponding

---

[1] p. 74.

[2] This throws light on a passage in the account which Pope gave to Arbuthnot of his visit to Letcombe on 4 July 1714: 'When we mentiond the wellfare of England he laughed at us, and said Muscovy would become a flourishing Empire very shortly. He seems to have wrong notions of the British Court, but gave us a hint as if he had correspondence with the king of Sueden.' Though Pope is giving particulars in the way of a News Letter, we now know that this passage is not whimsical but has to be taken seriously (Pope to Arbuthnot, 11 July 1714: *Life of Arbuthnot* by G. A. Aitken, 1892, p. 70).

[3] p. 64; cf. p. 60.

[4] *Correspondence*, ii. 265.

as I have been always. The Tories have lived all this while on whipt cream, and now they have even lost that.'[1] During these years of depression his thoughts habitually turned to the great days of his activities and ambitions. In time he made new friends and found new interests, but for six years the set of his mind was backwards. At the end of 1719, when he wrote the dedication to Gyllenborg, he could still say that the public wind was full in his teeth.[2] A few months earlier he had told Bolingbroke that there never was a more important period in England than the last years of the reign of Anne, and, in a passage which shows how he was still thinking of his abandoned History, and gives his views on how history should be written, he had urged Bolingbroke to describe the events of these years fully and exactly.[3] He completed his *Enquiry*, as we now know, as late as 1721. But by that time a change was taking place. He was breaking his resolution of never meddling with Irish politics.[4] ' As the world is now turned,' he writes in December 1719, ' no cloister is retired enough to keep politics out, and I will own they raise my passions whenever they come in my way.'[5] If the change could be dated definitely, we might ascribe it to the legislation which took away the jurisdiction of the Irish House of Lords. The ' Act for the better securing the Dependency of the Kingdom of Ireland upon the Crown of Great Britain' was passed in March 1720; and the letter to Ford in which he speaks of it shows the new spirit:

' I do assure you I never saw so universall a Discontent as there is among the highest most virulent and antichurch Whigs against that Bill and every Author or Abetter of it without Exception. They say publickly that having been the

---

[1] p. 66.  [3] *Correspondence*, iii. 31.  [4] p. 60.
[2] p. 83.  [5] p. 82.

most loyall submissive complying Subjects that ever Prince had, no Subjects were ever so ill treated.'[1]

Swift was finding a theme which was to waken him to new activity—the rights of the Irish People. He was soon to write *The Drapier's Letters*. He ceases to look back, and his experiences of government as he had known it under Queen Anne are henceforward to be found only in reflection, as in *Gulliver's Travels*.

We learn one or two new points about *The Drapier's Letters*. Swift's earliest reference to Wood's coinage in all his correspondence was made to Ford on 13 February 1724, when he says ' I can not tell whether I shall see you in the Spring, for I am afraid our Farthings will not pass in'.[2] He says nothing as yet about the role of Drapier, but he must have assumed it about this time, as when he next wrote to Ford, on 2 April, he speaks of his first *Letter* as being widely circulated throughout Ireland :

' I do not know whether I told you that I sent out a small Pamphlet under the Name of a Draper, laying the whole Vilany open, and advising People what to do ; about 2000 of them have been dispersd by Gentlemen in severall Parts of the Country.'[3]

The *Letter* must thus have been published as 'a pamphlet '[4] by the middle of March, and it was probably written in the latter half of February. Another brief statement shows Swift in touch with the Grand Juries who protected the printer :

' The grand Jury has been dissolved for refusing to present a Paper against Wood [i.e. *Seasonable Advice to the Grand Jury*]; a Second was called who are more stubborn.'[5]

[1] p. 86.  [2] p. 102.  shows that there is an earlier form
[3] p. 106.  of the first *Letter*; but it may not
[4] Mr. Herbert Davis in his  have been circulated.
edition of *The Drapier's Letters*  [5] p. 113.

This was written on the day before the second Grand Jury took the bold course of making a presentment not against the printer but against Wood and his patent. A minor point of interest is the spelling of 'Drapier'. The name occurs eight times in these letters to Ford, and the first four times it is spelled 'Draper', and afterwards a fifth time; 'Drapier' occurs only thrice, and not till four of the *Letters* had been published. Swift was not a stickler for spelling, but we are left wondering whether 'Drapier' was his own choice for his title pages, or whether it was the fancy of the printer.

But there is nothing of greater interest in these letters than the new and conclusive information which they supply about *Gulliver's Travels*. The date of composition was long a problem. Delany, who had the means of knowing but was careless, said confidently that the book was not written until some years after 1720.[1] Orrery and Deane Swift said equally confidently that it was written between 1714 and 1720; and two allusions in letters sent to Swift seemed to lend some support to this earlier date. When Bolingbroke said in his letter of 1 January 1722 'I long to see your Travels',[2] he might have implied that the book was finished; and when Vanessa in her letter of June 1722 showed that she was familiar with an episode in the Voyage to Brobdingnag,[3] she might be taken to have read the book in manuscript. So long as the evidence was of this kind, and so long as the evidence provided in plenty by the subject-matter of the book was neglected,[4] the view generally held was that *Gulliver's Travels* was completed by 1720, as if it was

[1] See p. 92, note 2.
[2] *Correspondence*, iii. 113.
[3] *Id.*, iii. 133.
[4] First adequately dealt with

by Sir Charles Firth in *The Political Significance of 'Gulliver's Travels'*, read to the British Academy on 10 December 1919.

the product of the six years of depression when Swift was settling down for life in Ireland, and as if, for reasons which were never explained, it should then have been kept for six years unprinted. Swift had given no help in his correspondence. Though Bolingbroke and Vanessa might allude to *Gulliver's Travels*, he himself had never once mentioned it in any known letter.

He had mentioned it in his letters to Ford, to whom he also spoke about it when they met in Ireland. What he wrote about it—all that he is known to have written about it while he was engaged on it—is here set down together with the dates:

15 April 1721.—I am now writing a History of my Travells, which will be a large Volume, and gives Account of Countryes hitherto unknown ; but they go on slowly for want of Health and Humor.

22 July 1722 (Lough-Gall).—The bad Weather has made me read through abundance of Trash, and this hath made me almost forget how to hold a Pen, which I must therefore keep for Dublin, Winter and Sickness.

19 January 1724.—I was at a Loss about one of the Letters, at first, but after found it was to you, and that you are a Traytor into the Bargain : else how should he [Bolingbroke] know any Thing of Stella or of Horses. Tis hard that Folks in France will not let us in Ireland be quiet. I would have him and you know that I hate Yahoos of both Sexes, and that Stella and Madame de Villette are onely tolerable at best, for want of Houyhnhnms.

— My greatest want here is of somebody qualifyed to censure and correct what I write, I know not above two or three whose Judgment I would value, and they are lazy, negligent, and without any Opinion of my Abilityes. I have left the Country of Horses, and am in the flying Island, where I shall not stay long, and my two last Journyes will be soon over.

13 February 1724.—He [Bolingbroke] raillyes me upon my Southern Journey, says, and swears it is no Pun, That Stella fixed my Course, talks of the Houyhnhnms as if he were

acquainted with them, and in that shows you as a most finished Traitor, for which you make very indifferent Excuses.

2 April 1724.—I shall have finished my Travells very soon if I have Health, Leisure, and humor.

14 August 1725 (Quilca).—I have finished my Travells, and I am now transcribing them; they are admirable Things, and will wonderfully mend the World.

16 August 1725 (Quilca).—I am amusing my self in the Quality of Bayliff to Sheridan, among Bogs and Rocks, over-seeing and ranting at Irish Laborers, reading Books twice over for want of fresh ones, and fairly correcting and transcribing my Travells, for the Publick.

From these passages it is now clear that Swift was at work in earnest in 1721, that he had written the draft of the first two Voyages before the end of 1723, that he wrote the fourth Voyage next and had completed the draft by January 1724, and that he was then engaged on the third Voyage. At the beginning of April he expected to finish the book 'very soon'. But in February or March he had begun *The Drapier's Letters*, and he was occupied with them till the end of the year. The revision of the *Travels* and the incorporation of new material, suggested partly by the circumstances which had called forth the *Letters*, may be assigned to 1725. By August of that year he had finished his *Travels* and was transcribing them.[1]

'Simplicity without which no human performance can arrive to any great perfection'—these are his own words.[2] The simplicity of his style did not come by chance. He had long thought of a satire in the form

---

[1] He had completed the transcription by 29 September, when he wrote to Pope: 'I have employed my time, besides ditching, in finishing, correcting, amending, and transcribing my Travels, in four parts complete, newly augmented.' *Correspondence*, iii. 276.

[2] In his *Letter to a Young Clergyman*.

of travels, but once he had found his design he did not write in haste. He was engaged on *Gulliver's Travels* for four years. He wrote it in draft, then he made additions and corrections, and then a fair copy. Revision was an important stage in the process of composition.

Much of the revision, and possibly most of it, was done at Quilca in County Cavan, the country 'cabin' of Thomas Sheridan, to which he retired with Stella and Mrs. Dingley towards the end of April 1725, with the hope—we may assume—of a clear stretch for undisturbed writing. It was as bad a summer as he had known. 'I can do no work this terrible weather, which has put us all seventy times out of patience',[1] he wrote to Sheridan in June. But he found 'some agreeablenesses'[2] in the wild country, and his health was better than it had been in Dublin. There is a rising note of cheerfulness in the letters which he wrote at this time, but to nobody, not even to his absent host, did he mention *Gulliver* before he told Ford that he had finished it. His nearest approach to mentioning it is in a letter to Pope where he speaks of grand designs that are all in prose.[3] To others he would say that when he could not stir out because of the weather he was reading some easy trash merely to divert himself; he even asked Sheridan to send him a large bundle of school exercises, good as well as bad, to correct.[4] Possibly no one except Stella knew how busily he was passing his time in that wild country and that bad summer. In his last letter to Ford, in March, he had spoken of the Drapier and not of Gulliver. He had his recurring fits of deafness, but he completed the task which he had set himself, and his spirits were high when, with the frankness which he seems to have

[1] *Correspondence*, iii. 241.    [3] *Id.*, iii. 257.
[2] *Id.*, iii. 237.       [4] *Id.*, iii. 247.

reserved for Ford, he announced on finishing his *Travels* that 'they are admirable things and will wonderfully mend the world'.

The little that Swift's friends in England knew about *Gulliver* while it was being written, they learned from Ford. Swift roundly declares him a traitor for telling Bolingbroke about the Houyhnhnms, but bore him no ill will. The Houyhnhnms and the Yahoos were, in the main, the work of 1723, the year in which Stella paid her long visit to Woodpark, and Ford must have divulged the secret on his return to England at the end of the year. That Bolingbroke regarded it as a secret is shown by his discreet silence in the letter which he wrote to Swift on the same day as he wrote to Ford rather foolishly about the Dean and Stella and horses.[1] Even his statement in January 1722 'I long to see your Travels' may be explained by a hint from Ford that the book was begun.[2] Likewise when Pope said in September 1725 'your Travels I hear much of',[3] he had heard of them from Ford; and then in reply Swift, for the first time, wrote openly to Pope about them, in the well-known letter in which he speaks of his hatred of that animal called man and his love of John, Peter, and Thomas.[4] The secret appears to have been well kept in Ireland. Sheridan in September 1725 could understand an allusion to the Yahoos.[5] But there is no evidence that any one ever saw the manuscript except Ford; and there is none that he saw it till it was finished, unless Swift's complaint that he has no one qualified to censure and correct what he writes be taken to imply that Ford had performed that service when in Ireland.

[1] p. 238.
[2] Bolingbroke wrote to Ford on the same day: see p. 235.
[3] *Correspondence*, iii. 269.
[4] *Id.*, iii. 277.
[5] *Id.*, iii. 267.

When the book was published by Motte on 28 October 1726 it was found to contain unauthorized alterations as well as errors of the press, and Ford was moved to make a list containing, as he says, 'every single alteration from the original copy'.[1] What the printer had received and tampered with was a transcript; had it been Swift's manuscript, the handwriting would have stultified the elaborate secrecy with which the work had reached the printer.[2] Whether Swift brought the transcript with him from Ireland, or whether it was made in England,—and the making of it in England would help to account for the delay between Swift's arrival in March and the negotiations with Motte in August,—the original manuscript was in Dublin at the end of the year when Ford compared it with the printed text. From Dublin on 3 January 1727 he wrote to Motte, probably at Swift's instigation, pointing out the 'many gross errors of the press' and referring to the serious alterations. Most of the minor faults were corrected in Motte's 'second edition' of 1727, but the major faults remained, and Swift could still speak of the mangled and murdered pages. When therefore Faulkner, the Dublin printer, proposed in 1733 to bring out a collected edition of his works, he welcomed the opportunity of seeing *Gulliver* printed as he had written it. But by that time the original manuscript was lost. Swift writes to Ford as if he did not think of its recovery, even as if he knew it to be destroyed. So he applied to Ford for an interleaved copy of the book, in

[1] p. 156.

[2] Even had it been the custom in those days for 'copy' to be sent out with proofs, the printer was not expected to know to whom to return the 'copy' of *Gulliver*. Swift certainly did not see any proofs. We assume that the 'copy' was retained in the printing-house, or destroyed. Some of the minor errors may have been introduced in the transcript.

which Ford had noted all the corruptions. 'I think', he writes, 'you had a Gulliver interleaved and set right in those mangled and murdered pages.' And again, 'I thought you had entered in leaves interlined all the differences from the original manuscript'.[1]

The two letters, now printed in full, in which he speaks of this copy are important for the history of the text. Somehow Swift believed that the alterations were made by Andrew Tooke, the son of his old friend Benjamin Tooke, afterwards Master of the Charterhouse, a writer on 'English Particles', and well known by name throughout the eighteenth century as the compiler of 'Tooke's *Pantheon*'. Swift did not appreciate his skill in particles. 'The whole sting is taken out in several passages, in order to soften them. Thus the style is debased, the humor quite lost, and the matter insipid.' And thus Swift wrote of the famous and coveted first edition. It is *Gulliver's Travels* as issued by Faulkner in 1735 that is the first authentic edition, finally approved by its author. Its value has been demonstrated since the text has been submitted to critical study ;[2] and Swift's two letters to Ford confirm its authority.

These letters likewise give some little help with the difficult problem of the Swift canon. We can now say definitely that *The Right of Precedence between Physicians and Civilians* is not his; and we must question his authorship of *The Puppet Show*. Swift wrote many things which he never intended to be

<hr/>

[1] pp. 154, 161.

[2] As in the edition of *Gulliver's Travels* by Mr. Harold Williams, 1926, which is of the greatest value for the study of the text. Mr. Williams prints Ford's list of errors (sent to Motte on 3 January 1727) and the additional corrections in Ford's interleaved copy. Both the list and the copy are in the Forster Library, South Kensington.

printed; but we have also to bear in mind that his was a name to which inferior matter was too readily attached.

'There is an honest humersom Gentleman here who amuses this Town sometimes with Trifles and some Knave or Fool transmitts them to Curl with a Hint that they are mine.' [1]

There were others who were not so honest. Nothing that passes as his can be accepted without scrutiny. It was a consequence of the pains which he took to remain hidden by having his genuine pieces transcribed in an unknown hand and dropped unseen at the printer's. The penalty of anonymity is false attribution.

He forgot how busy he had been in the Queen Anne days, and much that he remembered to have written then he thought not worth preserving. When Faulkner's edition of his works was being considered, Ford sent him a list of his pamphlets and papers; and he replied:

'In Your Catalogue of Pamphlets there are some I do not remember, I mean, *Journy to Paris*, *Remarks about Greg*, *Peace and Dunkirk*, *Windsor Prophesy*, *Pretenders Letter to a Whig Lord*. I fancy I did not write any of these. And, as for the rest, they were temporary occasional things, that dye naturally with the Change of times, and therefore I do not think any Printer in London, much less here, would concern himself about them.' [2]

Having these views on the wisdom of including 'temporary occasional things' in a collected edition to be issued under the author's name, he was prepared to reject even *The Conduct of the Allies*, so far had twenty years of Dublin removed him from the old world of his ambitions and his power. But we should not have

[1] p. 87.  Cf. *Correspondence*, iii. 125, 126, and 212.    [2] p. 163.

expected him to have no recollection of so many pieces, among them *The Windsor Prophecy*. They had cost him little effort.

Ford had six of Swift's poems in manuscript. Two of them—*The South-Sea* or *The Bubble*, and *To Charles Ford on his Birth-day, 1723*—are in Swift's autograph, and the importance of any original copy need not be emphasized. The others are in the handwriting of Ford. All are printed in this volume at the conclusion of the letters. The editorial problems which they present are described in the introductory notes.

The task of editing a familiar correspondence abounding in references to current events and common acquaintances can never be easy. These letters of Swift have presented a succession of problems which no doubt seem simple when solved; but that so many of them have been solved is largely due to the late Dr. Elrington Ball, both to the information which he made public in his six volumes of Swift's *Correspondence*, and to the information which he personally provided, till within a few weeks of his death, from the stores of his knowledge of Irish social history. Assistance has invariably been given generously, and three other friends must be mentioned in particular. To Sir Charles Firth the editor has never appealed in vain. Mr. Harold Williams, whose edition of *Gulliver's Travels* is soon to be followed by his edition of Swift's Poems, has always been ready to discuss any point, and has read the book in proof. Mr. Herbert Davis has been consulted on matters connected with *The Drapier's Letters*.

Lastly the editor has to thank the owners of the letters which were dispersed by auction and now by their courtesy are in a sense restored to the original collection. They are named in the notes to each letter that they have supplied, whether by photograph, or transcript, or access to the manuscript. They have done Swift a service, and they will have the thanks of all his friends.

D. N. S.

MERTON COLLEGE, OXFORD.

*September,* 1934.

Simple contractions of common words have been expanded when there can be no question of the full spelling; but contractions of which the expanded form is not certain, and all titles, such as L$^d$ for Lord, are given as they are in the manuscript.

# I

London. Nov^br. 12. 1708.

ONE Reason why I can not believe a word of what you say about your self, is because you write to me; for if you were not very ill entertaind, and much in the Spleen, you would neglect me as you did here, except¹ when you were in those Circumstances, which was just all the time that you were neither eating, drinking, sleeping, nor seeing the Opera, and if I had a mind to be rigorous I would substract a good deal even from each of those. When you talk morally about M^rs Tofts,² L^dy Mounthermer,³ and the rest, I think upon what S^t Evremont says of Devotes, that when they call their Sins to mind in order for Repentance, the truth of the Matter is, they take a delight in remembring them.⁴ I laugh at what You say of the glorious Life you led here, when I remember how often You told me it was a Life You wisht to Your Enemyes. But I have observed from my self and others (and I think it the wisest Observation I ever made in my Life) that Men are never more mistaken, than when they reflect upon passt things, and from what they retain in their Memory, compare them with the Present. Because, when we reflect on what is past, our Memoryes lead us onely to the pleasant side, but in present things our Minds are chiefly taken up with reflecting on what we dislike in our Condition. So I formerly used to envy

¹ MS. 'expect'.
² Katherine Tofts, of Drury Lane Theatre.
³ The youngest daughter of Marlborough, Lady Mary Churchill, married 2 March 1705 to Lord Monthermer, who succeeded his father as second Duke of Montagu 9 March 1709.
⁴ 'Une Dévotion nouvelle plaît en tout, jusqu'à parler des vieux Pechés dont on se repent.' Saint-Evremond, *Œuvres Meslées*, 1709, iii. 56 'Que la Dévotion est le dernier de nos Amours'.

B

my own Happiness when I was a Schoolboy, the delicious
Holidays, the Saterday afternoon, and the charming
Custards in a blind Alley; I never considerd the Con-
finement ten hours a day, to nouns and Verbs, the
Terror of the Rod, the bloddy Noses, and broken
Shins.—This is exactly your Case, as I find by your
Recollections, and in short I never knew a more imperfect Repentance, or more agreable to what I expected
from You. Thus much for You, Now for Publick
Affairs. On the Prince's death,[1] the Ministry resolved
to bring L^d Sommers to the Head of the Council, and
[p. 2.] make L^d Wharton|Lieu^t of Ireland, therefore L^d Pemb—
must be made Admirall. The Thing we all reckon is
determind; But L^d Pemb— is unwilling, and would
stave it if he could. If this Scheam holds, either my
Journy to Vienna[2] will vanish, or at least be upon such
a Foot as I would have it, unless my old Friends turn
Courti[e]rs every way, which I shall not wonder at, tho
I do not suspect. If they do, I will return to Laracor,
and in my way talk moralls, and rail at Courts, at
Wood-Park,[3] till You are weary.

To my great Surprise I had tother day a Letter from
M^r Domvil,[4] thô he faithfully promised to write to me.
It was dated from Geneva.

[1] Prince George of Denmark,
consort of Queen Anne, died 28
October 1708.

[2] Swift had hoped to go to
Vienna as Queen's Secretary with
the Earl of Berkeley: see *Correspondence*, ed. Elrington Ball, i.
117, 120, 132. 'I was a little
tempted to pass some time abroad,
until my friends would make me
a little easier in my fortunes at
home. Besides, I had hopes of
being sent in time to some other
Court, and in the meanwhile the

pay would be forty shillings a
day' (letter to Archbishop King,
6 January 1709).

[3] Ford's residence, eleven miles
from Dublin on the road to Trim,
two miles north of Dunboyne.
For a description and illustration
see Sir Frederick Falkiner's essay
on 'The Portraits of Swift',
*Prose Works* ed. Temple Scott,
xii. 68–70.

[4] William Domvile, member
for co. Dublin in the Parliament
of 1715–27, frequently mentioned

Here was some time ago publisht an Essay upon Enthusiasm,[1] which all my Friends would persuade me to have been the Author of; sed ego non credulus illis;[2] For upon my word I was not.  Some other Things people have been fathering on me with as little Truth, for I have publisht nothing since I saw you.

Pray give your self the Trouble of presenting my most humble Service to your Mother and Sister.

If you had told me you began to take a Relish in planting and improving the Scene,[3] I should begin to have favorable Thoughts of your Conversion.

*Address :* For M^r Ford, at M^r Westgarth's
House on Ormond Key
in
                                Dublin
        Ireland

*Added by another hand :* at m^r tody in sheep streete.

*Postmark :* $\frac{NO}{13}$

## II

London. Mar. 8. 170$\frac{8}{9}$

I am of late grown into debt with severall Correspondents, and You among the rest,[4] which I can

in the *Journal to Stella.* Swift heard from him on 10 November and replied on 2 December : see 'List of Letters' in *Correspondence,* i. 382–3.

[1] *A Letter concerning Enthusiasm,* by Shaftesbury, included in his *Characteristicks,* 1711. Swift denies all knowledge of it in the 'Apology' prefixed to *A Tale of a Tub,* 1710.  He imputed it to Ambrose Philips (*Correspondence,* i. 111) and Robert Hunter (*ibid.,* 136).

[2] Virgil, Eclog. ix. 34.

[3] At Woodpark.  Swift had been planting and improving the scene at Laracor ; see Forster, *Life of Swift,* 1875, 121–4.

[4] Swift had heard from Ford on 19 January : see 'List of Letters', *Correspondence,* i. 383.

impute to nothing but my having so little to do which has taken up all my Time, nothing being so great an Engrosser of it as Idleness.  I shall be very far from endeavoring to persuade you that you are not happy; onely I cannot apprehend the Reason of your dating your Happiness from February last year : that being not the Period distinguisht either by your coming to or leaving London.  I believe by this Time you are satisfyed that I am not grown great, nor like to do so very soon : for I am thought to want the Art of being thourow paced in my Party, as all discreet Persons ought to be, and some time this Summer you may not improbably see me alighting at your House in my way to Residence ;[1] and you will find, when I promised to take you into my Family, it was with a politick Design to strengthen my Title of being taken into Yours. Whether I am agreeably entertained here or no, I would not tell you for the World, unless I were assured I should never be blesst again with a Return to Ireland.  I must learn to make my Court to that Country and People better than I have done, thô to lett you into one Secret, (and it is a great one) I doubt at my return I shall pass my Time somewhat different from what I formerly did, wherein I will explain my self no further than by telling you of the humor of a Gentleman I knew, who having eat Grapes in France, never lookt up towards a Vine after he came back for England.  And if you find I pass for a morose Man, find some Excuse or other to vindicate me.  But the fault will not be Ireland's, at least I will persuade my self so ; For I am grown so hard to please, that I am offended with every unexpected Face I meet where I visit, and the least Tediousness or Impertinence gives me a Shortness of Breath, and a Pain in my Stomack. [p. 2.] Among all the Diversions | you mention among you,

---

[1] At Laracor, about two miles south of Trim.

I desire to know whether a Man may be allowed to
sitt alone among his Books, as long as he pleases.
You destroy my Opinion of your Content, by the
abundance of your Moral Reflections, which you may
find have given me the Spleen, and which I observe
men seldom trouble themselves about when they are as
they would be.

The Account you give me of Peoples Inclinations
with relation to the Test, agrees with what I have from
all the best Hands.    I believe little can be attempted
that way among you this Session.    I know not what
may be done in the next Parliament, of which I suppose
you will endeavor to be a Member.[1]

My Journy to Vienna is dropt as you are pleased to
wish. We all advised My L^d Berkeley against it, tho in
my own particular, I should not have disliked it.    I
thought I could be more usefull abroad, than I believe
I shall ever be at home ; and I was not unwilling to
be at as great a Distance as I could from the Factions
of the Age.    My onely dreed was the Ill Payment
from the Court, which might have utterly ruined me.[2]
No, the Report of my Answering Tindall's Book[3] is
a Mistake ; I had some thoughts that way, but they
are long layd aside.

[1] In his *Letter Concerning the
Sacramental Test*, dated 'Dublin,
December the 4th, 1708', Swift
had said that the party in favour
of the repeal of the Test 'will
hardly, I am confident, amount to
above Fifty Men in Parliament,
which can hardly be worked up
into a Majority of Three Hundred' (ed. 1709, p. 16).    He
expected that Wharton would
dissolve the Irish Parliament at
once, but it was not dissolved till
May 1713 ; and at that time

Ford was Gazetteer in London.
[2] See Letter I, p. 2, n. 2.
[3] *The Rights of the Christian
Church asserted against the Romish
and all other Priests*, 1706, followed by a *Defence*, 1707, and a
*Second Defence*, 1708. Swift had
begun an answer after Easter
1707 and before the publication
of the first *Defence*, but he soon
abandoned it.    The fragment he
had written was published by
Faulkner in 1758 as *Remarks upon
a Book intituled The Rights*, &c.

I have had a second Letter from Mr. Domvile,[1] who
is still at Geneva, and tells me, he is grown a Whig in
Point of Government, by observing the Plenty, Spirit,
and Trade, and Improvement wherever Liberty pre-
vails. I approve of his Conversion; and would have
him stick there, without proceeding further. How
liberall you are in your Pity, to bestow it from Dublin
upon him in Geneva, which I am told is the pleasantest
Place almost in Europe to pass away the Time.

Pray present my most humble Service to M[rs] Ford,[2]
and your Sister, and to M[r] Elwood,[3] if he comes in
your way; that is a Man I have an esteem for, and in
my London Phrase, will suffer his Acquaintance.

*Address :* For Charles Ford, Esq[r], at
        Lucas's Coffee-House
        in
                        Dublin
        Ireland

*Postmark :* $\frac{MR}{8}$

## III [4]

London. Sep[tr]. 8. 1711

I HAVE two Letters[5] of yours to acknolidge, one of
a very old date, and when I was going to write, your
second stopt me, because you gave me a Commission

[1] Received 12 February; Swift
replied 31 March. Cf. p. 2, n. 4.
[2] Ford's mother.
[3] John Elwood, sometime Vice-
Provost of Trinity College, Dublin, and University member in
the Parliaments of 1713–14 and
1727–60; died 1740.
[4] The 'List of Letters' (*Corre-*
*spondence,* i. 383–4) shows that
Swift had heard from Ford on
24 April 1709 and replied on
28 April. Both letters are lost.
[5] These two letters also are
lost. Ford had left London for
Ireland at the end of June: see
*Journal to Stella,* 24 June 1711.

in it about your Lotteryes. Ben Took[1] has been out of Town these three weeks, and at last I had no Patience, but was resolved to write to You, and let you know I will obey your Commands when he comes home. The last Lottery you know has been all drawn already; and I am apt to guess that this Curiosity of desiring the Lists[2] is not yours, but a near Relation's of the other Sex; For I cannot imagine what use they will be to You. You know L$^d$ Abercorn's Second Son[3] has got a Prize of 4000$^{ll}$ besides two small ones.—Now to your former Letter, where you say the Publick requires my Leisure. The Publick is a very civil Person, and I am it's humble Servant, but I shall be glad to shake hands with it as soon as I can. Tis probable I may sett out for Ireland about the same Time You begin your Journey here. I tell the great Men so, but they will not believe me. You are in the right as to my Indifference about Irish Affairs, which is not occasioned by my Absence, but contempt of them; and when I return my Indifference will be full as much. I had as live be a Beau in Dublin as a Politician,[4] nay, I had as lieve be an Author there; and if ever I have any thoughts of making a Figure in that Kingdom, it shall be at Laracor.

[1] Benjamin Tooke (*c.* 1642–1716), bookseller at the Middle Temple Gate. He published for Swift the third part of Temple's *Miscellanea*, 1701, and of Temple's *Memoirs*, 1709, and arranged for the publication of the fifth edition of *A Tale of a Tub*, 1710, and *Miscellanies*, 1711 (see his letter to Swift, *Correspondence*, i. 185–6); and Swift got him appointed printer of the *Gazette* in July 1711. He acted for Swift in money transactions (see *Journal to Stella, passim*, and Bodleian

MS. Montagu d. 1. 152).

[2] The amounts of the prizes and the numbers of the successful tickets in the 'Two Million Lottery' drawn at Guildhall from August 1 to 15, 1711, are given in *The Evening Post*, August 4–16. See also the *Gazette*, August 16–18.

[3] The Hon. John Hamilton (1694–1714). Cf. *Journal to Stella*, 29 August 1711.

[4] Cf. *Twelfth Night*, III. ii. 34 —one of Swift's few allusions to Shakespeare.

I will talk Politicks to the Farmers, and publish my
Works at Trim.—Thanks of the Convocation to me !¹
Why, the whole Sett of Bishops except four or five are
angry with me, because the D. of O's merit is lessened.
However they had the Grace to write L$^d$ Tr a Letter of
thanks signed by 17 Bishops: but I was not mentioned.
My L$^d$ Tr lent it me.—I will not say any thing to You
in defence of the A.Bp Dubl—² but I must believe
they were all mistaken, for Raillery is very little understood in Ireland.   You know, you and I do not always
agree in eodem tertio.   One thing is that I never
expect Sincerity from any man; and am no more angry
at the Breach of it, than at the colour of his Hair.
That same A.Bp told me in severall Letters that he
would shortly mention something about my self, which
would be to my Advantage ; I have heard from others
that he resolved to provide for me before any man.
Two days ago he performs his Promise, which consists
of two Parts, first to advise me to get some Preferment
now I have so many Friends.   Secondly, because I
have Parts and Learning, and a happy Pen, he thinks
it my Duty to engage in some usefull Subject of
Divinity untouched by others, which he doubts not,
I should manage with great Success &c.   He was
afraid, I expected something from him : He had got
some other View : and so takes care to undeceive me.³
[p. 2.] Now do | You imagine I take this ill, or think the
worse of him for it ? or would avoid his Company if
I liked it, for such Trifles as this.   Perhaps indeed

---

¹ For his share in procuring
the remission of the First-Fruits.
His memorial to Harley, Earl of
Oxford and Lord Treasurer since
May 1711, is preserved among
the Harley papers (*Portland
Manuscripts*, iv. 609).  See *Corre-*
*spondence,* i. 267–78, and *Journal
to Stella*, 14 August 1711. The remission was granted before Ormond
was declared Lord Lieutenant.
² Archbishop King.
³ King's letter (1 Sept. 1711) is
printed in *Correspondence,* i. 285–6.

I may answer so as to let him see I very well understand him,[1] and so we shall go on as before.

I have been at Windsor these six Sundays past, except one ; and I stayd there once a fortnight together. I go this afternoon[2] again, with L^d Treas^r, and I believe shall continue there a Week ; For our Society[3] meets this day Sennight at M^r Secr^ty's Lodgings there. Was that Society begun before you left us ? I think it was, and so will say nothing of it.— You hear I suppose, that Prior has been in France ; tis certainly true ; and I believe you may reckon that we shall soon have a Peace.[4] How do the Whigs in Ireland relish a Bishop's being L^d Privy Seal ?[5] They rejoice at it here, as a Thing that will one day ly against the present Ministry. We are weary of expecting Removals in the Excise, Customs, &c. yet they say something must be done before the Sessions. I was last night at the Christning of M^r Mashams young Son,[6] L^d Treas^r and L^d Rivers stood Godfathers, and M^rs Hill Godmother, the Dean of Rochester[7] did the

---

[1] Swift answered from Windsor, 1 October 1711 : *Correspondence*, i. 291–2.

[2] Saturday ; he returned to London with Oxford on the Monday, but went back to Windsor the following Saturday with St. John : see *Journal to Stella*.

[3] First mentioned in the *Journal to Stella*, 21 June 1711 : ' It seems, in my absence, they had erected a Club, and made me one ; and we made some laws to-day, which I am to digest or add to.' The *Journal* contains a brief reference to the meeting of Saturday, 15 September 1711, at Mr. Secretary's (i.e.

St. John's) lodgings. Out of the Society grew the Scriblerus Club.

[4] Prior was in Paris negotiating peace, July 12 to 24 : see *Portland Manuscripts*, v. 34–42.

[5] John Robinson (1650–1723), Bishop of Bristol, had been made Lord Privy Seal on 23 April 1711 ; afterwards plenipotentiary at Utrecht, and Bishop of London, 1714.

[6] A fuller account is in the *Journal to Stella*, 7 Sept. 1711.

[7] Samuel Pratt (1659–1723), Dean of Rochester since 1706, and Clerk of the Closet.

Office, there was no other Company but L^d Duplin ¹
and L^d Harley.² It was at Kensington. What abundance of Lords have dyed since You left us. L^d Jersey ³
would have had the Privy seal if he had lived a few
hours longer, the M—rs were a month bringing the
Qu— to consent. She is a little stubborn now and
then, or they would have us think so, thô I believe the
former. She is now in a Fit of the Gout. I find no
body expects she can live long ; and that is one great
Reason why they would hasten a Peace.

I have not time at present to write you more Politicks
nor have you been long enough absent to want much
Information. Tis thought by State Astronomers that
we shall have a scribbling Winter ; but perhaps I shall
then be far enough off. Pray let me know how I am
to direct to You ; I send this inclosed to M^r· Deering,⁴
of whom I am a very humble Servant. M^r· Philips ⁵
goes constantly to L^d T^r's Levee ; and I believe will
get something : I took Occasion to mention him as
favorably as I could. I can give You no account of
the Spectator ; for I never go to a Coffeehouse, and
seldom see them any where else. M^r· Lewis ⁶ is your

---

¹ George Henry Hay, Vis-
count Dupplin (1689–1758), the
Lord Treasurer's son-in-law. He
had married Abigail, Oxford's
younger daughter, in 1709. He
was one of the twelve peers
created at the close of 1711
(Baron Hay of Pedwardine), and
succeeded his father as eighth
Earl of Kinnoull in 1719.

² Edward Harley, the Lord
Treasurer's son.

³ Edward Villiers, first Earl
of Jersey. He died 26 August :
see the *Journal to Stella*.

⁴ Charles Deering, or Dering,

M.P. for Carlingford, 1703–13.

⁵ Ambrose Philips. On 30
June Swift had written in the
*Journal to Stella* : ' This evening
I have had a letter from Mr.
Philips, the pastoral poet, to get
him a certain employment from
Lord Treasurer. I have now had
almost all the Whig poets my
solicitors ; . . . but I will do nothing for Philips ; I find he is
more a puppy than ever, so don't
solicit for him.'

⁶ Erasmus Lewis, Under
Secretary of State at this time to
the Earl of Dartmouth, and from

humble Servant, and talks often of you with great
kindness.   I am at least twice oftner with the M——rs
than when you was here, yet you see nothing comes of
it, nor I believe will ; but every body else pretends to
believe otherwise : And this is all I shall say of my
self.   Adieu.

*Address :* To Charles Ford Esq^r·

## IV^1

Chester.[2] June 7, 1713.

*Written on the way to Dublin.   He speaks of the discomfort of the journey and says,*
If dissolving the Union [3] could be without ill consequence to the Ministry, I should wish for it with all
my heart.   But I have been too long out of London
to judge of politicks.

## V

Laracor.[4]   July. 9. 1713

I AM extreamly obliged to you for writing to me so
often, but I beg you will suspend or leave it off, when
it begins to be too troublesome.   I believe I have had

the beginning of August 1713 to
William Bromley.

[1] This letter, 'one page 4to ',
was exposed for sale at Messrs.
Christie's on 4 June 1896, but
is said to have been 'not sold ',
and has disappeared.   The extract is reprinted from the sale
catalogue.

[2] Swift set out from London
on Monday 1 June, reached
Chester on the 6th, and left for

Holyhead on the 8th : see *Journal
to Stella, ad fin.*

[3] At Chester Swift had received
news, perhaps from Ford as well
as from Erasmus Lewis, of the
motion in the House of Lords on
1 June to bring in a Bill dissolving the Union with Scotland : see
*Correspondence,* ii. 40.

[4] Swift was installed Dean of
St. Patrick's on Saturday 13 June,
and left for Laracor on the 25th.

your 6 Letters, for 3 came here, and I think I left as many in Dublin. I stayd there no longer than Business forced me. I received no Visits but one day, for I was very ill, and I payd none at all, but stole down here to ride and drink bitter Draughts. I am somewhat better, I thank God, but have still a very disordered [1]

I am tempted to think, that if the Tract [2] I left with M$^r$ L— [3] had been published at the time of the Peace, some ill Consequences might not have happened. L$^d$ T— said both to others and my self, that he did not care whether this Parlm$^t$ passt the Commerce or no, and that the next should have the Honor of it. But your Steps are sometimes so odd that I could not account for them while I was among you, much less at this distance, and you change so fast, that whoever is a Month from you is wholly a Stranger to Affairs. [4] I do not at all like the generall Face of them ; and if Domvile [5] would tell you the Advice I gave him you would think me a very desponding Person, and L$^d$ T$^r$ would call me the greatest of his four Cowards [6] if he knew it. A Country Vicar must quote Texts. Two men shall be in the Field, the one shall be taken, [p. 2.] and | the other left ; but how soon, or which shall be taken, and which left, is a shuddering Question. [7] If I am called for this Winter, I will come and take what share my Health will permit me, otherwise I will stay

---

[1] Sentence unfinished ; 'head' ?
[2] The tract afterwards entitled, inaccurately, *The History of the Four Last Years of the Queen*, first published 1758. Cf. letter to Vanessa, 8 July 1713, 'if the thing you know of had been published just upon the peace, the Ministry might have avoided what hath since happened'.
[3] Erasmus Lewis.

[4] The Treaty of Commerce with France was rejected on 18 June by 194 votes to 185. Sir Thomas Hanmer spoke against it and carried about forty votes over to the opposition : see below.
[5] See Letter I, p. 2, n. 4.
[6] Another of Oxford's four cowards was Dartmouth : see *Correspondence*, ii. 65.
[7] Oxford and Bolingbroke.

where I am, and learn by Habitude to render this Country supportable.    Neither shall the Promises I received of a thousand Pounds to pay my debts,[1] draw me over to sollicite, except I am commanded to come. In that Case, I will shew my Courage : though I know the Malice of a victorious Faction would not overlook me.    Atqui sciebat quæ sibi barbarus tortor pararet.[2] I sent the Book to M[rs] Barnard,[3] but I never saw your Mother ; I was not able to do it.    I write this Post to M[r] Manley.[4]    I am apt to think he is too obnoxious, and too much at mercy at present, to do any thing of that kind, if he were disposed to it.    I dare not write more, it is as much as my Head is worth, and that at present is not worth very much ; but my Heart is good, and that must answer for the defects of its Superior, as Servants are forced to do sometimes for their Masters. —S[r] T. Hanmer positively assured me that he was perfectly satisfied with every Part of the Commerce Treaty, after a full hearing of the Arguments for and against it in the House : So that nothing is strange.

*Address, on separate cover :*

To Charles Ford Esq[r]
at His Office at Whitehall
London

*Postmark :* $\frac{IY}{20}$

[1] ' I thought I was to pay but six hundred pounds for the house ; but the Bishop of Clogher says eight hundred pounds ; first-fruits one hundred and fifty pounds, and so, with patent, a thousand pounds in all' (*Journal to Stella*, 23 April 1713) ; cf. *Correspondence*, ii. 32, and *Imita-tion of Horace, Epist.* I. vii.

[2] Horace, *Odes* iii. v. 49, 50.

[3] Perhaps the Mrs. Barnard who was Swift's nurse in his last days : see W. Monck Mason, *Cathedral Church of St. Patrick*, 1820, p. 412.

[4] Isaac Manley, Postmaster-General in Ireland since 1703.

## VI

Laracor.   July. 30. 1713.

I HAD both your Letters.   I here send you inclosed one to L<sup>d</sup> Bol.¹ which you may seal, and get sent to him if it be in the manner you approve.   I hope you may succeed, for M<sup>r</sup> L— may twenty ways do you good Offices in it ; and if you get in, I hope you will prove a Man of Business.   I am still riding in the Country, and I thank God, am much better.   I am not of your Opinion about coming over till I am called ; and called I am not yet, as I think ; for though M<sup>r</sup> L— tells you the Ministry desire it, it does not so absolutely appear to me.²   You may be sure I should be glad to come on many Accounts, and because I should hope they would perform their Promises in giving me money to pay my Debts.   I alway[s] intended to come in October ; but not sooner without sending for.   My Service to all Friends.

I am [of] your Opinion about the Chancellor.³   I believe he is yet very happy, for his Longings were violent.

I write this Post to M<sup>r</sup> L—.⁴

*No address.*

¹ The letter to Bolingbroke appears not to be extant, and the post that Ford sought is not known.

² In a letter to Swift written on the same day Erasmus Lewis said, ' My Lord Treasurer desires you will make all possible haste over, for we want you extremely '. He wrote again more strongly on 6 August.   Swift set sail from Dublin on Saturday 29 August, and reached London on Tuesday 9 September.

³ The Lord Chancellor of Ireland, Sir Constantine Phipps, appointed 1710.   He had been counsel for Sacheverell.

⁴ Lewis would appear to have destroyed all the letters he received from Swift.   In January 1715 he wrote to Swift, ' if you have not already hid your papers in some private place in the hands of a trusty friend, I fear they will fall into the hands of our enemies '.

## VII

PRAY be so kind to direct the inclosed[1] to the Reverend M[r] Archdeacon Wall, over against the Hospitall in Queen-street Dublin. I hope they sent you my Scrutore. I gave the Key of it at Oxford to M[r] Trap,[2] to deliver to You. I am going on with the Discourse of which you saw the Beginning[3]; but not a Word of it for your Life. Did I steal away without telling you? No I remember I told you where to direct to me. I am at a Parsons House 52 miles from You,[4] putting some Papers in order. And you may be as mad as you all please for me. I write this Post to M[r] L—. I drink nothing but ale, and read and write and walk all day. I reckon I shall get the Spleen, but that is nothing.

[1] Printed in *Correspondence*, ii. 147–9. The Rev. Thomas Wall, or Walls, Archdeacon of Achonry, and vicar of Castleknock; he assisted Swift in the management of his affairs in Dublin.

[2] Joseph Trapp, the first Professor of Poetry at Oxford 1708–18, chaplain to Sir Constantine Phipps 1710, and, through Swift's influence, chaplain to Bolingbroke 1712 (*Journal to Stella*, 17 July 1712).

[3] *Some Free Thoughts upon the Present State of Affairs*, first printed in 1741. See Letter IX, *ad init.*

[4] 'I was six weeks compassing the great work of leaving London, and did it at last abruptly enough' (*Correspondence*, ii. 147). Swift arrived in Oxford on Monday, 31 May, and left on 3 June for the rectory of Letcombe Bassett

on the Downs near Wantage (*Portland Manuscripts*, vii. 185–6). He remained at Letcombe till 16 August. The parson was John Geree (1672–1761), who is said to have 'lived formerly in Sir William Temple's family'; a Fellow of Corpus Christi College, he was appointed to the college living of Letcombe in 1707 and held it till 1761. On 8 June Swift wrote to Vanessa, 'I am at a clergyman's house, an old friend and an acquaintance whom I love very well; but he is such a melancholy thoughtful man, partly from nature, and partly by a solitary life, that I shall soon catch the spleen from him' (*Correspondence*, ii. 142). Geree ran a 'school' for young gentlemen and at this time had 'only four, besides a nephew' staying with him (id. 135).

I long till your Session is over, but what have I to do with Politicks.   Our Strawberryes are ruined for want of rain, and Our Parsons Pigs have done ten Shillings worth of Mischief upon Goodman Dickens's Corn.   Tis thought the Tyth-farmer must answer for it.   I was tother day to see Parson Hunsden [1] at lower Letcomb. He is very ill with a Ptisick, but his Wife looks strong and lusty.   Will you have any more of this ?   Well, Chuse, and adieu.   I sent last Post a Letter to J. Barb— [2] under your Cover.

June 12th 1714.

Our publick news is that Princess Sophia is dead. [3]

*Address :* To Charles Ford Esq[r], at
His Office at White-hall
London

*Postmarks :* W[ant]age *and* $\frac{11}{IV}$

## VIII

Jun. 16. 1714

I THANK you kindly for your Letter, it was welcom because it came from You, but I value not your News a farthing, nor any publick You can tell me.   I hear you grow madder and madder ; that I can know at the distance I am.   I would ensure a Pitcher for a year that a child carryes nine times a day to a Well, sooner than

[1] John Hunsdon (1649–1715), of Queen's College, Oxford, vicar of Letcombe Regis since 1676. He died in the following March.

[2] John Barber (1675–1740), Swift's printer, Lord Mayor 1733.

[3] She had died 28 May.

your M—ry. Trap has the Key of my Ecritoire, and was desired to give it you.    Pray God bless you—adieu.

I write this Post to M^r. L. D^r A.,^1 and others.

*Address:* To Charles Ford Esq^r, at
His Office at Whitehall
London

*Postmark :* $\frac{18}{IV}$

## IX

HERE it is,^2 read it, and send it to B—^3 by an unknown hand, have nothing to do with it, thô there be no Danger.    Contrive he may not shew it M^r L— yet how can you do that ?    For I would not have him know that you or I had any concern in it.    Do not send it by the Penny post, nor your Man, but by a Porter when you are not at your Lodgings.    Get some Friend to copy out the little Paper, and send it inclosed with the rest, and let the same Hand direct it, and seal it with an unknown Seal.    If it be not soon printed, send to Dunstons ^4 in the name desired.—Spend an hour in reading it, and if the same word be too soon repeated, vary it as you please, but alter your Hand. adieu. Jul. 1. 1714.    I would fain have it sent on Saterday night, or Sunday ^5 because of the date, that it might not be

---

^1 The letter to Dr. Arbuthnot is printed in Aitkin's *Life of Arbuthnot,* 1892, 61–3, and in *Correspondence,* ii. 152–3 ; the letter to Lewis is not known.

^2 *Some Free Thoughts upon the Present State of Affairs.* For reasons shown in the subsequent letters, the text that was printed in 1741 differs seriously from what Swift sent to Ford.

^3 Barber, the printer.

^4 St. Dunstan's Coffee-house, Fleet Street.

^5 Sunday was 4 July.

suspected to come from here.   If you think any thing in the little Letter suspicious, alter it as you please.

*Address :*  To Charles Ford Esq<sup>r</sup>
at His Office at White-Hall
London

*Postmarks :*  Wantage *and* $\frac{2}{IY}$

## X[1]

# (Ford to Swift)

London July 6.

I<small>F</small> B.[2] be not a very great Blockhead, I shall soon send you a letter in print, in answer to your last.   I hope it may be next post, for he had it on Sunday.   I took care to blot the e's out of on*e*ly, and the a's out of Sche*a*me, which I suppose is the meaning of your question whether I corrected it.   I don't know any other alteration it wanted, and I made none except in one Paragraph that I chang'd the present to the past tence four times, and I am not sure I did right in it neither.   There is so great a tenderness and regard shewn all along to the —[3] that I could have wish'd this expression had been out, [the uncertain timorous nature of the—]   But there was no striking it out without quite spoiling the beauty of the passage, and as if I had been the Author myself, I preferr'd beauty to discretion.   I really think it is at least equal to any thing you have writ, and I dare say it will do great service as matters stand at present.   The

[1] British Museum, Add. MS. 4804, ff. 181–2 *v.*; first printed by Hawkesworth, *Letters*, vol. i, 1766.
[2] Barber.  Swift has written

'arber' above the line.
[3] The Queen.  The 'expression' is not found in the printed text of 1741.

Collonel [1] and his friends give the game for lost on their side, and | I believe by next week we shall see L. B.[2] at the [p. 2.] head of affairs.    The B$^p$. of Roc—r [3] is to be L$^d$ Privy Seal.    They talk of several other alterations as that my L$^d$ Trevor is to be President of the Council, L$^d$ Abingdon Chamberlain, L$^d$ Anglesey L$^d$ L$^t$ of Ireland, that M$^r$ Bromley is to go out, and a great many more in lesser employments.    I fancy these reports are spred to draw in as many as they can to oppose the new Scheme.    I can hardly think any body will be turn'd out of the Cabinet, except the T—r, and the P—y S—l.[4]    Perhaps my L$^d$ Pau—t [5] may lay down.    Certainly the Sec—ry[6] may continue in if he pleases, and I don't hear that he is dispos'd to resign, or that he is so attach'd to any Minister, as to enter into their resentments.    What has John of Bucks [7] done ? and yet the report is very strong, that he is to be succeeded by my L$^d$ T—or.    The Duke of Shrewsbury was one out of eight or nine Lords, that stood by my L$^d$ Bol—ke yesterday in the debate about the Spanish Treaty, and spoke with a good deal of spirit. Is it likely he is to be turn'd out of all ? The Lords have made a Representation to the Queen, in which they desire her to surmount the insurmountable difficultys the Spanish Trade lyes under by the last Treaty.[8]    It is

[1]  The Earl of Oxford.
[2]  Lord Bolingbroke.
[3]  Atterbury.
[4]  The Earl of Dartmouth, Lord Privy Seal.
[5]  Earl Poulett, Lord Steward of the Household.
[6]  William Bromley, Secretary of State (Southern Department).
[7]  The Duke of Buckingham, Lord President of the Council.
[8]  On 2 July the Lords took into consideration the three explanatory articles which had been added at Madrid to the Treaty of Commerce with Spain signed at Utrecht, and for which Bolingbroke and Arthur Moore were mainly responsible; and after a long debate, in which Oxford said that the articles were not beneficial, it was resolved 'to address her Majesty, that she would be pleased to cause all the papers relating to the negociation of the treaty of commerce with Spain to be laid before them, together with the names of the

thought there was a Majority in the House to have
[p. 3.] prevented such a Reflection upon the | Treaty, if they had
come to a division.  The clamour of the Merchants, Whig
and Tory, has been too great to have pass'd a Vote in
vindication of it, as it stands ratifyed, but my L^d
Anglesey and his Squadron seem'd willing to oppose
any censure of it, and yet this Representation was
suffer'd to pass no body knows how.  To day they are
to take into consideration the Queen's answer to their
Address, desiring to know who advis'd her to ratify the
Explanation of three Articles.   She sent them word she
thought there was little difference between that, and
what was sign'd at Utrecht.   When they rise, I will
tell you what they have done.   The last money Bill
was sent up yesterday, so that in all probability the
Parliament will be up in two or three days,¹ and then
we shall be entertain'd with Court Affairs.   I hope you
got mine last post, and one a fortnight ago.   Will the
change of the Ministry affect Elwood² ?   He is in pain
about it, and I am told the people of Ireland are making
a strong opposition against the present Provost.

The consideration of the Queen's answer is deferr'd
till to morrow.   I am now with my L^d Guildford,³ and
three other Commissioners of Trade, who were examin'd

persons who advised her Majesty
to that treaty'.   The Queen's
answer was reported on the 5th,
but was regarded by many as un-
satisfactory, whereupon it was
agreed that 'a representation be
made to her Majesty, to lay before her the insuperable difficulties
that attended the Spanish trade,
on the foot of the late treaty'.
See Boyer's *Political State*, July
1714, pp. 564–72.
¹ Parliament was prorogued
on 9 July.

² See Letter II, p. 6, n. 3.  He
hoped to succeed Dr. Benjamin
Pratt, Provost of Trinity College,
Dublin.   Pratt was then in
London, waiting in vain for a
bishopric.
³ Francis North, second Baron
Guilford, President of the Board
of Trade.   No reason for 'rapture' is discoverable in the report
of the examination of Moore and
the other Commissioners given
in the *Political State*.

to day at the Bar of the H: of L^ds.  They are prodigiously
| pleas'd with what has been done, but I don't under- [p. 4.]
stand it well to give you an account, for the rapture they
are in hinders them from explaining themselves clearly.
I can only gather from their manner of discourse that
they are come off without censure.

*No address.*
*Notes in Swift's writing* :
    (*at beginning*) M^r Ford ^1
                 Affairs go Worse—
    (*on p.* 4)  Jul. 6. 1714
                 Ch— F—


## XI ^2

# (Ford to Swift)

London July 10

WHAT answer shall I send?  I am against any
alteration, but additions I think ought by no means to
be allow'd.   I wish I had call'd sooner at S^t Dunstan's,
but I did not expect it would have come out till
thursday, and therefore did not go there till yesterday.
Pray let me know what you would have done.   B.^3 was
a Blockhead to shew it at all, but who can help that ?
Write an answer either for yourself or me, but I beg
of you to make no condescentions.

    Yesterday put an end to the Session and to your pain.
We gain'd a glorious victory in the House of Lords the
day before.   The attack was made immediately against
A. M—re, who appear'd at the Bar with the other

---

^1 'Ford' after 'Lewis' crossed    4804, ff. 183–4; printed by
out.                         Hawkesworth, 1766.
  ^2 British Museum, Add. MS.    ^3 Barber.

[p. 2.] Commissioners of Trade. The South Sea Company | had prepar'd the way ¹ by voting him guilty of a Breach of trust, and uncapable of serving them in any office for the future. This passed without hearing what he had to say in his defence, and had the usual fate of such unreasonable reflections. Those who propos'd the resolutions were blam'd for their violence, and the person accus'd appearing to be less guilty than they made him, was thought to be more innocent than I doubt he is. The Whigs propos'd two Questions in the H: of L^ds against him and lost both, one by 12 and the other I think by 18 votes.

Court affairs go on as they did. The cry is still on the Captain's ² side. Is not he the person B. means by one of the best pens in England? It's only my own conjecture, but I can think of no body else. Have you [p. 3.] the Queen's Speech, the L^ds Address &c. or | shall I send them you, and do you want a comment? Have Pope and Parnell been to visit you as they intended? ³ I had a letter yesterday from Gay who is at the Hague,⁴ and presents his humble service to you. He has writ to M^r Lewis too but his respect makes him keep greater distance with him, and I think mine is the pleasanter letter, which I am sorry for. We were alarm'd by B. two days ago. He sent Tooke word our friend was ill in the country, which we did not know how to interpret till he explain'd it. It was M^rs M—⁵ he meant, but she

---

¹ 'for a censure' crossed out after 'way'. The action of the South Sea Company is described in the *Political State*.

² Bolingbroke's.

³ Pope and Parnell went over from Binfield to Letcombe on Sunday 4 July, and stayed with Swift some days. Pope describes the visit in an amusing letter

written to Arbuthnot on 11 July.

⁴ Gay was now Secretary to Lord Clarendon, envoy extraordinary to Hanover. They reached the Hague on 4 July, and left it for Amsterdam on the 8th. Gay's letter to Ford is printed on p. 221, but it does not mention Swift.

⁵ Mrs. Manley, author of *The New Atlantis*, Swift's successor on

is in no danger.   Pray write immediately, that there may be no further delay to what we ought to have had a week ago.

*No address.*
*Note in Swift's writing (p. 4):* M^r F—d.
℞ Jul. 12
1714


*Enclosure* ^1

Lambeth Hill, July 6. 1714.

S^R

I thankfully acknowledge the receipt of a Packet sent last Sunday : I have shewn it only to one Person, who is charm'd with it, and will make some small Alterations and Additions to it, with your leave : You will the easier give leave, when I tell you, that it is one of the best Pens in England.   Pray favour me with a Line. I am

S^r Yr most Obedient Serv^t
Jn°. Barber

*Address :* To Samuel Bridges,^2 Esq^r;
at S^t. Dunstan's Coffee-house
Fleet-street

*Notes in Swift's writing (p. 4):* July. 6^th. 1714
J— B—r, Letter
about the Pamphlet
*and* B—r

Jul. 6. 1714.

*The Examiner.* She was now living in poverty at Finchley : see her two letters to Oxford, 14 June and 30 August 1714, *Portland Manuscripts,* v. 458, 491, and

*Life of John Barber,* Curll, 1741, pp. 24, 44.
^1 British Museum, Add. MS. 4804, f. 175.
^2 Ford's pseudonym.

## XII

July. 11. 1714

I THANK you for your long kind Letters. B—[1] writt to me since, but took no notice of any thing come to his hand, perhaps he will not venture without advice, and advice will ruin it. Why did you not blot out whatever you had a Mind ; as for Service it will do, a Fiddlestick. It will vex them, and that's enough. Your Letters will make good Memoirs ; I have putt up your last among my Papers, I have had all you sent me before.[2]—No, I hope and belive Elwood [3] will be safe ; but who knows any thing in such a Confusion. Some of the Changes you mention, were what we were scheaming severall months ago ; particularly that of L^d Tr—or and upon second reading, I think none else ; for the rest seems wild to me, but strange things may happen in our land in less than six weeks.
The inclosed. To the Rev^rd M^r Archdeacon Wall
over against the Hospitall in Queen Street
Dublin.[4]

Wall tells me Parvisol [5] is playing the Rogue with me in my Accounts, and run in great Arrears. I shall be ruined with staying here.

*Address :* To Charles Ford Esq^r,
at His Office at White-hall
London

*Postmarks :* Wantage *and* $\frac{12}{IY}$

[1] Barber's letter, 6 July, is printed in *Correspondence*, ii. 172–3.

[2] Ford's letter of 6 July, the first now preserved. The letter of 10 July had not yet been received.

[3] See Letter X, p. 20, n. 2.

[4] This letter, 3 July, is printed in *Correspondence*, ii. 164–6.

[5] Isaiah Parvisol, appointed by Swift on 16 May 1713, as 'my Proctor to sett and let the Tyths of the Deanery of St. Patricks' :

## XIII [1]

# (Ford to Swift)

London July 15. 1714.

You see I was in the right; but I could wish the booby had not convinced me by naming my Lord Bolingbroke,[2] and then I should have dealt well enough with him. Since it has happened so, the best remedy I could think of, was to write him a very civil answer; in which, however, I have desired to see the alterations: this is mentioned with great respect to my Lord. Though he is promised to have it again to-morrow, it is probable he may be disappointed, and there may be time enough for me to receive your directions what I shall do, when I get it into my hands. If the alterations are material, shall I send it to some other printer as it was first written? Reflect upon every thing you think likely to happen, and tell me beforehand what is proper to be done, that no more time may be lost. I hate the dog for making his court in such a manner.

I am very sorry you have had occasion to remove your premier minister.[3] We are told now, we shall have no change in ours, and that the Duke of Shrewsbury will perfectly reconcile all matters. I am sure you will not believe this any more than I do; but the Dragon [4]

see *Journal to Stella*, 16 May 1713. For 'Wall', see Letter VII, p. 15, n. 1.

[1] Original not known; printed by Deane Swift, *Letters*, 1768.

[2] Ford must have enclosed a second letter from Barber.

[3] Parvisol; see Letter XII, p. 24, n. 5.

[4] 'The Dragon, Lord Treasurer Oxford, so called by the Dean, by Contraryes, for he was the mildest, wisest and best Minister that ever served a Prince'—Note by Swift on a letter from Erasmus Lewis, 17 July 1714 (Brit. Mus. Add. MS. 4804, f. 189).

has been more chearful than usual for three or four days ; and therefore people conclude the breaches are healed. I rather incline to the opinion of those who say he is to be made a Duke, and to have a pension. Another reason given why there is to be no change is, because the Parliament was not adjourned to issue new writs in the room of those who were to come in upon the new scheme, that they might sit in the House at the next meeting. But I can't see why an adjournment may not do as well at the beginning as at the end of a session ; and certainly it will displease less in January or February, than it would have done in July. The Whigs give out the Duke of Marlborough[1] is coming over, and his house is actually now fitting up at St. James's. We have had more variety of lies of late than ever I remember. The history we were formerly talking of would swell to a prodigious size, if it was carried on.[2] There was a fire last night on Tower-Hill,[3] that burnt down forty or fifty houses. You say nothing of coming to town. I hope you don't mean to steal away to Ireland without seeing us.

[1] Marlborough and the Duchess were reported in the newsapers to be at Ostend on 18 July. They landed at Dover on 2 August, and arrived in London on Wednesday 4 August.

[2] Swift supplemented his *History of the Four Last Years of the Queen* (see Letter V, p. 12, n. 1) by writing *Memoirs relating to that Change which happened in the Queen's Ministry in the year 1710*, dated October 1714, printed 1765, and *An Enquiry into the Behaviour of the Queen's Last Ministry*, dated June 1715, but finished 1721, and printed 1765. See Letter XV, p. 29, n. 4, and Letter XXXIX, p. 93, n. 3.

[3] 'This morning about Two of the Clock a Dreadful Fire began at a Cane Chair-Makers in Gravel Lane in Hounds-Ditch, they being Boiling of Varnish ; and before it could be Extinguished Burnt down near 20 of those Houses, besides 5 next the Street in Hounds-Ditch.' — *Dawks's News Letter*, 15 July 1714. *The Evening Post* says 'above Thirty Houses, besides many more very much damaged'.

## XIV[1]
# (Ford to Swift)

London July 17. 1714.

A SECOND to-morrow is almost past, and nothing has been yet left at St. Dunstan's. B.[2] will lose by his prodigious cunning; but that is nothing to the punishment he deserves. Had it been only his fear, he would have chosen somebody else to consult with; but the rogue found out it was well written, and saw the passages that galled. I am heartily vext at the other person, from whom one might have expected a more honourable proceeding. There is something very mean in his desiring to make alterations, when I am sure he has no reason to complain, and is at least as fairly dealt with as his competitor. Besides, a great part of it is as much for his service as if he had given directions himself to have it done. What relates to the Pretender is of the utmost use to him;[3] and therefore I am as much surprized at his delay, as at his ungenerous manner of treating an unknown author, to whom he is so much obliged. But perhaps I may wrong him, and he won't desire to turn the whole to his own advantage. If it had come to me yesterday, or to-day, I was resolved to have sent it to some other printer without any amendment; but now I shall wait till I have your directions. I wish you had employed somebody else at first; but what signifies wishing now? After what

[1] Original not known; printed by Deane Swift, *Letters*, 1768.

[2] Barber; the 'other person' is Bolingbroke.

[3] e.g. 'He is likewise said to be of weak intellectuals, and an unsound constitution.' Neither Swift nor Ford knew that Bolingbroke was at this time treating with the Pretender. Swift did not doubt 'the security of the Protestant Succession in the House of Hanover'.

B. writ in his last, I can hardly think he will be such a —— as not to let me have it : and in my answer I have given him all manner of encouragement to do it. He has as much assurance as he can well desire, that the alterations shall be complied with, and a positive promise that it shall be returned to him the same day he leaves it at St. Dunstan's.

I can't imagine why we have no mischief yet. Sure we are not to be disappointed at last, after the bustle that has been made. It is impossible they [1] can ever agree, and I want something to make my letters still entertaining. I doubt you will hardly thank me for them, now the parliament is up ; but as soon as any thing happens you shall know it.

The Queen has not yet appointed the time for removing to Windsor. My Lord Chief Baron Ward [2] is dead, and we have already named seven successors, among whom is our Lord Chancellor Phips. Frank Annesley was to have had his place under my Lord Anglesey,[3] so that it is well for him we have provided him with another for life.

---

[1] Oxford and Bolingbroke.

[2] Sir Edward Ward, Chief Baron of the Exchequer since 1695. He was succeeded by Sir Samuel Dodd.

[3] Anglesey was expected to succeed Shrewsbury as Lord Lieutenant of Ireland : see Letter X, and *Portland Manuscripts*, vii. 192. Phipps (Letter VI, p. 14, n. 3) was succeeded as Lord Chancellor by Alan Brodrick, and returned to practice at the English bar. Francis Annesley (1663–1750), who was Anglesey's cousin, was a Bencher of the Inner Temple, and at this time M.P. for Westbury ; in May 1711 he promoted the Bill for the building of the fifty new churches in London, and saw it through the House of Commons, and thereafter he was one of the Commissioners for the building of the churches.

XV

July. 18<sup>th</sup>. 1714

HERE's a Splutter with your nasty Pamphlet ; I fancy, one of L<sup>d</sup> B—'s alterations will be to soften a Particular that seems to fall hard upon him : *Whether others have not contended for a greater Part in the Direction of Affairs* &c., *than either Friendship, Gratitude, or*¹ &c. The Word *Gratitude* seems hard there, and may be left out ; but I will not have any thing harder on the Dragon than it is ; and if you dislike the Alterations, take back the Thing, and either burn it or send it to some other Printer as you think best. If the last, leave out the Word *Gratitude*, and let all the rest be as at first except what you think fit to change, for I rely altogether on your Judgment ; and will not write one word more about it, say what you will. The D— of Shr— would certainly be a proper man to reconcile People, but I doubt it is too far gone : The D— would make a great Figure in doing it ; but he wants the Circumstances of Courage and Truth. L<sup>d</sup> Bol— writt to me last Post ² and hints quite otherwise that Things are as bad as ever, or worse ; so he did in an Ironicall message he sent me by B—r.³ Barb— has writt to me thrice this last week and never said a Word of the Pamphlet, so I hope neither he nor L<sup>d</sup> B— smoak. As to my coming to Town, I have no Thoughts of it, unless they send for me, as I am sure they will not ; or unless they make me Historg<sup>r</sup> ⁴

---

¹ This passage is not in the printed text.

² Letter of 13 July, *Correspondence*, ii. 177–8.

³ In Barber's Letter of 6 July, *Correspondence*, ii. 172–3.

⁴ Swift had thoughts of the office of Historiographer Royal as early as 1710 (letter to Addison, 22 August 1710). Thomas Rymer, who had succeeded Shadwell, died on 14 December 1713, a few months after completing the fifteenth volume of his monumental *Fædera* ; and on 5 January Bolingbroke wrote to

which I am sure they never think of, and I shall not ask. I intend to take a Ramble into Herefordshire &c.[1] about a fortnight hence, and for ought I know to Ireland about Michalmas. The Letter I writt to the Dragon[2] was in the Style of a Parting. He has shewn [p. 2.] | it to D$^r$ Arb$^t$— and pretends to be pleased with it: I nippt him a little in it. I believe you never paid the Sempstress in Westminster hall, nor took my Hankerchiefs. I ow her 3 or 4 shillings of an old Debt. She must stay till next Sessions like her Betters.

M$^r$ L—[3] writes me word that 50$^{ll}$ should be got from

the Duke of Shrewsbury urging Swift's claims. On 15 April Swift himself addressed a Memorial to the Queen, 'humbly desiring her Majesty will please to appoint him her historiographer'. On 17 July Arbuthnot reported that he had spoken to Lady Masham to ensure that the Queen should have a right notion of his application, and had spoken also to Bolingbroke. But the post had by this time been filled by the appointment, on 12 July (Brit. Mus. Addit. MS. 4572, f. 108), of Thomas Madox, author of *The History and Antiquities of the Exchequer of the Kings of England*, 1711. Swift, who had been satirizing the follies of antiquaries in the *Memoirs of Scriblerus*, knew nothing of the merits of Madox's great work; in a letter to Vanessa (1 August) he spoke of Madox as 'a worthless rogue that nobody knows'. As his Memorial and his correspondence show, his own work as Historiographer would have been a History of his Own

Times, and in particular of the later years of Queen Anne. See Letter XIII, p. 26, n. 2.

[1] Swift had planned 'a ramble for some weeks about Herefordshire', on his way back to Ireland. His grandfather had been vicar of Goodrich in that county; and Brampton Castle, the Earl of Oxford's seat, was another attraction. When Oxford was expected to retire to Brampton on his fall, Swift arranged to visit him; but neither the visit nor the ramble took place (*Correspondence*, ii. 163, 166, 198, 209).

[2] On 3 July 1714. He 'nipped' in this admirable letter when he said 'in your public capacity you have often angered me to the heart, but as a private man never once'. Arbuthnot wrote on 10 July that 'the Dragon shewed me your letter, and seemed mightily pleased with it' (*Correspondence*, ii. 160, 175).

[3] Erasmus Lewis: see Letter XXIII, p. 51, l. 7, and *Correspondence*, ii. 157.

the Secr^tys to finish that Troublesom Business you know of. I have desired D^r A— to speak to L^d B. for his part,[1] and it would be kind in M^r L— to speak to M^r Bromly for tother part. What can I do? I have no money; and I think it would be hard if they do not sett me right in such a Trifle as they promisd.

Upon second thoughts, how comicall a Thing was it to shew that Pamphlet to L^d Bol— of all men living. Just as if *the Publick Spirit* had been sent to Argyle for his Approbation[2]—adieu.

*Address:* To Charles Ford Esqr
    at his Office at White-hall
        London

*Postmarks:* Wantage *and* $\frac{19}{IY}$

## XVI[3]

# (Ford to Swift)

London July 20

WHO would ever do any thing for them, when they are so negligent of their own interest? The Captain must see what use it would be to him to have it publish'd, and yet he has not return'd it. You have another copy

---

[1] Arbuthnot replied on 17 July that he had spoken to Bolingbroke: 'As to the fifty pounds, he was ready to pay it; and if he had had it about him, would have given it me.'

[2] In *The Publick Spirit of the Whigs* Swift had dealt with his old friend the Duke of Argyle and the Scottish peers who were for dissolving the Union, in four paragraphs which brought the printer (Barber) and publisher (Morphew) into trouble and had to be cancelled. See *Life of Barber*, Curll, 1741, pp. 5–7.

[3] British Museum, Add. MS. 4804, ff. 193–4; printed by Hawkesworth, 1766.

by you, I wish you would send it, and if you don't care
it should appear in your own hand, I will get it transcrib'd.
My Secretary is a boy of ten or eleven years old, and no
discovery can be made by him.   I don't know what my
L$^d$ Bo— may do, but I dare say Bar— do's not suspect
from whence it comes.   However I wonder he has not
mention'd it to you.

I thought you had heard the Historiographer's place
had been dispos'd of this fortnight.   I know no more
of him who has it, than that his name is Madocks.   It
would be imprudence in them to send for you, but
[p. 2.] I hope you will come.   A reconcilement | is impossible,
and I can guess no reason why matters are delay'd,
unless it be to gain over some Lords who stick firm to
the Dragon, and others that are averse to the Captain.
The D. of S—y declares against him in private conversation, I suppose because he is against every chief Minister,
for it's known he has no kindness for the Collonel.
L$^d$ Ang— rails at the Chancelor, for some opinion the
Attorney and Solicitor G$^l$. have given relating to Ireland.[1]
Who can act, when they have so much caprice to deal
with.

M$^r$ L. says he will speak to M$^r$ Bromley for his
part, and will engage it shall be paid as soon as L$^d$
Bolingbroke has given his.[2]   But it was mention'd before
my L$^d$ Treasurer, and he immediately took the whole
upon himself.   If they liv'd near one another, and
a house between them was on fire, I fancy they would
contend who should put it out, till the whole street was
burnt.   M$^r$ L— goes into Wales[3] the week after the

[1] On the question whether the
Lord Mayor of Dublin (Tory)
could hold office for another year,
the Corporation (Whig) having
refused to elect as his successor
any of his three nominees.   See
*Correspondence,* ii. 72, 101, 122;
*Portland Manuscripts,* v. 370,
473; and Elrington Ball, *The
Judges in Ireland,* ii. 48–50.

[2] See Letter XV, p. 31, n. 1.

[3] Lewis belonged to Abercothy

next.   I shall have the whole Town to myself.   Now
it's my own, I begin not to value it.   Pope and Parnell
tell me you design them a visit.[1]   When do you go?
If you are with them | in the middle of a week, I should [p. 3.]
be glad to meet you there.   Let me know where you
are to be in Herefordshire, and I will send you some
claret.   It is no compliment, for I am overstock'd, and
it will decay before I drink it.   You shall have either
old or new, I have too much of both.   I paid the
woman for your handkerchiefs, but should not have
given her so much, if she had not assur'd me you agreed
with her.   I think you may very well strike off the old
debt, and she will have no reason to complain.   So
I told her, but if you would have me I will pay her.

Pray send me the other copy,[2] or put me in a way
of recovering the former.

*No address.*
*Note in Swift's writing (p. 4):* ℞ Jul. 22. 1714
Ch— F—

## XVII [3]

# (Ford to Swift)

London July 22[d].

PRAY send me the other copy, and let us have the
benefit of it, since you have been at the trouble of
writing.   Unless ———[4] be serv'd against his will, it is

in Caermarthen.  On 6 July he
had written to Swift, 'I believe
I shall not go to Abercothy, otherwise I would attend you' (to
Herefordshire presumably), and
had asked if they could meet at
Bath in August.

[1] At Binfield; see Letter XI,
p. 22, n. 3.
[2] Of *Some Free Thoughts.*
[3] British Museum, Add. MS.
4804, ff. 199–200; printed by
Hawkesworth, 1766.
[4] Bolingbroke.

not like to be done at all, but I think you us'd to take
a pleasure in good Offices of that kind, and I hope you
won't let the cause suffer, tho I must own in this
particular, the person who has the management of it,
do's not deserve any favour.   Nothing being left for
me at St. D—n's, I sent to B.[1] for an answer to my
last.   He says it is not yet restor'd to him, as soon as
it is, I shall have it.   This delay begins to make me
think all Ministers are alike, and as soon as the Captain
is a Collonel, he will act as his Predecessors have done.

[p. 2.]    | The Queen goes to Windsor next tuesday,[2] and we
expect all matters will be setled before that time.   We
have had a report, that my L^d P—y S—l [3] is to go out
alone, but the learned only laugh at it.   The Captain's
friends think themselves secure, and the Collonel's are
so much of the same opinion that they only drink his
health while he is yet alive.   However it's thought he
will fall easy with a pension of 4000 a year, and a
Dukedom.   Most of the stanch Torys are pleas'd with
the alteration, and the Whimsicals [4] pretend the cause
of their disgust was because the Whigs were too much
favour'd.   In short we propose very happy days to ourselves as long as this Reign lasts, and if the *uncertain
timorous nature of* —— [5] do's not disappoint us, we have

---

[1] Barber, the printer.

[2] 27 July.   She did not leave
London; on that day she was
present at the protracted meeting
of Council at which Oxford
ended his political career.

[3] Dartmouth.

[4] The group led by Sir
Thomas Hanmer: see Letter V,
p. 12, n. 3.   Cf. Swift's *Some Free
Thoughts* : 'that race of politicians, who in the cant phrase are
called the *Whimsicals*, was never

so numerous, or at least so active,
as it hath been since the great
change at court; many of those
who pretended wholly to be in
with the principles upon which
Her Majesty and her new servants
proceeded, either absenting themselves with the utmost indifference, in those conjunctures where-
on the whole cause depended, or
siding directly with the enemy'.

[5] See Letter X, *ad init.*

a very fair prospect. The Dragon and his Antagonist meet every day at the Cabinet : they often eat, and drink, and walk together as if there was no sort of disagreement, | and when they part, I hear they give one [p. 3.] another such names, as no body but Ministers of State could bear without cutting throats. The D. of M——gh is expected here every day. Dʳ Garth says he comes only to drink the Bristol waters for a Diabetis.¹ The Whigs are making great preparations to receive him, but yesterday I was offer'd considerable odds that not one of those who go out to meet him, will visit him in half a year. I durst not lay, tho I can hardly think it. My Lᵈ Marr² is marryed to Lʸ Frances Pierrepoint, and my Lᵈ Dorchester³ her father is to be marry'd next week to Lady Bel Bentick. Let me know if you go to Pope's, that I may endeavour to meet you there.

*No address.*
*Note in Swift's writing (p. 4) :* Mʳ F—d
℞ Jul. 24.
1714

---

¹ *Dawks's News Letter* of 20 July had announced that Marlborough was ' expected here in a day or two, designing for the Bath, being something Indisposed '. There was much speculation about his return, which was given out to be delayed by bad health and bad weather. On 31 July *The Weekly Packet* said that he had deferred his return, ' finding the Design for which he was coming over discover'd '. He crossed on the day after the Queen's death. See Letter XIII, p. 26, n. 1.

² The Earl of Mar, appointed third Secretary of State in September 1713, married as his second wife Lady Frances Pierrepoint (sister of Lady Mary Wortley Montagu) on 20 July 1714.

³ The Marquess of Dorchester, created Duke of Kingston 1715, married as his second wife Lady Isabella Bentinck, fifth daughter of the Earl of Portland, on 2 August 1714.

## XVIII [1]

# (Ford to Swift)

London July 24.

WE expected the great affair [2] would have been done
yesterday, and now every body agrees it will be to
night. The Bishop of London,[3] L$^d$ Bathurst,[4] Mr.
Bridges,[5] S$^r$ W$^m$ Wyndham,[6] and Campion,[7] are nam'd
for Commissioners of the Treasury, but I have not
sufficient Authority for you to depend upon it. They
talk of the D: of Ormond for our L$^d$ L$^t$. I can't get
th[e] pamphlet [8] back, what shall I do? I wish y[ou]
would send me the other copy. My L$^d$ Anglesey go's
next monday to Ireland. I hear he is only angry with
the Chan—r, and not at all with the Captain.[9]

*Address :* To the Rev$^d$
        D$^r$ Swift Dean of S$^t$ Patrick's
*No postmark.*
*Notes in Swift's writing (p. 4) :* Mr F—
                    ℞ Jul. 26. 1714
            *and* July. 24$^{th}$. 1714
                    Ch— F—

---

[1] British Museum, Add. MS.
4804, f. 201; printed by
Hawkesworth, 1766.

[2] The dismissal of Oxford,
which did not take place till 27
July. The Treasury was not put
into commission; the Duke of
Shrewsbury succeeded Oxford on
the 30th.

[3] John Robinson. See Letter
III, p. 9, n. 5.

[4] Allen Bathurst, one of the
twelve peers, created 1 January

1712; the friend of Swift and
Pope.

[5] James Brydges, son of Lord
Chandos of Sudeley, created Earl
of Carnarvon October 1714, and
Duke of Chandos 1719; 'the
princely Chandos', the supposed
original of Pope's Timon.

[6] The Chancellor of the Exchequer, since August 1713.

[7] Henry Campion, member at
this time for Sussex. He was a
leading member of the October

## XIX

July. 25th 1714.[1]   I had yours[2] and accordingly inclose the Pamphlett, and do with it as you please.   It will now do nothing to the Cause for I hear from others hints of what you say plainly, that the Dragon must out.   I was three days last week at Oxford with L[d] H. and his L[dy], at D[r] Stratfords,[3] and they all said the same thing ; and sett as hard on L[dy] M— [4] as on L[d] Bol.   I find you are not much displeasd ; nor I perhaps with the Dragons being out ; but with the manner of it ; and the dispositions of those who come in ; and perhaps their Crede Scheam.[5]   I shall not go to Pope's[6] but entre nous I will sett out for Ireland to morrow Sennight.[7]   Say nothing of it yet.   D[r] A. knows nothing of the Histor.'s place being disposed of ; and has gravely mentiond it to L[d] Bol— who

---

Club, the extreme wing of the Tory party ; see the list of its 159 members in Boyer's *Political State of Great Britain*, February 1712, pp. 117–21.

[8] 'pamphlet' (i.e. *Some Free Thoughts*) obliterated in MS.

[9] i.e. angry with Phipps, not with Bolingbroke : see Letter XVI, p. 32, n. 1.

---

[1] The MS. appears to have '1712'.

[2] The letter of 22 July. The Pamphlet is the second copy of *Some Free Thoughts*.

[3] Lord and Lady Harley were at Christ Church from 17 to 23 July as the guests of his old tutor Dr. William Stratford, Canon of Christ Church. Swift returned to Letcombe on the 23rd. See his letter to Arbuthnot from Oxford, 22 July, and the Stratford Papers, *Portland Manuscripts*, vii. 195.

[4] Lady Masham.

[5] The Schism Act, which required 'every schoolmaster and person teaching youth in a private family as a tutor or schoolmaster' to be a member of the Church of England.   Bolingbroke was responsible for it ; Oxford did not like it, and refrained from voting. The Bill passed the Commons, where it was introduced by Wyndham, by 237 to 126, and passed the Lords (15 June) by the narrow majority of 77 to 72.

[6] See Letter XVI, *ad fin*.

[7] Monday 2 August. Swift remained at Letcombe till 16 August.

intended as gravely to speak to D. Shrew[y].[1] I am satisfied ; let them take their own Course ; perhaps it may produce a History they will not like. And I will tell you one Hint when I have more time. Have you got the Cambrick Hanckercheifs ? otherwise you have paid her for nothing.[2] I wish you would send them down by the Carrier on Wednesday morning early. Barber will tell you where. No, Send them by your Man to Robert Stone[3] at the Saracen's head in Friday street near Cheapside, directed to me.—I think when you send the inclosed to a Printer you should prefix the following Letter,[4] which should be printed before it.

Mr (name his name). The annexed Papers were sent a month ago to a very cautious Printer, with leave to shew them to any one Friend he had a Mind : The Person he shewed them to has kept them ever since in order to make some Alterations, and the time is almost lapsed wherein they might have done any Service. I shall no longer wait the Leisure either of that Printer or his Friend ; If you do not think them worth a

[1] As Lord Chamberlain, Shrewsbury had the disposal of the Historiographer's place. See Letter XV, p. 29, n. 4.

[2] See Letter XVI, *ad fin.*

[3] The Wantage carrier. According to the 'List of all the Stage Coaches', &c., in *New Remarks of London*, 1732, p. 395, the Wantage wagon left the Saracen's Head, Friday Street, on Wednesdays. There was a second Wantage wagon which left the Oxford Arms, Warwick Lane, on Thursdays.

[4] The events of the following week put an end to all thoughts of publishing *Some Free Thoughts*, and it remained unpublished till 1741. From the 'Advertisement to the Reader' prefixed to this edition, it would appear that the pamphlet was then printed from the manuscript which had been sent to Barber, and that this manuscript had not been returned to Swift. The differences between the printed text and the allusions in these letters may be attributed to Bolingbroke's revision. There is no reason for holding that the printers used the second copy forwarded to Ford on 25 July.

Publication, pray return them immediatly.    I am S^r &c.

And you may chuse the same or any other place to have them sent to you.    They will cost some time transcribing ;    and I think it is not prudent to let them be in my Hand.

*Address :* To Charles Ford Esqr,
　　　　　　at His Office at White-hall
　　　　　　　　　London

*Postmark :* $\frac{26}{IY}$

## XX[1]

# (Ford to Swift)

London　July 31.
Three in the afternoon

I DON'T doubt but you have heard the Q— is dead,[2] and perhaps we may be so unfortunate before this comes to you.    But at present she is alive, and much better than could have been expected.    I am just come from Kensington, where I have spent allmost these two whole days.    I am in great hast, but till dinner comes up, I will write to you, and give you as full an account as I can of her illness.    Her disorder began between eight and nine yesterday morning.    The Doctors order'd her head to be shav'd, and while it was doing, she fell into a Fit of Convulsion, or as they thought an Apoplexy.    This lasted near two hours, and she was

---

[1] British Museum, Add. MS. 4804, ff. 218–19 *v.*; printed by Hawkesworth, 1766.

[2] The Queen died about seven in the morning, Sunday 1 August. For other accounts of her last hours see *Wentworth Papers*, 1883, pp. 407–8, Boyer's *Political State*, July 1714, pp. 627–35 (reproduced in *The Historical Register*), and *Portland Manuscripts*, v. 480.

speechless, and shew'd little sign of life during that
time, but came to herself upon being blouded.   As
soon as she recover'd, my L^d Bol— went to her, and
told her the P—y Council was of opinion, it would be
for the publick service to have the D. of Shrewsbury
made L^d Treasurer.   She immediately consented, and
gave the Staff ¹ into the Duke's hands.²   The Great
Seal was put to the Patent by four a clock.   She con-
[p. 2.] tinued ill | the whole day.   In the evening I spoke to
Dr. A— ³ and he told me he did not think her distemper was desperate.   Radcliffe ⁴ was sent for to
Cass—n about noon, by order of the Council, but said
he had taken Physick, and could not come.   In all
probability he had sav'd her life, for I am told the
late L^d Gower ⁵ had been often in the same condition

---

¹ 'The Third *Great Officer* of
the Crown is the *Lord High
Treasurer of England*, who re-
ceives this High Office by delivery of a *White Staffe* to him
by the King, and holds it *durante
bene placito Regis*' (Edward
Chamberlayne, *Angliæ Notitia*,
1674, p. 152).

² 'The same Nobleman was, at
once, . . . Lord Treasurer, Lord
Chamberlain, and Lord Lieutenant of Ireland' (*Political
State*, p. 630).

³ Arbuthnot.

⁴ Radcliffe had been Anne's
doctor in her youth, but she disliked him and abandoned him in
1694, though he continued to be
doctor to her son, the Duke of
Gloucester (d. 1700). Ford is
alone in saying that he was now
summoned 'by order of the
Council'. The *Political State*

says by the Duke of Ormond ;
Radcliffe himself thought by Lady
Masham. When the message
came he was at his seat at Car-
shalton, near Croydon, suffering
from a severe attack of gout, and
he knew, from a report sent to
him by Mead, that nothing more
could be done. On 7 August he
wrote that 'ill as I was, I would
have went to the Queen in a
Horse-Litter, had either her
Majesty, or those in Commission
next to her, commanded me so to
do'. The affair appears to have
preyed on his mind. He died
three months later, on 1 November. See also Pittis, *Dr. Radcliffe's Life and Letters*, pp. 72–6,
and *Wentworth Papers*, p. 410.

⁵ Sir John Leveson-Gower,
created Baron Gower of Sitten-
ham 1703. He died 1709, aged
34.

with the gout in his head, and Rad— kept him alive many years after. This morning when I went there before nine, they told me she was just expiring. That account continued above three hours, and a report was carryed to town that she was actually dead. She was not prayd for even at her own Chapel at St. James's, and what is most infamous Stocks rose three per cent upon it in the city.[1] Before I came away she had recover'd a warmth in her breast and one of her arms, and all the D$^{rs}$ agreed she would in all probability hold out till to morrow, except Mead who pronounc'd several hours before she could not live two minutes, and seems uneasie it did not happen so. I did not care to talk much to A— because I heard him cautious in his answers to other people, but by his manner I fancy he do's not yet absolutely dispair. The Council sat yesterday all day and night, taking it by turns to go | out and refresh themselves. They have now [p. 3.] adjourn'd upon what the D$^{rs}$ said till five. Last night the Speaker[2] and my L$^d$ C. Justice Parker[3] were sent for, and the Troops from Flanders.[4] This morning the Hanover Envoy[5] was order'd to attend with the black box,[6] and the Heralds to be in a readiness to proclaim the new King. Some of the Whigs were at

[1] South Sea Stock $81\frac{1}{2}$–$84\frac{3}{4}$, Bank Stock $120\frac{1}{2}$–$123\frac{1}{4}$ (*The Evening Post*, 29–31 July).

[2] Sir Thomas Hanmer. He was in Wales and did not return till the 4th (*Political State*, August 1714, p. 144). Bromley's letter summoning him is printed in *The Correspondence of Sir Thomas Hanmer*, ed. Bunbury, 1838, p. 169.

[3] Sir Thomas Parker, Lord Chief Justice 1710–17, afterwards Lord Chancellor and Earl of Macclesfield.

[4] Seven of the ten battalions in Flanders were recalled; they arrived 15 and 16 August (*Political State*, July 1714, p. 632, and August, p. 176).

[5] Kreienberg.

[6] Containing the names of the nineteen peers nominated by the Elector as Lords Justices, who with the seven great officers named in the Act of 1705 formed the Regency.

Council yesterday, but not one fail'd to day, and most of the Members of that Party in each House are already come to town. If any change happens before the Post go's out, I will send you word in a Post[s]cript, and you may conclude her alive, if you hear no more from me and have no better authority than Post Letters to inform you of the contrary. For God's sake, don't think of removing from the Place where you are till matters are a little setled. Ireland is the last retreat you ought to think of, but you can never be better than you are now till we see how things go.

I had yours with the printed Pamphlet as well as the other, and should have sent it away to morrow. [p. 4.] Pray let me hear from you. [*Six lines heavily obliterated.*[1]] Have you had all mine? I have fail'd you but one post, (I think it was the last,) for a fortnight or more.

Eleven at night.

The Queen is something better, and the Council is again adjourn'd till eight in the morning.

*No address.*

*Note in Swift's writing (p. 4) :*  M^r. F—d
  R̸ Aug. 1. 1714
  Qu— dying

---

[1] Ford has scribbled out some words, and disguised others by inserting letters or writing new words over them. The passage, as Swift found, is very difficult to read, but runs thus: 'Bar— was order'd by my L^d Bol— to go down & endeavour to bring you to town. He undertook for the — if this had not happen'd. I really believe he is very sincere in what I hear he has profess'd of you. B— I suppose will tell you all. He told me, and I desired him to write you word of it.'

## XXI

Aug. 3. 1714

You are more constant than all my Correspondents together ; and I wonder you are not ashamed of it. We had an account of the Queen at noon on Sunday by a Servant of L^d Bol—s who rode through Wantage to M^r Packer.¹ It was what I monthly expected, thô not daily, and I laughed at their new Ministry for that very Reason, before this happened ; I fancy the Qu— dyed about 5 on Sunday morning. She was alive at two, as we hear by a Postscript to the Postmasters Letter at Wantage. I writt a week ago to M^r Dawson ² at the Castle of Dublin, to desire he would renew my Licence of absence when it expires, which will be the End of this Month ; Lest it should miscarry, I beg you will write to him to the same Purpose, and desire his Answer, which will serve us both. I desire it may be a Licence of Absence in generall, without specifying England ; because, who knows, &c. My Trunk with Cloaths and Linnen is gone to England,³ and I am here in Rags, intending to have sett out yesterday for Ireland ; if the Dragon's Fall had not first stopt me, and then the Qu—'s Death.—Were the Whigs at Council when D— Sh— was recommended to be Tr—⁴

¹ Robert Packer, of Shellingford Castle, near Faringdon. His wife and Bolingbroke's were sisters, daughters of Sir Henry Winchcombe. He was member for Berkshire from July 1712 (in succession to Bolingbroke, called to the Upper House) till his death in April 1731.

² Joshua Dawson, Under-Secretary at Dublin Castle, M.P. at the time for Wicklow Borough.

Swift's letter 29 July is printed in *Correspondence*, ii. 204–5.

³ A mistake for ' Ireland '.

⁴ According to Boyer's *Political State*, July 1714, p. 629, and *Wentworth Papers*, p. 408, Somerset and Argyle were present (30 July) when Shrewsbury was unanimously recommended to be Lord Treasurer. But in answer to Swift's question Ford says (5 August) that ' the Whigs were

You want hands. I think Ratcliff[1] acted right, they would never distinguish him by any honorary Pension, but send for him at a Plunge when he could onely lose Credit. For the Qu—'s case seems not to have been the Gout in her Head, But Histericks, Convulsive, or Apoplectick, but I judge at distance. Poor Ar—[2] was glad to hope as long as possible. The Manuscript you have, may lye by now : Some Hints in it may serve for a help to future Memoirs, or burn it, as you please.[3] I have [been] plaguing my self to read 5 or 6 lines you blotted out. That is human Nature. I have done the Imitation of Hoc erat in votis.[4] Tis pretty well, and will serve in some scurvy Miscellany. Pray send me the Gazette of Tuesday next, if it contains any thing materiall of these Things. adieu.

*Address, on separate cover :*
To Charles Ford Esqr, at
His Office at White-hall
London

*Postmarks :* Wantage *and* $\frac{4}{AV}$

not in Council, when he was recommended ', though in his previous letter (31 July) he had said ' Some of the Whigs were at Council yesterday, but not one fail'd to day '. It would appear that in saying ' the Whigs were not in Council ' he was thinking of the Whigs as a body. See Lecky, *England in the Eighteenth Century,* ed. 1892, i. 205.

[1] See Letter XX, p. 40, n. 4.

[2] Arbuthnot.

[3] In his next letter Swift asks Ford to return the manuscript.

[4] Horace, *Satires,* ii. vi. This is the Imitation beginning

I often wish'd, that I had clear
For Life, six hundred Pounds a
    Year,

first printed in *Miscellanies. The Last Volume,* 1727, pp. 33–41. It was added to by Pope, and published in folio in 1738.

## XXII [1]

# (Ford to Swift)

London Aug: 5th 1714

I HAVE writ to Dawson [2] for a license of absence for you, but you know you must take the oaths in Ireland within three months. There are a great many here in the same circumstances, and in all probability some of them will desire an Act of Parl[t] to have leave to do it here. In that case it will be no difficult matter to have you included. M[r] L— [3] tells me he writ to you to come up to town, and I see no reason why you should not. All matters go on very quiet, and we are not apprehensive of any disturbances. Stocks never rose so much in so few days.[4] This is imputed to the hatred of the old Treas—r and the Popularity of the new one. The Whigs were not in Council, when he was recommended.[5] L[d] B— propos'd it there, as well as to the Queen, and I hope they two are upon very good terms, tho M[r] L— seems positive of the contrary. I never heard of any pique the D: had to him, but that he was to be chief Minister, and that being at an end, why may not they be reconcil'd? The Dragon was thought to shew more joy upon proclaiming the King, than was consistent with the obligations he had receiv'd from ——— [6]. He was hiss'd all | the way by [p. 2.] the mob, and some of them threw halters into his

---

[1] British Museum, Add. MS. 4804, ff. 228–9 v.; printed by Hawkesworth, 1766.

[2] Ford's letter to Dawson, 5 August, was in the Public Record Office, Dublin (Elrington Ball).

[3] Lewis's letter, 3 August, is printed in *Correspondence,* ii. 211.

[4] South Sea Stock rose from 81½ on 30 July to 89½ on 5 August and to 92½ on 6 August; Bank Stock from 120½ to 127¼ and 130 (*The Evening Post*).

[5] See Letter XXI, p. 43, n. 4.

[6] The Queen.

coach.[1]   This was not the effect of Party, for the D:
of Or—d was huzza'd throughout the whole city, and
follow'd by a vast crowd to his own house, tho he us'd
all possible endeavours to prevent it.   There was an
attempt to affront the Captain in the Cavalcade, but it
did not succeed, and tho a few hiss'd, the acclamations
immediately drown'd their noise.   Not a single man
shew'd the least respect to the Collonel and last night my
L[d] Bingley [2] was beaten by mistake coming out of his
house.   I doubt he has disoblig'd both sides so much,
that neither will ever own him, and his enemys tell
storys of him that I shall not believe, till I find you
allow them.   The L[ds] Justices made a Speech to the
Parl[t] to day.   If it comes out time enough I will send
it you, but I hear it only contains their proceedings
upon the Queen's death, that they have yet receiv'd
no directions from the King, and to desire the Commons to continue the funds, which are expir'd.   I am
told our R—ts [3] are already divided into four Partys.

[1] '[1 August] . . . the Heralds
at Arms proclaim'd His present
Majesty *George*, King of *Great
Britain* . . . before the Gate of
the Royal Palace, at *St. James's*,
at *Charing-Cross*, at *Temple-Bar*,
at the End of *Wood street* in
*Cheapside*, and lastly at the *Royal
Exchange*.  Great numbers of the
Nobility and principal Gentry
assisted at each Proclamation, and
attended in their Coaches during
the whole Solemnity, as did also,
in the City, the Lord Mayor and
Court of Aldermen; the Streets
being crowded with vast Multi-
tudes of People, who made joyful
Acclamations.  No manner of Disturbance was given to the Ceremony; nor was any Disorder

committed in it; save only, that
some of the Mobb hiss'd at and
insulted the Lords *Ox—d* and
*Bo—ke*' (Boyer's *Political State*,
August 1714, p. 119).

[2]  Robert Benson, created Baron
Bingley July 1713, Chancellor of
the Exchequer 1711 to 1713
(succeeded by Wyndham).  'On
Wednesday last [4 August] Mr.
Man, the woollen draper, went
to the Earl of Oxford's house in
York Buildings, and called his
Lordship all to naught, so soon
as he went out of the house he
met the Lord Bingley and insulted him' (News-letter, *Portland Manuscripts*, v. 485).

[3]  Regents.

The greatest use they have yet made of their Power
is to appoint my L$^d$ Berkeley[1] to command the Fleet
which is to bring over the King, and to make the
D: of Bolton[2] L$^d$ L$^t$ of Hampshire.    I send you
a Gazette, tho I am asham'd to have it seen.[3]    I had
writ a great deal more of the Queen's illness, an
account of her Birth &c.    But I could not find out
M$^r$ L— and had no body to consult with, and there-
fore chose rather to | say too little, than any thing I [p. 3.]
doubted might be improper.    Yesterday the Duke of
Marl—gh made his Publick Entry through the city.[4]
First came about 200 horsemen three in a row, then
a Company of train bands with drums &c.    His own
Chariot with himself and his Dutchess.    Then my
Dutchess[5] follow'd by 16 Coaches with 6 Horses, and
between 30 and 40 with two horses.    There was no
great mob when he pass'd through the Pellmall, but
there was in the city, and he was hiss'd by more than
huzza'd.    At Temple Bar I am assur'd the noise of
hissing was loudest, tho they had prepar'd their friends

[1] James, third Earl of Berke-
ley, son of Swift's old friend : cf.
Letter I, p. 2, n. 2, and *Journal
to Stella*, 15 Feb. 1711.    He was
First Lord of the Admiralty under
George I.

[2] Charles Paulet, second Duke
of Bolton, Lord Chamberlain
1715–17, Lord Lieutenant of
Ireland 1717–19.

[3] Ford's account of the
Queen's illness and death, in the
*Gazette* of 31 July to 3 August,
runs to only a dozen lines: 'This
Day, at half an Hour past Seven
in the Morning, died our late
most Gracious Sovereign Queen
Anne, in the Fiftieth Year of her
Age, and the Thirteenth of Her

Reign ; a Princess of exemplary
Piety and Virtue.    Her Majesty
complained on Thursday last of
a Pain in Her Head : The next
Day She was seized with Convulsion Fits, and for some time
lost the use of Her Speech and
Senses, which, tho' She afterwards
recovered upon the Application of
proper Remedies, She continued
in a very weak and languishing
Condition till She expired.'

[4] See Letter XIII, p. 26, n. 1,
and Letter XVII, p. 35, n. 1.    For
other accounts of Marlborough's
entry see *The Flying-Post*, 3–5
August 1714, and Boyer, *Political
State*, August 1714, p. 141.

[5] The Duchess of Montagu.

to receive him, and the gathering of others was only
accidental.   You may guess how great a Favourite he
is by some old storys of his behaviour at the Camp
when ——— [1] was there, and afterwards at Han——r, and
by the share he and his Family have in the Regency.[2]
But to be sure this discreet action will endear him
more than any subject in England.   We had bonfires
&c. at night.   From the List of L^ds Justices, and some
other things, we imagine to ourselves there wo'n't be
many changes, but that the vacancys for some time will
be fill'd up with Whigs.

What I blotted out in my last was something that
pass'd between the Captain and B——r relating to you.
After I had writ, they told me all letters would be
open'd, which made me blot out that passage.   B——r
[p. 4.] says he gave you some account of it tho not a | full
one.[3]   I really believe L. B—— was very sincere in the
professions he made of you, and he could have done
any thing.   No Minister was ever in that heigth of
favour, and L^y M ———[4] was at least in as much credit as
she had been in any time of her life.   But these are
melancholy reflections, pray send me your Poem Hoc
erat &c.[5] or bring it up yourself.   B—— told me he

[1] The King. He had not been
informed by Marlborough and
Eugène of their plans for the
campaign of 1708 and refused to
act on the offensive; and in May
1710 he resigned his command.

[2] Neither Marlborough nor the
Earl of Sunderland, his son-in-law,
was included in the Regency.
But the King's first official act
when the news of Anne's death
reached Hanover was to appoint
Marlborough Captain-General.

[3] In his letter of 3 August
(*Correspondence*, ii. 212–13) Barber had said: 'Lord Bolingbroke
told me last Friday that he would
reconcile you to Lady Somerset,
and then it would be easy to set
you right with the Queen, and
that you should be made easy
here, and not go over.   He said
twenty things in your favour, and
commanded me to bring you up,
whatever was the consequence.
He said further, he would make
clear work with them.   But all
vanished in a minute.'

[4] Lady Masham.

[5] See Letter XXI, p. 44, n. 4.

had been several hours with the Captain upon a thing
that should have come out, but was now at an end.[1]
He did not tell what it was, and I would not ask many
questions for fear of giving him suspicion.

*No address.*
*Note in Swift's writing (p. 4):* Aug. 5. 1714
C. F.

### XXIII

Aug. 7th. 1714

The Inclosed,[2] | To the Reverend Mr
Arch-deacon Wall, over against the Hospitall
in Queen-street.   Dublin.

I HAD your long kind Letter of the 5th : I never once
dreamt of taking the Oaths : but the sooner I do it
the better : and travelling will soon grow bad ; so that
I design to sett out on Monday sennight the 16th
instant, and if they want me, I can return in Winter,
when I suppose you will have a new Parlmt, for this is
not for your Purpose.   To include my self in an Act,
will not be decent, unless I were unable to travell ;
and besides I have some good Friends among the Lds
who would be glad to mortify me with their Negative.
I have writt this Post a very long Letter to Ld Bol—[3]
and told him my Call for Ireland ; and that I would
come back if I were wanted.   I wish he and the Dragon

---

[1] Swift's *Some Free Thoughts.*
[2] Printed in *Correspondence*, ii.
226 ; dated 8 August.
[3] Printed in *Correspondence*, ii.
222–6 ; written in answer to
Bolingbroke's letter of 3 August
beginning ' The Earl of Oxford
was removed on Tuesday ; the
Queen died on Sunday.   What a
world is this, and how does Fortune banter us '.   In this long
and important letter Swift re-
viewed the events of the last few
months and spoke of his relations
with both Bolingbroke and Oxford, ' having been for two years
almost the only man who went
between you '.   Bolingbroke replied on 11 August denouncing
Oxford, and expressing warm
affection for Swift.

would write.  I believe M^r L is in the right about the Captain and D. of Shr—  I have been long afraid that we were losing the Rabble ^1———As for L^d Bingl— ^2 I will not be [h]is Guarantee.——I think the Regents agree pretty well in their Choice of Persons, and that we are this moment under the Height of a Whig Administration.  You do not mention Addison ; who M^r L says is Secretary to the Regency.^3  Your Gazette is perfectly right, and what is said of the Queen very decent and proper :  had there been more it might have been better ; and indeed I know no body has a better Style for Letters or Business than you :  which considering your Lazyness, you may be said to have acquired in spight of your Teeth.  I do not conceive the D. of M. will be a Favorite.  I believe your Dutchess lookt very sawcy and handsom.  When did the Rabble get this Trick of Hissing ; they learnt it at the Play-house in the upper Gallery.  How a div–l do you gather from the List of R—ts that there will not be many removalls ; they are all of the rankest Whigs, except 4 or 5 Proselytes, which is worse ; at least such as quarrelled about the Peace and Treatyes, and Danger of the Succession.^4

I will bring you my Poem my self—when I return [p. 2.] from Ireland :  It is | not yet sufficiently corrected to my Mind, thô I have labored it much.  But I am not now that way turned.  I am breeding another Pamphlet, but have not writt a Word of it.  The Title will be something like this—Some Considerations upon

---

^1 In his letter to Bolingbroke (7 August) he says ' I only doubt my friends, the rabble, are at least grown trimmers '.

^2 See Letter XXII, p. 46, n. 2.

^3 Stated in Lewis's letter of 3 August, on which day Addison was appointed (*Political State,* August 1714, p. 142).

^4 The ' Proselytes ' among the nineteen Regents nominated by the Elector were ' Whimsicals ' or Hanoverian Tories—the Archbishop of York, the Duke of Roxburgh, and the Earls of Anglesey, Nottingham, and Abingdon.

the Consequences apprehended by the Qu—s Death.[1]
If I have humor I will write it here and upon the Road,
and send it you from Ireland.

If you have the Manuscript I sent you last, pray
return it me by next Post, for I may have use for some
Passages in it.[2]

I must desire you to receive 50ll from Mr Thomas[3]
of the Treasury ; which belongs to a Clergy-man in
Ireland, to whom I have this Post sent a Bill.   With
part of this money, pay your self the 20 Guinneas I ow
you, and for the Handkerchiefs you bought, there
will then remain six or seven and twenty Pounds ; out
of which pay thirty Guinneas to Mr Barber, besides for
hatts, Nightgown, Books &c. whatever his Account is.
How will you do this ? Why : he is to receive 30ll of
mine from the South-Sea,[4] which I hope will overdo it
a great deal, and keep the Remainder in your Hands.
Take up Barbers Note for the thirty Guinneas and
cancell it.   Can you do this silly debt without perplex-
ing your self ?

And pray tell Mr Thomas I writt to him
this Post under cover to Mr L—

*Address :* To Charles F[. . . . .]
his Office at [. . . . .]

*Postmarks* torn off.

[1] Swift did not proceed far
with this pamphlet. The fragment was published in 1765. The
MS., dated 9 August 1714, is in
the Forster collection, and has
been used for Temple Scott's
edition, vol. v. 421-4.

[2] *Some Free Thoughts*, second
copy : see Letter XIX, p. 38, n. 4.

[3] William Thomas, secretary
to the Earl of Oxford. The

clergyman was the Rev. Thomas
Fetherston, Prebendary of St.
Patrick's. See Thomas's letters
to Swift, *Correspondence*, ii. 157
and 167 ; also 203.

[4] Swift had £1,000 in South
Sea Stock : see his letter of 20 July
authorizing the accountant of the
Company to pay to Barber the
half-year's interest, *Correspondence*, ii. 188.

## XXIV

Aug. 12. 1714

I HAVE received the Pacquet ;[1] by the same Token, some scoundrel of the Post office either here or there, scratched out your name, and indorsed it, *this is no right Frank, but must pay 2 shill.* I have orderd my Man to inquire to morrow, whether it were done at Wantage.— Sure the Dragon intends to strike in with the new World ; by his treating the Kings.[2] He thinks he has a kind of Merit by his ill Usage, and may think right for ought I know. I sett out early on Monday next[3] for Ireland, be so kind if any Letters come to me inclosed to You or M[r] L— to send them to Dublin ; but not till you are sure I am as far as Chester.— Confound all Politicks. Have I had enough of them or no ? We had news here that L[d] Bol— was sent to the Tower, and this Night a Servant from Wantage brings word, that a Stranger who spread that Report there, is taken up for it. You are to know that Wantage is a Whig Town. You are incorrigeable in that Fault of giving more than I would have. Between

---

[1] Containing, presumably, the second copy of *Some Free Thoughts.*

[2] Swift echoes a phrase in a letter of 10 August from Lewis, 'If the Dragon declares against the Man of Mercury (i.e. Bolingbroke), he may strike in with the *tertium quid* that will probably arise' (*Correspondence,* ii. 228). In addition to showing joy upon proclaiming the King, Oxford had on 6 August drafted a letter to the King expressing his zeal and devotion (*Portland Manuscripts,* v. 484).—The reading is difficult ; perhaps 'friends' or some such word has been omitted after 'Kings', and 'treating' is not certain. Cf. Ford's reference to Oxford's 'entertainment' in Letter XXVI, p. 57, ll. 6–12.

[3] 16 August. He reached Dublin on Tuesday, 24 August.

the Time that I desired your Wine and your granting
it me, things altered so, that I shall hardly have a Tast
of it ; But I sent M^r Geree a Chest of Florence,[1] and
have drunk it out since I came here ; so yours must
requite him. I knew not how to buy, nor since the
Change where to beg ; and living without it would
hurt my Health. Be assured I will never repay you.
I have writt a good piece of the Thing I told you I
was breeding.[2] I shall be quiet some time or other.
I reckon the King has by this time received his Con-
doleance and Congratulation, Grief in one hand &c,
Or rather Joy in one hand, and Gladness in the other.
The Dragon told me confidently and often, that all
foreigners Peers, such as Portland &c ceased to be
Peers, on the Queen's Demise : by the Act of Settlement. Sure he was mistaken.[3] I had a short melancholy Letter from D^r Prat,[4] he and the rest are hardly
used. How shall I look Elwood[5] in the Face. I have
no Interest even with the Footmen of any body now in
Power. This is a bad Stroak for the H. of L^ds in
Ireland ; and consequently for our Friends here. I
sollicited that matter 800 times ; but that cursed Delay
ruined all.

[1] See Letter XVI. Geree had
acknowledged on 24 April 'the
noble present of wine' which
Swift had sent him when arrang-
ing for his visit to Letcombe :
see Letter VII, p. 15, n. 4, and
*Correspondence*, ii. 134.

[2] *Some Considerations*, &c.

[3] The Act of Settlement 1701
(12 & 13 William III, c. 2)
enacted that 'no Person born out
of the Kingdoms of England
Scotland or Ireland or the Domi-
nions thereunto belonging although he be naturalized or made
a Denizen (except such as are
born of English parents) shall be
capable to be of the Privy
Councill or a Member of either
House of Parliament or to enjoy
any Office or Place of Trust
either Civill or Military or to
have any Grant of Lands Tene-
ments or Hereditaments from the
Crown to himself or to any other
or others in Trust for him'.

[4] See p. 20, n. 2.

[5] See Letter II, p. 6, n. 3, and
X, p. 20, n. 2.

Adieu, and now I am going, believe I love you very well—

*Address :* To Charles Ford Esq^r, at his
Office at White-hall   London

*Postmarks :* Wantage *and* $\frac{13}{AV}$


## XXV [1]
# (Ford to Swift)

London Aug: 12

OUR Justices sit several hours every day, without affording us the least news.   I don't hear any thing they have done worth mentioning except some Orders they have given about the dispute in the City of Dublin.[2]   You may be sure they are not such as will please our friends, but I think you and I agreed in condemning those Proceedings in our own people. My L^d Derby [3] is made L^d Lieut^t of Lancashire.   That and Hampshire are the only vacant Employments they have fill'd up, I suppose under pretence of their being maritime Countys.   If the Whigs had directed the List of Regents Marl— Sund— and Whar— had not been left out.   There are five Torys too that would not have been in.[4]   Tho they were a little whimsical for three or

---

[1] British Museum, Add. MS. 4804, ff. 236–7; printed by Hawkesworth, 1766.

[2] See Letter XVI, p. 32, n. 1. 'Orders are sent to Dublin to require Sir Samuel Cook and the aldermen of that city to meet, and elect forthwith a Lord Mayor and Sheriffs, and the Lords Justices and Council are to approve of the persons so elected'

(*Portland Manuscripts,* v. 486). See also Boyer, *Political State,* August 1714, p. 172, and October, p. 340.

[3] James Stanley, tenth Earl of Derby. For 'Hampshire' see Letter XXII, p. 47, l. 4.

[4] See Letter XXIII, p. 50, n. 4. Cf. letter by Lord Berkeley of Stratton, 3 August 1714, in *Wentworth Papers,* p. 409: 'It

four days about the Succession, they seem'd to recant
and own themselves in an | Error by later Votes. Every [p. 2.]
one of them approv'd the Peace, and were for the
Address at the end of the last Session that it was
safe, honourable, and advantagious. Considering what
Ministers were employed here by the Court of Hanover,
and that the King himself had little information but
what he receiv'd from them, I think his List shews
no ill disposition to the Torys, and they say he is not
apt to be hasty in removing the persons he finds in
Employment. The Bill is brought in for granting
him the old Dutys for the Civil List.[1] One Wikes of
Northampton mov'd to tack the place Bill to it, but no
body seconded him, and he was extremely laugh'd at.[2]
He happens unluckily to be a Tory.

Did you receive your Papers last post? The first
copy is not yet left at St. D—n's,[3] should I send to
B—r for it, in L. B's name? I have writ to him to
bring in his Bill, and as soon as he comes I will pay
him.[4] I suppose I shall see him to morrow. I wish
you a good journey to Ireland, but if I hear Saterday's
post comes into | Wantage on Sunday, I may trouble [p. 3.]
you again. Pray let me know when you land in
Ireland, that I may write to you if any thing happens

was a surprise to me, and I fancy
will not be less soe to himself,
not to see My Lord Wharton's
name in the list, and My Lord
Sunderland look'd very pale when
the names were read '.

[1] The grant amounted to
£700,000. A Tory motion that
the sum should be raised to
£1,000,000 was allowed to drop.

[2] 'Hereupon *John Wykes,* Esq;
Member for the Town of *Northampton,* proposed the *Tacking* to
it the *Bill,* which had so often
miscarry'd, *for limiting the
Number of Officers in the House
of Commons*: But no Body
seconded that Motion' (*Political
State,* August 1714, pp. 151–2).
The name is given as William
Wykes, or Wickes, in the Parliamentary Returns.

[3] See Letter IX, p. 17, n. 4.
The second copy of *Some Free
Thoughts* had been returned by
Ford, the first remained in
Barber's hands.

[4] See Letter XXIII, *ad fin.*

worth while.   I shall be very impatient for what you
promise me from thence.[1]   I should be very glad to
hear from you while you are on the road.

L^d Anglesey came to town last tuesday.   They are
all here now, except Pembroke and Strafford.[2]

Charles Eversfield[3] is making his Court to the
D: of Somerset, and Argyle.   He declares he will keep
his place if he can, and that he will not stir for
Campion's election in the County of Sussex.   Campion
and he have had some high words upon that account.
L^d Orford[4] told the Commis^rs of the Admiralty, they
were ignorant, negligent of their duty, and wanted zeal
for the King's service.

*No address.*

## XXVI[5]

# (Ford to Swift)

Aug 14^th

I HOPE you did not pay the two shillings for Postage.
If you did, pray send me the cover, that I may enquire
into the meaning of it.   I suppose you expect news
upon Crags's return from Hanover,[6] but I don't hear

[1] *Some Considerations*, &c.: see
Letter XXIII, p. 51, n. 1.

[2] The Earl of Anglesey re-
turned from Ireland, Tuesday
10 August.   He was one of the
Regents nominated by the Elec-
tor ; so also the Earl of Pembroke.
The Earl of Strafford, who as
First Lord Commissioner of the
Admiralty was a Regent *ex officio*,
was at the Hague : see *Wentworth
Papers*, p. 414.

[3] Charles Eversfield was at
this time member for Horsham.
In June 1712 he had been made
Treasurer and Paymaster of the
Ordnance.   For Campion see
Letter XVIII, p. 36, n. 7; he was
not re-elected for Sussex.   They
had both been leading members
of the October Club.

[4] Edward Russell, Earl of
Orford, one of the Lords Justices,
First Lord of the Admiralty
1709–10 and 1714–17.

[5] British Museum Add. MS.
4804, ff. 240–1 ; printed by
Hawkesworth, 1766.

[6] James Craggs, the younger,
had been sent to Hanover on 31
July (before the Queen's death)
with a letter from the Council to

a word more than what you have in the L^ds Justices
Speech.   Yesterday morning after he came the Whigs
look'd dejected, and our friends very much pleas'd, tho
I don't know any reason for either, unless it was expected
by both sides that he would have brought Orders for
Alterations.   It seems the Dragon's entertainment was
upon a family account upon the agreement between
L^d Harley and L^d Pelham,¹ and only those who were
concern'd in their affairs were invited.   But slighter
grounds would have serv'd to raise a story at this time,
and it was sufficient that my L^d Townesend and L^d
Cooper² din'd at his house.   However we look upon
him as lost to | our side, and he has certainly made [p. 2.]
advances of civility to the Whigs, which they have
return'd with the utmost contempt.   I am told Dismal³
begins to declare for his old friends, and protests he
was really afraid for the Protestant Succession, which
made him act in the manner he did.   The forreign
Peers are certainly deprived of their right of voting by
the express words of the Act of Succession,⁴ and it
appears it was the intention of the Legislature at that
time, for Prince George of Den—k was excepted by

the Elector desiring him to hasten
over to England, and arrived
back on 13 August.
   ¹ Oxford's son, Edward Harley, had married Henrietta, only
child of John, Duke of Newcastle
(d. 1711) on 31 October 1713:
see Swift's poem 'To Lord
Harley, on his Marriage'. The
greater part of Newcastle's estates
had gone to his nephew, the
second Lord Pelham (created
Duke of Newcastle 1715). The
agreement between Harley and
Pelham is briefly described in
Erasmus Lewis's letter to Swift of

17 July (*Correspondence*, ii. 183).
   ² Viscount Townshend succeeded Bolingbroke as Secretary
of State on 17 September; Lord
Cowper, afterwards Earl Cowper,
succeeded Lord Harcourt as Lord
Chancellor on 22 September.
Both were Lord Justices.
   ³ The Earl of Nottingham.
Swift had given him this name
in 1712: see 'Toland's Invitation to Dismal' and 'A Hue and
Cry after Dismal', and cf. *Journal
to Stella*, 17 July 1712.
   ⁴ See Letter XXIV, p. 53, n. 3;
and cf. *Wentworth Papers*, p. 413.

name. But it's thought the Lords will interpret it otherwise when it comes to be tryed. They don't lose the other Privileges of Peerage, and their Posterity born here may sit in the House. The same clause extends to the House of Commons, and no Foreigner can enjoy any Employment civil or military. They may be favourable to the Lords, who are all Whigs, but I doubt poor Duke Disney will lose his Regiment.[1]

I suppose B<sup>r</sup> has given you an account of L. B's [p. 3.] Pamphlet.[2] If you and he are not come to | an eclaircissement upon it, shall I send to him for it ? I long for the other. Yesterday the Commons voted Nem. Con. to pay the Hanover Troops that deserted us in

---

[1] Henry Desaulnais, a French Huguenot who took the name of Desney or Disney. He fought at Blenheim and Malplaquet in the First Foot Guards, took part in General Hill's expedition to Canada in 1711 (see Josiah Burchett, *Transactions at Sea*, 1720, p. 781), and was at this time Colonel of the 36th Foot. In a letter written from Edinburgh, 26 August 1714, he says—'I have done all that lay in my power that nothing might be laid att my charge all my officers and recruites being att the garison, and Gen<sup>ll</sup>. Wetham [i.e. Wightman] being so kind as to keep me here there being no likeliwood of any disturbance on these parts and the Clause against us's not being yet explain, so that I shall stay here some time longer with him till I see how matters goe on your part of the world' (letter in possession of editor). His commission was renewed by George I,

but he sold his colonelcy on 25 July 1715. On 25 December 1725 he became Colonel of the 29th Foot—1st Batt. Worcestershire Regiment—in succession to Lord Mark Kerr (Charles Dalton, *George the First's Army*, 1910, i. 365 and ii. 400). He died on 21 November 1731, aged 56, and was buried in the east cloister of Westminster Abbey, where there is a tablet to his memory, in the same grave as his life-long friend General Withers. Gay's poem *Mr. Pope's Welcome from Greece* explains how he came to be called 'Duke':

Withers the good, and (with him ever join'd)
Facetious Disney greet thee first of all :
I see his chimney smoke, and hear him say,
'Duke ! that's the room for Pope, and that for Gay.'

In a letter of 28 December 1705 he adds to his signature 'elias

1712.[1] To day S^r W^m Wyndham, Campion, and two
or three more gave some opposition to it, for which
they are extremely blam'd. I think they had acted
right if they had spoke against it yesterday, but it
seems they were not then in the House. They had
not strength enough to day to come to a division.
Once more I wish you a good journey, and a quick
return, and I hope you will find things go better than
you expect.

*No address.*
*Note in Swift's writing* (*p.* 4) :   Aug. 12, and 14, 1714
Ch. F—
Memd. I left
Ledcomb[2] Aug. 16. 1714
in order to Ireld.

1^d Duke'. He was elected to the
Society (Letter III, p. 9, n. 3) on
29 November 1711; 'we all
love him mightily', said Swift,
and again 'a fellow of abundance
of humour; an old battered rake,
but very honest, not an old man,
but an old rake' (*Journal to
Stella*, 14, 15 March 1713). But
Lady Mary Wortley Montagu
had another opinion of him:

> She ended, and assumed Duke
> Disney's grin,
> With broad plump face, pert
> eyes, and ruddy skin,
> Which shewed the stupid joke
> which lurk'd within.

('Unfinished sketches of a large
Poem', *Works*, ed. 1817, v. 176.)
[2] Swift's *Free Thoughts* as revised by Bolingbroke. But Barber
had not spoken of it in his letter

to Swift of 3 August. The 'other'
which Ford longs for is *Some
Considerations.*

---

[1] When Ormond, who had
succeeded Marlborough, acted on
St. John's secret instructions to
'avoid engaging in any siege or
hazarding a battle till you have
further orders from her majesty'.
On 13 August 1714 Horatio
Walpole moved 'to impower the
Lord High Treasurer, or Commissioners of the Treasury for the
Time being, to issue the Sum of
65022*l.* 8*s.* 8*d.* (being the Arrear
due to the Troops of *Hanover*,
for their Service in the *Low
Countries* in the Year 1712)'.—
Boyer, *Political State*, August
1714, p. 155.
[2] 'Ledcomb' written over
'Wantage' crossed out.

## XXVII

Dublin. Sept<sup>r</sup>. 1714.[1]

I HAVE been hindred by perfect Lazyness, and Listlessness, and anneantissement to write to You since I came here ; which was Tuesday the 24 instant. I am now hunting after a Horse to ride. I know not what to say to You. I cannot think nor write in this Country : My time passes in doing nothing, which makes me so busy that I have not leisure for any thing else. I have not added one Syllable to the Thing I was about ;[2] which at London or Letcomb would have now been finished. Tell Barber I will write to him in a few days. I have already to M<sup>r</sup> L—.[3] I cannot stop my Ears when People of the wisest sort I see (who are indeed no Conjurers) tell me a thousand foolish Things of the Publick : But I hope I shall keep my Resolution of never medling with Irish Politicks. It is hoped by those of our Side, that the K— will not answer altogether the Expectation of the Whigs, the Chancellor here[4] tells me he has been informed so from England. But I can believe nothing at this distance, when I know that there is no trusting to any thing three yards from the Court. I wish the Honeymoon may not make the Parlm<sup>t</sup> give up any thing they will repent of. I shall judge of what will happen by the great or little Pains to manage by the Court against next Elections ; without much Pains and Pence the Whigs cannot have a

---

[1] 'September' ought to be 'August', as is shown both by 'the 24 instant' and by the London postmark (August '30' or '31'). The letter was posted at Trim. Hitherto no letter by Swift has been known between 15 August (when he wrote to Oxford just before leaving Letcombe) and 14 September (when he wrote to Bolingbroke from Dublin).

[2] *Some Considerations.*

[3] The letter to Barber (if written) and the letter to Lewis are not preserved.

[4] Sir Constantine Phipps.

Majority ; and without a Majority, I think they cannot prudently take any large steps.

This is the Summ of my Politicks :  L$^d$ B— would [p. 2.] fain have me come over soon.$^1$   I will not do it, till I am fully convinced that my coming may be of use. For I care not to fight against Sea and Wind so late in my Life ;  and having been beaten with all Advantages on our side, makes me a greater Coward$^2$ than ever. L— and you shall deal very fairly with me ;  For my Fortunes will not suffer me to make an idle Journey. And therefore when I am presst to go over, I will have both your impartiall Opinions, if you will give them to me.   Being in England onely renders this Place more hatefull to me, which Habitude would make tolerable. I can say no more now, and what I have said is not worth a Rush.   Pray order Barber to settle my Accounts, and let him send them to me—

Y$^{rs}$.

I believe the Bp of Clogher $^3$ is in
Town, and D$^r$ Prat $^4$ or others know
where to send it to Him.

*Address, on separate cover :*

To Charles Ford Esq$^r$,<br>
at His Office at Whitehall<br>
London

*Postmarks :* Trim *and* $\frac{3[?]}{\text{AV}}$

---

$^1$ In his letter of 11 August (*Correspondence,* ii. 229) Boling-broke had said : ' Go into Ire-land, since it must be so, to swear, and come back into Britain to bless, to bless me and those few friends who will enjoy you.'

$^2$ Cf. Letter V, p. 12, n. 5.

$^3$ St. George Ashe, bishop of Clogher 1697–1717. He had been Swift's tutor at Trinity College, Dublin, of which he was appointed Provost in 1692.

$^4$ See Letter X, p. 20, n. 2.

## XXVIII

Dublin.   Sep^ber. 27. 1714

I have had your three Letters,[1] and have no Excuse
for not acknoledging them beside the generall Languor
this Country gives one, and the want of Matter to
furnish what may be worth any body's reading ; For if
an Account of the Factions here deserved writing, you
may be pretty confident I mingle not with them, thô
after fourty miles riding over Welch mountains,[2] I
might amuse my self with two Parsons whom I met
with a Friend, I might amuse my self with giving half
an hours way to their Impertinences.   I know not how
your Speculations and Conjectures tend, or what Hopes
you can form, for my Part since their Treatment of
L^d Bol—[3] and some other Proceedings I expect the
worst the[y] can compass, and that they will be able to
compass it ; if the Crown thinks fitt at the Head of the
Stocks to exert it self upon the next Elections.   If any
thing witholds the Whigs from the utmost Violence, it
will be onely the fear of provoking the Rabble, by
remembring what passt in the Business of Sacheverell.
Our L^d Chancellor has writt for leave to go for
England and waits it impatiently because he knows he
must be out, which is not yet done by some Incident,

[1] Not now known.

[2] Presumably between Chester
and Holyhead.

[3] Bolingbroke was removed
from his office of Secretary of
State on 31 August 'with parti-
culer Marks of Displeasure ; three
of the Lords of the Regency, *viz.*
the Dukes of *Shrewsbury* and
*Somerset,* and the Lord *Cowper,*
having taken the Seals from him,
and lock'd and seal'd up all the
Doors of his Office in the *Cock-
pit*' (*Political State,* August
1714, p. 186).

which it seems you had not heard of when You writt your Letter.[1] I believe [h]is elder Brother on your side[2] will hardly meet with better Quarter, let him make what submissions he pleases ; I believe every thing you can say of him, and that nothing but Guinneas can influence him. Give my service to M^r Domvile,[3] I am glad I had Credit enough to make a Letter from me do him a Pleasure ; He is but an half dippt Whig ; pray advise him to a little Violence on one side or other, else he will be a very insignificant Gentleman. There is a way of charming an Ague into Dogs ; can you not contrive to charm your Infectious Distemper from the Cows and Sheep into Whigs, a much more infectious Cattle.

Yes, I have other Reasons for Staying in Ireland besides saving money, or else I should have none at all. I would first know how your Elections are like to run ; | besides, I stay here out [of] a *Publick Spirit* ; [p. 2.] And I stay here because of L^d Bol's Treatment ; And I stay here to forget England and make this Place supportable by Practice, and because I doubt whether the Present Government will give me a Licence. These I take to be good Reasons ; However, if I can get leave, I will come when I am calld, and not till then.—I know not why you should give up till you are forced.[4] I remember the Whig Ministers advised all their Friends against it some years ago. I think the King is now arrived,[5] (for I know no News) and one would see the new World a little before one left

---

[1] Sir Constantine Phipps was not succeeded by Alan Brodrick, afterwards Viscount Midleton, till 30 September. See *Political State*, September 1714, p. 280, and October, p. 338; and Letter XIV, p. 28, n. 3.

[2] Lord Harcourt. See Letter XXVI, p. 57, n. 2.
[3] See Letter I, p. 2, n. 4.
[4] The office of Gazetteer.
[5] The King arrived at Greenwich on 18 September and made his entry into London on the 20th.

it.   Judge Nutley[1] is just come over to us; I onely
talkt a minute to him at his Coach side; He and most
of us despond; Quo fata vocant[2]—adieu.

What do you talk of writing in this Country, I can
as easily fly.

—28th.   By the Bonfires I guess the Pacquets are
come in, but I have not yet received my Letters, if
there be any for[3] me.

*No address : separate cover lost.*

## XXIX[4]

# (Ford to Swift)

### Paris Oct: 23. [O.S. 12, 1716]

If I was to see you again, you would give twice as
much as you offer'd six weeks ago[5] not to have seen
me.   By the same rule you might afford something
not to hear from me, but the enclos'd[6] came this
morning to me, and I could not send it away without
adding a few lines in the cover.   They are not to put

[1] Richard Nutley, born London 1673, M.A. Oxford 1694, member of the Middle Temple 1698, practised at the Irish Bar and was member of parliament for Lisburn from 1703 to 1711, when he was appointed a Puisne Justice of the Queen's Bench in Dublin.   He was superseded on 30 September 1714 by James Macartney, a political opponent whom he had replaced in 1711. He returned to practice at the bar and died in 1729. See F. Elrington Ball, *The Judges in Ireland*, ii. 39, 72, 86.

[2] Cf. Virgil, *Aeneid*, vi. 147, x. 472.

[3] MS. 'from'.

[4] British Museum, Add. MS. 4805, f. 27; printed by Hawkesworth, 1766.   The date has hitherto been given as 'October 28'.

[5] Ford had spent July and August in Ireland, and set out for Rome at the beginning of September.

[6] Bolingbroke's letter to Swift of 23 [O.S. 12] October 1716.

you again into the spleen, but only to ask how you do, and how you employ yourself. Do the great designs go on at Laracor,[1] or have the rains put a stop to your improvements, as well as to my journey? It will cost you but a penny, and a few minutes to answer these questions, and in return you shall know any thing you desire to know of me in my travels. I shall go on as soon as we have five or six days sunshine to dry the roads, and make the finest country in the world support-able. I am laugh'd at here when I talk of travelling, and yet of waiting for fair weather, but to me the journey is the greatest part of the pleasure; and whereas my companion[2] is continually wishing himself at Rome, I wish Rome was a thousand leagues farther off that I might have more way to pass in France and Italy. If you will do me the favour to write to me direct to be left with M$^r$ Cantillon Banker in Paris.[3]

*Address :* To the Rev$^d$.
D$^r$ Swift Dean of S$^t$ Patrick's
at his house in
                 Dublin,
    par Londres    Ireland

*Postmark :* $\dfrac{\text{OC}}{23}$

*Notes in Swift's writing (p. 4) :* The Squire.
                     ℞ Nov$^{br}$. 7$^{th}$. 1716
         *and*    Paris. Oct$^{br}$. 23$^d$. 1716

---

[1] Swift was enlarging the glebe at Laracor by the purchase of twenty acres, but his improve-ments were checked less by rain than by the law's delays.

[2] 'Mr. Wight.' Ford has left a long account of 'an adventure that happened to M$^r$ Wight and me at Siena' on Oct. 12, 1717.

[3] In the enclosed letter Boling-broke asked Swift to address letters for him 'A Monsieur Charlot, chez Monsieur Can-tillon, banquier, rue de l'Arbre Sec' (B.M. Add. MS. 4805, f. 26).

## XXX

Laracor. or Trim.    Aug. 20<sup>th</sup>. 1718

I MET your Letter at Gallstoun,[1] but intending to leave it before next Post, I could not write till now. I am here upon a Clergy business called a Trienniall Visitation, which begins to morrow. I intend to be in Town next week, and shall see you the morning after I come, thô I expect you will give me more Spleen than ever. But every body now is as desponding as I have been always. The Toryes have lived all this while on whipt Cream, and now they have even lost that. I find you intend onely a Visit, and a short one too.[2] I keep much in the Country because it is more unlike Dublin than any thing I can find on this side the Water. I can give you no Arguments to live in Ireland, but what the Fox gave about his Tail. M<sup>r</sup> Rochfort[3] has a mind that you and I should pass a fortnight with him between this and Michaelmas, I know not how that will fall in with your Methods.

I send this by a Gentleman who is just going, so adieu.

*Address :* To Charles Ford Esq<sup>r</sup>, at his
　　　　　Lodgings at M<sup>r</sup> Shaw's house
　　　　　on Ormonde key
　　　　　　　　　Dublin.

[1] Gallstown, or Gaulstown, in Westmeath, about seven miles south of Mullingar, near Lough Ennell. It was the seat of Robert Rochfort, Chief Baron of the Exchequer, Ireland, from 1707 to 1714 (when he was removed along with Lord Chancellor Phipps and Judge Nutley); and of his eldest son George Rochfort, member for Westmeath in the parliaments of 1703–13 and 1713–14.

[2] Ford had returned from the Continent after the middle of July, and was still in Dublin at the middle of October: see *Correspondence,* iii. 18.

[3] George Rochfort.

## XXXI

Dublin.   Dec^{br} 20^{th} 1718

I HAVE but just received Yours of Nov^{br} 13^{th} for we had 11 Packets together.   I desire I may never hear more from you of the Person you reproach me with.[1] Since his coming from abroad I have had 20 Letters from him, teazing me to death to write to him about an Information he apprehends against him, and about his Family.   I had a great Respect and Friendship for his Wives Mother, and at last I was forced to let him know that my Head and Eyes were so bad I could not write, nor could tell him any thing of his Affairs, and desired to be excused.   He came to know me inspight of my Teeth, and writes to me inspight of my Teeth, and there 's an end.

I stayd to hear from You, that I might know you were in Town but what can you expect from hence, from a Place every way contemptible in it self, and yet more so in your Esteem.   What have I to say unless I should transcribe a Sermon or a Pamphlet.   It is a just Tax upon you in great Scenes to entertain us who are out of the World, but it is a cruell Tyranny to expect Returns.   We had been undone for Talk during the Northwest Winds if two Ladyes had not been carryed off and ravished in the Country.   M^{rs} Ford[2] is so great a Rambler since your Absence, that in ten Attempts I have seen her but thrice, and once more in a third Place, where she tells me of an Account from you that a certain Friend of ours complains of my Silence.   I suppose it is the Friend that saw me coming

---

[1] Knightley Chetwode, who had left Ireland in 1715 to join Ormond, and was now in London (*Correspondence*, ii. 298, 300; iii. 10, 20).

[2] Ford's mother. The ' Friend of ours ' has not been identified.

in the Cloud.   I wrote him a long Romantick Letter, and desired a Correspondence ; perhaps it miscarryed ; I have his Address and will write again, and so I will to my Sister O—[1] in a day or two, but she must stay [p. 2.] till I have done my Christmas Sermon.   It | seems the Politicians are so busy in Parliament matters, that I cannot yet get a Successor to D[r] Parnel in Finglas,[2] where I have prevailed to place one of my Grattans,[3] as soon as our great Viceroy[4] will have Leisure from the weighty Affairs of Europe to remove an Impediment.

Mons[r] Charelot[5] is in debt to me not I to him : I wish he would mind his Interest upon the Death of an old Dean, now that the Person who can make him easy is on the Spot.

If my Spirit of repining were at Leisure, I could use it much upon the Subject of your Parliamentary Debates. Perhaps the Toryes had a Mind it should go for the Court upon S[r] James Forbes's[6] Reasons.   For I have been told, that for two Years past it hath been the Politicks of that Party to let every thing go as it would, without interposing.   But I am more con-

---

[1] The Duchess of Ormond. The Duke was a member of the Society (see Letter III, p. 9, n. 3), and thus a ' Brother '.   Cf. the *Journal to Stella*, 7 Sept. 1711 : ' Mr. Masham being a brother of our Society, his son, you know, is consequently a nephew.'

[2] Thomas Parnell, vicar of Finglas since 1716, died at Chester in October 1718.

[3] John Grattan, vicar of Finglas 1719–20.

[4] The Duke of Bolton.   War was declared against Spain on 17 December.

[5] Bolingbroke : see Letter XXIX, p. 65, n. 2.   This veiled allusion may have some reference to his relations with the Ministry ; he was hoping to be allowed to return to England, and was reported in July to have supped with Stanhope in Paris : see *Stuart Papers*, vii. 48.

[6] Clerk of the Green Cloth in 1689, when he was knighted ; mentioned in letters by, or to, Prior, *Longleat Manuscripts*, iii. 281, 283, 304.   The Debates were on the war with Spain, which was opposed by Walpole.

cerned about Sheridan the Schoolmaster[1] plaguing me
with bad Verses during his Christmas Leisure ; and
about contriving how to hinder an old Knave of an
Alderman from cheating me in a Lease, and where to
find a proper Successor for Parvisol,[2] who dyed last
Month without any Notice taken of it either in Court·
or Parliament.   But I am at present casting about how
to get Acquaintance with one Boswell a Prentice boy,[3]
who acts Punch to Admiration, and besides I am under
great Difficultyes how to entertain seven Butchers and
Grocers with their Wives and Familyes at a Christmas
Dinner.   I am afraid all these Momentous matters are
as indifferent to you as the Sliding of a Duck.   I am
concerned for my Friend Hatton,[4] but not disappointed,
because it was what I expected, and said something to
you that way when you were here.   He and Carteret[5]
were the onely two young Lords that I threw away
some Esteem on, and I heartily repent it.

The Grattans[6] and Jacksons[7] would not believe that

[1] Thomas Sheridan (1687–
1738), grandfather of Richard
Brinsley Sheridan.   Cf. Swift's
poem, 'The Dean to Thomas
Sheridan', dated 'Sept.   15,
1718':

> But why should we fight thus,
>     my partner so dear,
> With three hundred and sixty
>     five poems a year ?

[2] See Letter XII, p. 24, n. 5.

[3] Apparently   Swift's   only
mention of him.

[4] William,   second   Viscount
Hatton (1690–1760); mentioned
as dining with Swift in the
*Journal to Stella*, 29 October
1711 ; probably the Hatton who
was supposed to be a suitor of
Vanessa, *Correspondence*, i. 307 ;

cf. *Vanessa and her Correspondence*,
ed. A. Martin Freeman, 1921,
pp. 63, 68.

[5] John, second Baron Carteret
(1690–1763), had joined the
Whig party since Swift's London
days, and was now steadily rising
to power ; in March 1721 he
succeeded Craggs as Principal
Secretary of State, and in 1724
resumed his friendship with Swift
as Lord Lieutenant of Ireland.

[6] Robert Grattan, prebendary
of Howth, and John Grattan (see
above), two of the seven sons of
Patrick Grattan, of Belcamp, Co.
Dublin.   See W. G. Carroll,
*Succession of Clergy in S. Bride*,
1884, pp. 19–20.

[7] John Jackson, vicar of Santry,

you remembred them but I assured them I gave you a Copy of their Names and Callings. Your other Friends are well, and Peter Ludlow[1] came to Town with his Lady who is soon to be brought to bed of [p. 3.] another Son. Jervas[2] must | positively be in London before Christmas day but is not yet preparing his Equipage. Remember me to John and Ben[3] when you see them.

Did I tell you that Oct<sup>r</sup> 28<sup>th</sup> I received a Letter

and his brother Daniel, cousins of the Grattans. They are the 'Robin and Jack and Jack and Dan' of Swift's Birthday Verses to Ford, 1723 (p. 195). See B. W. Adams, *History of Santry*, 1883, pp. 5, 68–70.

[1] Peter Ludlow, of Ardsallagh, between Trim and Navan, M.P. for Dunleer 1713–14, and for Meath in the parliament of 1715–27; died 1750. He was a connexion of the Fords, and the father of the first Earl of Ludlow. Mrs. Delany, in a letter of 26 July 1744, writes of him as 'a very ingenious gentleman with a vast deal of humour, but so reduced by the gout that he was carried in and out on men's shoulders: he is very musical and understands painting' (*Correspondence of Mrs. Delany*, 1861, vol. ii, p. 320; cf. p. 498).

[2] Charles Jervas, portrait-painter and translator of *Don Quixote*. He had painted Swift in his Whig days (*Journal to Stella*, 9 Sept. 1710); this portrait is now in the Bodleian Library. He painted him again

in Ireland. On 14 August 1725 Swift wrote to the second Earl of Oxford (original in possession of R. B. Adam, Buffalo, N.Y.), 'I hope the picture of me in your house is the same which Mr. Jervas drew in Ireland, and carried over, because it is more like me by several years than another he drew in London' (*Correspondence*, iii. 262). This second portrait has not been identified with any of the known portraits of Swift by Jervas, or ascribed to him. Sir Frederick Falkiner thought it was probably painted during Jervas's long visit to Ireland in the second half of 1716, when he painted Parnell: see 'The Portraits of Swift' in *Prose Works*, ed. Temple Scott, vol. xii, p. 13. But Swift preferred to remain at Trim in 1716 while Jervas was in Dublin (*Correspondence*, ii. 333), and the comparative intimacy of the allusions in this Letter and the next suggests rather that it was painted in 1718.

[3] John Barber and Benjamin Tooke.

from the Dragon.¹ Octʳ 28ᵗʰ it came to my hands, and
Novᵇʳ 15ᵗʰ he was to be back in Town, and I must
visit him for 3 days, and take a good Winter Journey
Ætat. suae² 51. 1 wrote him such an Answer as he
deserved, and stayd here, and saved 50ˡˡ — I have been
just dining in my Closet alone on a Bief Stake and Pint
of wine, in 7 Minutes by my Watch ; and this is what
I often do, to encourage Cheerfullness.   I am heartily
concerned for Lady Boling— but we have a story, that
some Proceeding in my Lᵈ had provoked her.³

On second thoughts I write this Post to my sister
O—

*Address :* To Charles Ford Esqʳ, at
             his Lodgings at the Golden
             Perewig in Pell-mell
                           London ⁴

*Postmarks :* D *and* $\frac{29}{\text{DE}}$

## XXXII

### Dublin.   Janʸ 6ᵗʰ 1718–19.

I ANSWERED your Former letter as I remember, the
very Post after I received it.   But there was at that
time a great delay for want of Packets on each side,
and so probably mine had not reached you.   After all
I am not satisfied, that it hath been my old Custom not
to write to you ; while you were abroad you could
not easily be come at, and except that Period, I deny

¹ Oxford's letter and Swift's
answer have both disappeared.
² A slip for ' meae ' ?
³ She had died on 25 October
1718.   She left nothing to her
husband, who was then living

with the Marquise de Villette, his
second wife from 1722.
⁴ Added in another hand—
'Gold    perreywig    over    gain
Rochd's.'

that we were long asunder. It is really a difficult matter to be a good Correspondent from hence, where their is nothing materiall to say, where you know very few, and care for nothing that can pass in such a Scene as this, nor I neither if I could help it. You know I chuse all the sillyest Things in the world to amuse my self, in an evil age, and a late time of life, ad fallendam canitiem quæ indies obrepit. Little trifling Businesses take up so much of my time, that I have little left for speculation, [in] which I could gladly employ my self, for my Eyes begin to grudge (that I may speak in Royall Style) me reading, and the Pen is not half so troublesom. But instead of that, I do every thing to make me forget my self and the World as much as I can; and this is a full and true Account of your Correspondent. Here is a Pamphlet come over, and they say privatly reprinted here, called an Apology for Alberoni,[1] they say 6 Editions are already printed in England, and that it is a wonderfull Piece of wit and Satyr. I have read it, and lament the Tast of the Age, as well as the Malice, for except the latter, I can impartially find nothing in it but great Impudence, Wickedness and wrong Representation. | I wonder when men sit down with a Resolution to stick at nothing how they contrive to be so very dull and unentertaining, but de his satis. M^rs Ford told me what you desired her about our absent returning Friend. I am glad he received my last Letter.[2] I never had his Answer, but that shall not hinder me from writing again.

[p. 2.]

Pray tell M^r Pope that I will never be angry with him for any Mark of his Kindness, and will therefore

[1] *A Modest Apology for Parson Alberoni . . . The Whole being a short, but unanswerable Defence of Priestcraft, and a New Confutation of the Bishop of Bangor,* dated 1719, but published December 1718 : see the *Post Boy* of 9–11 December. The author was Thomas Gordon.

[2] See Letter XXXI, p. 67, n. 2.

pardon his Concern, or rather thank him for it.   I hope
this is enough, and that he will not require me to assure
him he is misinformed, honest men know each other
better : and I believe you have heard me say that Lord
Oxford took it as the greatest Compliment ever made,
when I told him on Occasion that I never regarded
what I said to him, nor what I said of him.[1]

I have as great a desire as my Nonchalance will
permit me to pass some Months in England, but not
in London ; and if I can adjust matters to bear, I have
had some Intentions that it might be this Summer.
But my Resolutions are like the Scheams of a Man in
a Consumption which every returning fit of Weakness
brings to nothing.

Tell D[r] Arbuthnot, that I received his last Letter,[2] and
will write to him when he has recovered Breath to read
another of mine.

I am extremely sorry that the Clause to make voyd
the Test by a Certificate, &c. did not pass,[3] and I have
a true Veneration for those Prelates who stood for it ;
The first part of this Assertion is actually true.——I
writt to my sister O— the same Post that I did to
you, I hope my Letter did not miscarry.[4]

[1] Cf. Swift's letter to Oxford, 3 July 1714 (*Correspondence*, ii. 162): 'I will add one thing more, which is the highest compliment I can make, that I never was afraid of offending you, nor am now in any pain for the manner I write to you in.'

[2] Of 11 December (*Correspondence*, iii. 21–4).

[3] The 'Act for strengthening the Protestant Interest in these Kingdoms' had been introduced by Stanhope in December, when the reasons offered by Cowper, and some other Peers, 'had so much weight, that some clauses derogatory to the Test and Corporation Acts were agreed to be left out'. The prelates who spoke in favour of the Bill were the Bishops of Bangor (Hoadly), Gloucester (Willis), Lincoln (Gibson), and Peterborough (White Kennett). See *Political State*, December 1718, pp. 613–26.

[4] See Letter XXXI, p. 68, n. 1. The letter is not known.

I hope you have found your English Climate since you left us, as bad as ours. Jervas happened to read [p. 3.] the Story of Belphigor in an | Italian Machiavel, and not knowing it was already in English, very gravely translated and published it here,[1] so that I assure you he is an Author. I was not let into the Secret till lately, so this is entre nous, but it may serve for Pope to laugh at, if he can pretend to come by it any where else. Has Gay done nothing of late? He is too idle for a young Fellow, pray tell him so: And I think Pope should bestow a few Verses on his friend Parnels memory,[2] especially if it is intended (as I think I have heard,) that some of Parnels scattered Things are to be published together. Who is that same Eusden, they have made Laureat? is he a Poet?[3]

I am personally concerned for the Death of the K of Sweden,[4] because I intended to have beggd my Bread

---

[1] 'The Marriage of Belphegor, An Italian Novel, Translated from Machiavel' had been added to *The Novels of Quevedo, Faithfully Englished*, 1671, and reprinted in *The Works of the famous Nicolas Machiavel*, translated by Henry Nevile, 1675, pp. 524–9. Another version is given in Samuel Croxall's *Select Collection of Novels in Four Volumes . . . all new translated from the Originals, By Several Eminent Hands*, 1720, vol. i, pp. 265–79; and perhaps this version is by Jervas. The separate issue at Dublin in 1718 has not been traced. Jervas became quite a considerable author when he translated *Don Quixote*. He gave Pope lessons in painting. See Letter XXXI, p. 70, n. 2.

[2] At the conclusion of his notes to *The Iliad*, 1720, Pope says that Parnell entrusted him with the publication of his poems 'almost with his dying breath'. *Poems on Several Occasions. Written by Dr. Thomas Parnell, Late Arch-Deacon of Clogher: and Published by Mr. Pope* was published in December 1721, dated 1722. The verses which Pope there bestowed on Parnell's memory took the form of the famous dedication to the Earl of Oxford, which says more about Oxford than about Parnell.

[3] Laurence Eusden's appointment as Laureate in succession to Nicholas Rowe (died 6 December) is announced in *The St. James's Evening Post* for 16–18 Dec. 1718.

[4] Charles XII of Sweden was

at His Court, whenever our good Friends in Power thought fit to put me and my Brethren under the necessity of begging. Besides I intended him an honor and a Compliment, which I never yet thought a Crownd head worth, I mean, dedicating a Book to him.[1] Pray can you let me know how I could write to the Count of Gillenburg.

This is enough at present so adieu.

*Address :* To Charles Ford Esqr, at
his Lodgings at the blue
Perewig in Pell-mell
London

*Postmarks :* D and $\frac{12}{IA}$

## XXXIII

Dublin.    Feb. 16th 1718–19.

I CONTINUE in an ugly State of Health by the disorder in my Head, which Blister upon Blister and Pills upon Pills will not remove, and this whole Kingdom will not

killed at Fredrikshald on 11 December (N.S.) 1718. Swift had been invited to the Swedish court before 1710, but his intention of finding refuge in Sweden in the event of exile has not hitherto been known. He hinted at it in Letter XXI, p. 43, and in his talk with Pope recorded in Pope's letter to Arbuthnot of 11 July 1714.

[1] The book survives in the fragment called *An Abstract of the History of England*, published by Deane Swift in 1765–8 (vols.

viii and xiii). It had been begun about 1703. On 2 November 1719 Swift wrote a dedication to the Count de Gyllenborg. The dedication is in part an expansion of this sentence, written ten months earlier.

Gyllenborg had been Swedish ambassador in London from 1710 to 1717 when, on 30 January, he was arrested for complicity in the plot to support a new Jacobite rising with 12,000 Swedish troops. See *The English Historical Review*, 1903, xviii. 81–106.

afford me the medicine of an unfoundred trotting Horse.
I have yours of Jan^{ry} 13^{th} and ought to have answered
it immediately if I intended to talk to the purpose, for
there are such sudden whirles in your Court and Parliament, that Affairs are at an Issue before one can have
time to reason on them. It would be an admirable
Scituation to be neither Whig nor Tory. For a Man
without Passions might find very strong Amusements.
But I find the turn of Blood at 50 disposes me strongly
to Fears, and therefore I think as little of Publick
Affairs as I can, because they concern me as one of the
Multitude ; and for the same Reason I dare not venture
to play at threepeny Basset, because it is a Game where
Conduct is of no use, and I dare not trust to Fortune
as the younger Folks do, and therefore I divert my self
with looking upon others at Play mea sine parte pericli,[1]
which if a Man could do in what concerns the Publick,
it would be no ill Entertainment. But when the Diver-
sion grows to throw Fire-balls at Random, how can I be
certain that Ucalegon may not live at the Deanry-
house.[2]—There is a Proverb that shews what is the
Time when honest People come by their own. I wonder
whether that Proverb hath a Reverse. A Friend of
ours[3] proposeth to set up a School of Strong Believers,
and desires that his own Father now in London may be
at the Head of it. I just now think of carrying this
Proposal further, and there may be a Whig and Tory
side of the School. The Test of the latter was the
[p. 2.] K. of Sweden's Death, which the best | Scholars would
not allow till Friday last at seven Minutes past eleven.
The Whig Test shall be that no Further Attempts
shall be made against the Church.

I was so unfortunate to lose your note about the

[1] Lucretius, ii. 6.
[2] *Aeneid* ii. 311–12.
[3] Probably George Rochfort:

see Letter XXX. The next letter
speaks of his father as being in
London.

Chaise by an Excess of Care ; for I had mislayd it before, and keeping it in my Pocket to shew a Merchant, it is irrecoverably gone, which I forgot to tell you in my last. Jam quoque Mœrim vox fugit ipsa, lupi Mœrim videre priores [1] ; and my onely Merchant Friend Samson [2] I fear is dying of a Consumption. But I shall endeavor to patch up the Matter with somebody else. —Ask your sanguine black Friend at My Sister O's [3] how his match goes on, and tell him the Story of Picrochole out of Rablais,[4] which I think I mentioned in my last. I had lately a Letter from an Inmate of John's,[5] who tells me that poor Ben Took grows ill an[d] spleenatick, and talks of selling his share in the Patent &c. It seems that Inmate and Ben have referred a Case to me, which I entirely give against Ben ; for I am Party to the Bargain made by L<sup>d</sup> B.'s order when that Patent was granted ; and pray signify to that Person that I would write if I knew some Name to direct to. I do not find among those that talk news, any discourse of

[1] Virgil, *Eclogues*, ix. 53–4.

[2] Possibly the Michael Sampson who died in 1736 and is described in Vicars's *Prerogative Wills* as a Dublin merchant; but the date suggests ' Michael Sampson, esq.', who died in 1719 and was M.P. for Lifford.

[3] See Letter XXXI, p. 68, n. 1. The friend remains unidentified.

[4] *Gargantua*, xlix : ' Ainsi s'en alla le pauvre cholerique ; puis, passant l'eau au Port Huaulx, et racontant ses males fortunes, fut advisé par une vieille lourpidon que son royaume luy seroit rendu à la venue des cocquecigrues : depuis ne sçait on qu'il est devenu. Toutefois, l'on m'a dict qu'il est de present pauvre gaigne denier à Lyon, cholere comme devant. Et tousjours se guemente à tous estrangiers de la venue des cocquecigrues, esperant certainement, selon la prophetie de la vieille, estre à leur venue réintegré en son royaume.' Swift referred to the story in a letter written on the same day to Bolingbroke, now lost : see Bolingbroke's reply, *Correspondence*, iii. 28.

[5] John Barber's. In 1711 Swift had procured for Barber and Tooke the printing of the *Gazette*, and in 1713 they were made Queen's Printers, their term to begin after Baskett's had expired in 1739 ; but Baskett bought back the reversion. See *Life of Barber*, Curll, 1741, p. 7.

L^d Bolingbroke's Return, therefore I suppose that Matter is dropt. If his Lordship expects Mercy he must get ready a Sacrifice, wherein the Princes of the Earth seem to differ a little from God Almighty, who says, he will have Mercy and not Sacrifice.—This is all I can work out of an ill Head at present: I have a mind to drink the Waters of Aix la Chappelle¹ this Summer. Pray tell me the proper time to take them and my Journy. I will once desire you to present my humble Service to severall Persons by name, My L^d Kinoul, Dartmouth, Harly, Masham, Bingly, Arran, M^r Bromly, S^r Th. Hanmer, D^r Arbuthnot, M^r Pope, Gay, &c, but especially friend Lewis; not forgetting |

[p. 3.] L^d Bathurst. I can recollect no more at present, but I am in a humor of Civility; and my humble Respects to Sister O—.

My humble Service to M^r Prior. I expect his Works² daily, I think the Method must be to consign them to a Bookseller here, and I am sending for one Hide, who has dealt that Way already and is recommended to me as an honest man.

We have found out the Fellow that killd³ Harry Lutterel,⁴ but cannot hang him. No doubt you know the Story, but it is very odd that he who hired the

¹ In his letter to Prior of 28 April he says he 'cannot be at Aix-la-Chapelle in May, as I intended' (*Correspondence*, iii. 29). He would have met Bolingbroke.

² Tonson's monumental folio of Prior's *Poems on Several Occasions*, 1718. In the list of Subscribers Swift is entered for 'Five Books', for himself and others: see Letter XLIV, p. 106, and cf. Harold Williams, *Dean Swift's Library*, 1932, pp. 23, 77. The subscription was two guineas,

one down and the other on delivery. John Hyde (d. 1727) had brought out the Dublin edition of *The Conduct of the Allies*.

³ 'that killd' repeated in MS.

⁴ Colonel Henry Luttrell was shot dead before his house in Stafford Street, Dublin, in October 1717. See F. Elrington Ball, *History of County Dublin*, iv. (1906) pp. 14–16, and Macaulay's *History*, ch. xvii. It has hitherto been understood that the assassin was not discovered.

murderer should confess in hope of the Reward, which
however he must have had by the Letter of the Proclamation, if it were not for his Perjury in swearing before
against Lutterell's widow.

*Address:* To Charles Ford Esq^r, at his
Lodgings at the blue Perewig
in the Pell-mell

London

*Postmarks:* D *and* $\frac{23}{FE}$

## XXXIV

Laracor. May. 3^d 1719. Ireld.

I HERE send you inclosed an Answer to the Letter
you sent me, which you will please to conveigh.[1] You
see what a Master a man is of his Resolutions after 50.
But I am absolutely ordered to ride, and my Health
having grown somewhat better, I have bought a Horse
at a great Price, and am resolved to ramble about this
Scurvy Country this Summer, and take the Shame to
my self of being lazy and irresolute. One thing shook
my Measures, that M^r Dopping[2] who was to have been
my Companion is not thought strong enough by his
Physicians to undertake so long a Journey. I go soon
from Hence to M^r Rochforts,[3] so to L^d Anglesey's[4] &c.

[1] The answer was to Bolingbroke's letter of 6 March (*Correspondence*, iii. 24–8).

[2] Samuel Dopping, eldest son
of Anthony Dopping, Bishop of
Meath; mentioned several times
in the *Journal to Stella*, and on
15 May 1716 as 'Sam Dopping,
whom I love and esteem above
most men' (*Correspondence*, ii.

316). He was member for
Armagh from 1695 to 1714, and
for Dublin University from 1715
till his death in 1721. The long
journey was to have been to Aix-
la-Chapelle.

[3] At Gaulstown: see Letter
XXX, p. 66, note 1.

[4] At Camolin Park, County
Wexford.

I made twenty other Difficultyes not worth troubling you with. But I hope we shall see a quiet World, and then I will rouze up my self, if Health and Humor will permit me. I wrote last week to M$^r$ Prior$^1$ to send over His Subscribed Books, which has been a great Neglect in his Bookseller to omit : There is one Hyde a Bookseller in Damas-street$^2$ Dublin, who has a good Repute, and is used to that Business, and is content to under-

[p. 2.] take | delivering them, and receiving the other Guinea from the Subscribers. Pray speak to M$^r$ Prior—

You will not let us be quiet here one Moment with Your confounded Invasions. A great Whig Prelate$^3$ says, this is the Invisible, as tother was called the Invincible Armada. There is such Doubling and trebling of militia Guards, and such a Dread of the L$^d$ Lucan's Ghost,$^4$ and of the D. of O. who is likewise reported dead, that we cannot sleep in our Beds for them.—M$^r$ Charlot$^5$ still passes very ill among our comers from England.

Pray tell Ben Took if you see him, that I shall obey the Commands in his this days Letter, and I shall write to him soon ; His Friend Cap$^t$ Cock never called on

$^1$ On 28 April (*Correspondence*, iii. 29).

$^2$ Now Dame Street, the bookselling centre in the eighteenth century; see J. T. Gilbert, *History of the City of Dublin*, ii. 263, and Letter XXXIII, p. 78, n. 2.

$^3$ Archbishop King.

$^4$ Patrick Sarsfield, created Earl of Lucan by James II in 1691 for his brilliant services in Ireland, and mortally wounded at Landen in 1693, left a son who was popularly known by his father's title. He had come to Ireland in 1715. Boyer's *Political State* for April 1719, p. 408, reports that 'About this Time the Lord Lieutenant of *Ireland* received Letters from General *Wynne* at *Galway*, who by his Grace's Order had made search in those Parts for *Sarsfield*, commonly called Lord *Lucan*, that Information had been given him, that the said Lord had made his Escape out of that Kingdom, taking Shipping at *Killicolgan*, a Creek within 6 miles of *Galway*.'

$^5$ Bolingbroke.

me but just when he was going to sea, and I searched for him in vain at his old Lodgings.

If you visit L^d Ch. Baron Rochford, and he has not left London, it would be kind in you to desire he would order to buy and bring me over a good Beaver,[1] I have a tolerable large head, thô it be not a very good one at present ; and that Beaver will be a good riding one when I ride next year to see You.   Where is Friend L——,[2] I suppose diverting himself with L^d Lexinton[3] or Mansel,[4] or Dartmouth, in the Country, and I conceive you will pass this Summer in the same Manner. Adieu—

*Address :* To Charles Ford Esq^r, at
His Lodgings at the blue
Perewig in Pel-mel
London

*Postmarks :* D *and* $\frac{12}{MA}$

## XXXV [5]

Dublin. Dec^br. 8^th. 1719

I HAD yours of above six weeks ago, and your last yesterday.   I do not think that Men who want their Health, are answerable for Lazyness and Indolence.   If they keep the same Affection for their Friends, no more

---

[1] Swift's 'best', 'second best', and 'third best' beaver hats are mentioned in his will.

[2] Erasmus Lewis.

[3] Robert Sutton, second Baron Lexington, ambassador to Madrid for the treaty of Utrecht.  In his remarks on Macky's Characters of the Court of Queen Anne Swift credits him with ' a very moderate degree of understanding '.

[4] Thomas Mansell, first Baron, a Lord of the Treasury in Oxford's administration, one of the twelve peers created at the close of 1711. Swift's character of him is ' of good nature, but a very moderate capacity '.   He gave Swift a bad dinner (*Journal to Stella,* 31 March 1711).

[5] The original is in the Pierpont Morgan Library, New York.

in justice ought to be required.   Indeed I fear, when Life
grows indifferent every Thing grows so too.   I was
somewhat recovered from a long Disorder when a piti-
full broken shin, which I skillfully cookt up into a sore
of Importance, confined me above a Month, and is not
yet well, and my want of Exercise under it, has been of
ill use to my Head ; Thus in Excuse for my Silence,
I am forced to entertain you like an old Woman with
my Aylments.   But your Complaint is not dans les
formes.   You live in the midst of the World, I wholly
out of it, and therefore ought to be the Writer and
complain of you.   I am very confident, that in the
whole year I do not speak to above a dozen Persons,
and make choice onely of such with whom it is of no
manner of Consequence what I say to them, or what
they say to me.   When it happens otherwise I am not
at my Ease, and that is the true Reason why I cannot
think of a Journy to England till I get more Health
and Spirits.   I will tell you a grievous unhappyness
under the Sun, that when Time brings a man to be
hard to please, he finds the World less carefull to
please him.   Which however is less to be wondred at,
because it is what every man finds in himself.   When
his Invention decays, his Judgment grows nicer, and
thus he is left in the state of those who ruin their
Fortunes, and enlarge their Appetites.   Take this Philosophy in return of your Apology for writing a word
of Politicks.   But as the World is now turned, no
Cloyster is retired enough to keep Politicks out, and
I will own they raise my Passions whenever they come
in my way, perhaps more than yours who live amongst
them, as a great noise is likelyer to disturb a Hermit
than a Citizen.

   I began this a week ago,[1] and between disorder and

[1] The second paragraph cannot be earlier than 19 December :
see p. 83, n. 2.   The London
postmark is 1 January.

Interruption was not able to finish it.    I am heartily
glad M^r Dopping ^1 has found Benefit by his Journy.
It is impossible to describe to you how I have been
hindred from accompanying or following him.    This
silly station I am in engages | me in more trifling Busi- [p. 2.]
ness than a high Treasurer, and besides the publick
wind is full in my Teeth.    But however I will try next
Spring what can be done, thô I foresee a foolish Impedi-
ment already: But the Truth is, the fear of returning
in ten times worse humor than I should go, has been
my strongest discouragement, as a prudent Prisoner
would not chuse to be a day out of Jayl, if he must
certainly go back at night.    I here inclose a Letter to
Mons^r [    ]— ^2 and hope it will not miscarry like the
former.    I saw a very foolish Pamphlet of Steele's to
Lord Oxford without Method Argument or Style,^3 for
my own Part I wish the Bill had passt upon S^r James
Forbes's^4 Reason :  And I remember to have agreed
many years ago with some very great men, who thought
a Bill for limiting the Prerogative in making Peers
would mend the Constitution, but as much as I know
of this it was wholly naught, and there is one invincible
obvious Argument which Steel lightly touches ; That
the Lords degenerate by Luxury Idleness &c and the
Crown is always forced to govern by new Men.    I think
Titles should fall with Estates.    The ABD ^5 (who is half

---

^1 See Letter XXXIV, p. 79,
n. 2.

^2 'Char' obliterated followed
by a dash, i.e. Charlot.    This is
the letter to Bolingbroke of 19
December, *Correspondence*, iii. 40.

^3 *A Letter to the Earl of O—d,
concerning the Bill of Peerage,*
published on 7 December, the
day before the Bill, after having
passed the Lords, was rejected by

the Commons. It provided that
no more than six English peerages
should be added to the existing
number of 178, and that the 16
Scottish representative peers be
replaced by 25 hereditary peers.

^4 See Letter XXXI, p. 68, n. 6.

^5 The Archbishop of Dublin,
the 'great Whig Prelate' of
Letter XXXIV.  'King was
neither a Whig nor a Tory, but

a Tory) seems to be at a Loss what the Bill was intended for, and will not allow the common Reason.   I should not be sorry to know what is said on that Subject.   If you see Mr. Charleton[1] pray tell him I had his Letter, but have not seen the Doctor he mentions.   I hear My Sister O— has very ill Health, which is an Affliction she does not want.   I desire you will present my most humble Service to her and L^d A—[2] when you see them, and particularly to Mr. L— D^r. A—[3] &c, and to M^r. Pope and Gay.—I write nothing but Verses of late, and they are all Panegyricks.[4]—I like Mr. L—s manner of Life, strolling thro the Kingdom, better than any amongst you.

> *Address :* To Charles Ford Esq^r,
> at his Lodgings at the blue
> Perewig in the Pell-mell
> London

> *Postmarks :* D *and* $\frac{\text{I}}{\text{IA}}$

something of both.  His position, to put it briefly, was that the Revolution had been made by, and in the interests of, the Church of England party.  But he also held that in coming to Ireland the English colonists had forfeited none of their rights and privileges as Englishmen.   They had their own Parliament and their own Church, and in civil and ecclesiastical matters they were independent of England.  Holding this opinion, he offered a strenuous resistance to every attempt on the part of the English Ministry and the English Parliament to subordinate the Irish to the English Interest in the country'

(Robert Dunlop, *Cambridge Modern History*, vi, p. 482).

[1] Arthur Charleton, chaplain to the Duchess of Ormond, and to the Earl of Arran.   He was the son (b. 1685) of Andrew Charleton, Chancellor of Armagh Cathedral.

[2] The Earl of Arran, brother of the Duke of Ormond.

[3] Erasmus Lewis, Dr. Arbuthnot.

[4] Unidentified.   One of these 'Panegyricks' may be the version of Horace's Ode, iv. ix, addressed to Archbishop King, though there is good reason for assigning it to 1721.

## XXXVI

### Dublin Apr. 4<sup>th</sup> 1720.

I HAD your former Letter with the inclosed from our Mississipi Friend,[1] I can make no excuse for my not acknowledging it than my perpetuall ill Health. I should not scruple going abroad to mend it, if it were not for a foolish importunate Ailment that quite disspirits me ; I am hardly a Month free from a Deafness which continues another month on me, and dejects me so, that I can not bear the thoughts of stirring out, or suffering any one to see me, and this is the most mortal Impediment to all Thoughts of travelling, and I should dy with Spleen to be in such a Condition in strange Places ; so that I must wait till I grow better, or sink under it if I am worse. You healthy People cannot judge of the sickly. Since I had your last of Mar. 10<sup>th</sup> I have not been able to write ; and three Days ago having invited severall Gentlemen to dinner, I was so attacked with a fitt of Giddyness for 5 Hours, that I was forced to constitute a Grattan to be my Deputy and do the Honors of the House while I lay miserable on my Bed. Your friendly Expostulations force me[2] upon this old Woman's Talk, but I can bring all my few Friends to witness that you have heard more of it, than ever I troubled them with. I cannot understand the South-Sea Mystery, perhaps the Frolick may go round, and every Nation (except this which is no Nation) have it's Missisippi. I believe | my self not guilty of too much [p. 2.] veneration for the Irish H. of L<sup>ds</sup>, but I differ from

---

[1] Bolingbroke, who had speculated in Mississippi stock and in May 1720 acquired La Source, his 'hermitage' near Orleans. See his letter to Ford of 29 January 1720, printed on p. 233. His letter to Swift of this date, and Ford's letter on forwarding it, are both lost.

[2] 'force me' repeated in MS.

you in Politicks, the Question is whether People ought
to be Slaves or no.[1]  It is like the Quarrell against
Convocations ; they meet but seldom, have no Power,
and for want of those Advantages, cannot make any
Figure when they are suffered to assemble.  You fetter
a Man seven years, then let him loose to shew his Skill
in dancing, and because he does it awkwardly, you say
he ought to be fetterd for Life.  Scotland is poorer and
more Northward than this Island, yet were satisfied with
their own Legislature till they were united on their
Conditions, which though I think too good for them,
yet they are proud enough to be ashamed of.  I do
assure you I never saw so universall a Discontent as
there is among the highest most virulent and antichurch Whigs against that Bill and every Author or
Abetter of it without Exception.  They say publickly
that having been the most loyall submissive complying
Subjects that ever Prince had, no Subjects were ever so
ill treated.  They tell many aggravating Circumstances
relating to the manner of rejecting their Addresses &c.
I who am to the last degree ignorant, was some time at
a Loss how the Commons at this Juncture when the
H. of L[ds] are not very gracious with them, and at all
times think not very well of their Jurisdiction, should
agree to extend it.  But it is easy to see why the
Ministry presst it, and as easy to guess what methods
a Ministry uses to succeed.

I cannot help the usage which honest M[r] Curl gives
me.[2]  I watched for his Ears in the Queens time, and

[1] The 'Act for the better
securing the Dependency of the
Kingdom of Ireland upon the
Crown of Great Britain' passed
through Parliament in March
1720.  It took away the jurisdiction of the Irish House of Lords.
See *Political State*, March 1720,
pp. 258–96, and Lecky, *Ireland
in the Eighteenth Century*, ii.
446 ff.

[2] The immediate occasion of
this allusion to Curll is not clear.
At the end of *A Defence of
English Commodities . . . written
by Dean Swift*, 'reprinted at

was I think once within an Inch of them.¹  There is an honest humersom Gentleman here² who amuses this Town sometimes with Trifles and some | Knave or Fool [p. 3.] transmitts them to Curl with a Hint that they are mine.   There is one about Precedence of Doctors,³ we do not know who writt it ; It is a very crude Piece, tho not quite so low as some others ; This I hear is likewise a Present of Curl to me.   I would go into any Scheam you please with Mʳ Congreve and Mʳ Pope and the rest, but cannot imagine a Remedy unless he be sent to Bridewell for Life.—You will present my humble service to My Lᵈ Arran and Lᵈ Harley and Lᵈʸ Harriette, and Friend L— and the rest.—I can write no more for my Head, and so much the better for you.

*Address :* To Charles Ford Esqʳ,
   at his Lodgings at the blue
   Perewig in Pell-mell
      London

*Postmark :* $\frac{11}{AP}$

London' July 1720 by J. Roberts (under whose name Curll issued many of his ventures), there is a list of books ' lately published, written by Dean Swift', including *Letters, Poems, and Tales* (Curll, 1718), *The Art of Punning* (Roberts, August 1719), and *The Right of Precedence* (February 1720 : see note 3).

¹ Cf. Swift's letter to Pope, 30 August 1716 : 'I had long a design upon the ears of that Curll, when I was in credit; but the rogue would never allow me a fair stroke at them.'

² Possibly Sheridan.

³ *The Right of Precedence between Physicians and Civilians Enquir'd into,* 'Dublin : Printed for John Hyde in Dame's-Street, and Robert Owen in Skinner-Row', 1720, and thrice 'Reprinted at London for J. Roberts', 1720.   Two of Roberts's three reprints contain this note : '*Dublin-Castle, Feb.* 3. 1720.   *Sir,* I here enclose to you a Pamphlet, written by Dr. *Swift,* in which you will find the *Humour* peculiar to that Gentleman.   *I am, Sir, Yours,* &c.'   This tract has been wrongly included in Swift's works since Nichols's *Supplement,*

## XXXVII[1]

WE were for some days in a good deal of pain about [you], but at last were assured you were safe in London.[2] I have been for some d[ays] out of Order with my old Deafness, which hath hindred me from going to [Da]wson-street.[3] I here send you the Thing I promised, as correct as I can [ma]ke it, and it cost me Pains enough, whether it be good or no.[4] The way to pub[lish] it will be to send it by the peny Post or an unknown Hand to some [. . .]er Printer, and so let him do what he pleases : only tear out this prose P[art an]d blot out the Subscription ; and then there can be no other Inconvenience than the Loss of the Copy.  When it comes out, buy one and send it franked and inclosed, immediatly, and I will send it to the Printer here.

You will let me know that      Dec^{br}. 15^{th}. 1720.
You have received this.

*Address :* To Charles Ford Esq^{r},
        at His Lodgings at the
        blue Perewig in Pell-Mell
              London

   *Postmarks :* Dublin *and* $\frac{26}{DE}$

1779.  It is of unequal merit; the best parts read like a parody.

[1] This 'letter' is written at the end of the original manuscript of the poem on the South-Sea Bubble. See p. 182.

[2] Ford had been in Ireland from July or August of this year, and returned to England sometime after 18 October (*Correspondence*, iii. 68), probably about the middle of November.  The London newspapers report a great storm on 19 and 20 November.

[3] The residence of Ford's mother.

[4] The poem.  The bursting of the Bubble and the financial crisis which followed had been the one topic of conversation while Ford was in Ireland.  This passage is interesting as evidence of the 'pains' which Swift took with his lightest verse, and of his methods for concealing his authorship.  Fortunately Ford did not

## XXXVIII

Dublin.   Apr. 15<sup>th</sup> 1721

You and I do not correspond upon equall Terms, for your Letters are usefull and entertaining, and often cost me nothing; whereas you are sure to pay for mine, which from such a Scene as this must be wholly useless and insipid.   I dined a few days ago with your People, who were in good Health, and assured me of Yours, and I believe you are now thorowly amused in the height of all these present Combustions; and I find the People here of each Party are as fully taken up as if it were there own Affair, and so far it is, that they are equally ruined with you, and at least as much and universally discontented.   Upon a Charitable Collection some days ago for the Poor Weavers, the Return of those who are starving for want of Work amounts to above 1600, which is pretty fair for this Town,[1] and one Trade, after such Numbers as have gone to other Countryes to seek a Livelyhood.—I sent M<sup>r</sup> Prior a Bill of 80<sup>ll</sup> above a Month ago, and desired he would let me know he had received it[2]; pray ask him the Question, and return the Answer your self.   Somebody or other told me that the Gentlewoman whose Bond I gave you was in prison for other Debts, and M<sup>r</sup>

follow his advice, but made a copy and preserved the original intact.

[1] 'The cry of the weavers of all sorts, linen, woollen, and silk, was intolerable. They sold and pawned all they had.... The numbers of the families belonging to the weaving trade in this condition upon inquiry are found to be near seventeen hundred, and the persons near six thousand, and no doubt but the other trades have their proportion of poor.'—Letter by Archbishop King, 8 April 1721, quoted by Elrington Ball, *Correspondence*, iii. 75, n. 2.

[2] See Letter XXXIV, p. 80, n. 2, and Prior's two letters of 28 February and 25 April, *Correspondence*, iii. 74, 76.

Charleton writt to me in her Favor; I am sure she is
an old Knave; but if you please to send the Bond
back by the first safe hand, I will use it against the
principall Rascall, who I find sculks about this Town.——
I have been employing my Credit by L^d Arran and
[p. 2.] other Means to get the D. of Gr—^1 to order | putting off
the Affair of the Printer till He comes over, but my
Sollicitor M^r Charleton^2 meets no Success; Surely tis
a small Favor, and I desired S^r Th. Hanmer might use
his Credit the same way: But I find there is less trusting in Friends than ever our Grandmothers warn us
again[st]; and the Term begins in ten days, and the
Matter will be resumed afresh, to great Expence and
more Vexation neither of which I am well capable of
bearing either by my Health or Fortune, and this
hinders me from going to England as I intended.—The
letter of Brutus to Cicero^3 should have been better trans-

---

¹ Charles second Duke of
Grafton, Lord-Lieutenant 1721–
4; he came over on 28 August.
His mother had married Sir
Thomas Hanmer as her second
husband.

The 'Affair of the Printer' is
the prosecution of 'E. Waters, in
Essex-Street, at the Corner of
Sycamore-Alley', for the publica-
tion of Swift's pamphlet *A Pro-
posal For the universal Use Of
Irish Manufacture, in Cloaths and
Furniture of Houses, &c. Utterly
Rejecting and Renouncing Every
Thing wearable that comes from
England*, 1720. Swift wrote to
Hanmer on 1 Oct. telling him
that 'the printer was tried with
a jury of the most violent party
men, who yet brought him in not
guilty, but were sent back nine

times, and at last brought in a
special verdict, so that the man
is to be tried again next term';
and on 22 Oct. Hanmer replied
that he had procured from his
step-son a promise to write at
once to the Chief Justice (*Correspondence*, iii. 64, 69). Swift's
comments on Hanmer in this
letter were mistakenly severe.
The affair dragged on till Grafton
came over, and then a *noli prosequi*
was granted. See Swift's account
in his letter to Pope of 10 January 1722, *Correspondence*, iii.
115–16.

² See Letter XXXV, p. 84, n.1.

³ Printed in *The London
Journal* for 1 April 1721 as the
main portion of one of 'Cato's
Letters'; reprinted in the *Political State* for April, and in *The*

lated ; Your Ministry seems to me to want Credit in
suffering so many Libells published against them ; and
here there is a worse Matter ; for many of the violent
Whigs profess themselves perfect Jacobites, and plead
for it the Miseryes and Contempt they suffer the by
Treatment of England.    We abound in Papers[1] as
well as you, and I have observed it to be one of the
Consequences of wretched Times, and it seems naturall
enough, that when People[2] are reduced to Rags they
should turn them to the onely Use that Rags are
proper for.—The sanguine Stile begins to revive, the
D. of Ormonde and his naturall Son were last week in
Ireland, and went over to the West, with the like Trum-
pery.    Sheridan put the Players upon acting a Puppet
shew, but | his Subject was ill chosen, and his Perform-  [p. 3.]
ance worse, and it succeeded accordingly ; yet gave
Occasion to a very pretty Copy of Verses on Puppet
shews[3] printed here but not published, yet I shall soon
get one, and would send it to you if I could Frank it ;

*Fourth Collection of Cato's Politi-
cal Letters,* 1721, pp. 3–12.
' Cato ' was John Trenchard and
Thomas Gordon.

[1] The chief Dublin periodicals
at this time appear to have been
*The Dublin Gazette, The Dublin
Courant,The Post-Man, Whalley's
News-Letter, Harding's Weekly
News-Letter, Pue's Occurrences,*
and *Dublin Intelligence.*    A few
odd numbers of the first five of
these published in April 1721 are
preserved among the Irish newspapers in the Gilbert Collection,
Dublin.    Other Dublin periodicals survive in odd numbers of a
slightly earlier date.

[2] ' kingdoms ' obliterated before ' People '.

[3] ' ThePuppet-Show ' was first
printed among Swift's Poems by
Faulkner, 1762, and has generally been accepted as his, the evidence for his authorship being
the similarity to the poem on the
South-Sea Bubble.    This passage
is stronger evidence against his
authorship ; Swift is not given to
mystifying Ford.    On the day
on which Ford received the letter
the poem was printed in *The St.
James's Post* with the heading
' The Puppet-Show, a Poem publish'd at Dublin '.    The subject
of the show was ' Punch turn'd
School-Master '.    Sheridan's Pro-
logue is printed in Concanen's
*Miscellaneous Poems,* 1724, pp.
398–400.

We cannot find the Author, and it is not Delany.[1]—Are not these fine materialls for a Letter; but I have no others.—I am now writing a History of my Travells, which will be a large Volume, and gives Account of Countryes hitherto unknown; but they go on slowly for want of Health and Humor.[2] I condole with you for the Death of Lady Newtoun.[3] They are bringing over her Body as I am told. Remember me to Mr Lewis and Pope and Gay. Some people complain for want of Mr Pope's 2 last Volumes of Homer[4]——and my remembrance to Dr Arbuthnot.

*Address :* To Charles Ford Esqr, at
his Lodgings at the blue
Perewig in Pel-mel
London

*Postmark :* $\frac{21}{AP}$

[1] Patrick Delany, the author of *Observations upon Lord Orrery's Remarks on Swift*, 1754. He came to know Swift in 1718, and was at this time a junior fellow of Trinity College. The best account of him is in F. Elrington Ball's *History of County Dublin*, Part vi (1920), pp. 130 ff.

[2] This is the first reference to *Gulliver's Travels*. It disposes of the opinion expressed by Deane Swift (*Essay*, 1755, pp. 278–81), and often repeated, that the book was finished in the winter of 1720. Orrery had suggested (*Remarks*, 1752, p. 196) that the book was written between 1714 and 1720, and Delany had asserted (*Observations*, 1754, p. 100) that it was not written 'until some years after' 1720.

[3] Emily, wife of Theophilus Butler, first Lord Newtown-Butler. She was the daughter of Ford's aunt, Mary Ford, who married James Stopford, of New Hall, co. Meath. Lodge's *Peerage of Ireland* (1754), ii. 339, says that she died 13 June 1722 and was buried the 15th in the family vault under St. Ann's Church, Dublin, and that her only son died 10 January 1721 and was also buried there. These dates cannot be reconciled with what we are told by Swift. The burial records of St. Ann's have perished and the existing extracts from them are said to leave the problem unsolved.

[4] Vols. v and vi of *The Iliad* were published as far back as May 1720.

## XXXIX

Dublin. Jun. 19<sup>th</sup> 1721

I SEND you here a Letter inclosed to Friend Charlotte,[1] and wish I had health or humor to have it done sooner, nor can I brag of either now, being hardly got out of an Ague, and am to morrow morning going in a Stage Coach for want of Horses to George Rochfort,[2] not being able to stir further by reason of that Scoundrel Circumstance of the Printer. I am now in the midst of Packing, and am awkward as an Alderman by long confinement. Your People are well, and were so kind to send frequent Messages to me while I was Sick.— I hear you are grown weary of prosecuting the South Sea, and our News writers bawl about that L<sup>d</sup> Mar and the D. of Ormond are to be restored, and folks tell me there is some Truth in it: I believe the Former but not the latter. I have finished that Tract you saw,[3] where you said I was mistaken about some Persons; I mean L<sup>d</sup> Poulet &c and I have some thoughts of

---

[1] Swift's letter is not known, but we have Bolingbroke's reply of 21 [O.S. 10] July, *Correspondence*, iii. 88.

[2] At Gaulstown: see Letter XXX. On 5 July Swift wrote to Vanessa, 'I had a weary journey in an Irish stage coach'; on which Mr. Elrington Ball remarks, 'It was probably of most primitive construction. The allusion is the earliest which I know to the use in Ireland of a public conveyance by a man of Swift's rank.'

[3] *An Enquiry into the Behaviour of the Queen's Last Ministry*, first published 1765. It is dated 'June 1715'; but Chapter ii, which is erroneously said to have been 'written about a year after' though it speaks of Oxford's 'two years residence in the Tower', can now be dated 1721. The *Enquiry* is Swift's last work as an historian of the reign of Queen Anne; and he would appear to have been stimulated to complete it by Ford's visit in 1720. The reference which we now read to Lord Poulett (Letter X, p. 19, n. 5) may be taken to have been amended according to Ford's criticism.

sending that and the other Thing which was sent to you before the Qu— died,[1] and have them both printed in a Volume by some Whig Bookseller, by sending it to him at a venture. L^d Anglesea is mortally fallen out with me about a passage in the Pamphlet of Irish Manufacture,[2] where he was meant, but with no Reflection further than differing in Opinion, he has not been to see me, and I him. He is for all the Hardships that have been put on this Kingdom. He sent me a Message, and I have returned him an Answer that will sting him.—Tis late, and I have not packt up my Shirts and Jesuits Bark.

*Address :*  To Charles Ford Esq^r, at
His Lodgings at the Blue
Perewig in Pell-mell
London

*Postmark :* $\frac{26}{IV}$

## XL

Sep^br. 30. 1721

I AM forced to put you to double Charges by sending the inclosed to Mons^r Charlotte :[3] this you might avoyd if you would let me know whom I could direct to that it might be francked, for I never pay for any of yours. I have been in the Country at M^r Rochforts above 3 Months, and from your Letter I conceived you would have been long before this in Dublin, and you

---

[1] *Some Free Thoughts :* see Letters VII, IX, &c.

[2] The passage beginning 'I was much delighted with a person who hath a great estate in this kingdom', in *A Proposal for the universal Use of Irish Manufacture.*

[3] Again only Bolingbroke's reply is known, 1 January [O.S. 21 Dec.] 1721/2, *Correspondence,* iii. 109.

left me so loose that I did not know how to send
sooner to M^r Charlotte, though I resolved to answer
him soon; I send this to M^rs Ford in Dublin, who
knows best what measures to take with you.   I shall
be in Dublin in a short time.[1]  A Friend is just going
to Dublin, who will take this with him, and the inclosed
must make up for the shortness of this.
     I am &c.

*Address :*   To Charles Ford Esq^r, at his
          Lodgings at the blue Perewig in
          Pell-mell
                              London
*No postmark.*


## XLI

### Lough-Gall. July. 22^d. 1722

I HAVE been here three Weeks with your Old Friend
M^r Cope,[2] who is the most domestick man you ever
saw, with a Wife whom he is so silly as to love, and
who deserves it as well as a Wife can ;  and with nine
Children, with whom he troubles himself as much and
his Friends as little as possible.  I have had little
Benefit of Summer since I left Dublin, the continuall
Rains have deprived me of riding and walking, and
I believe the Clymate has not got much Credit with

[1] Swift left Gaulstown the
next week, probably Tuesday
3 October.   He describes his
return journey in a letter written
from Dublin on 6 October, *Correspondence*, iii. 103.   His stay at
Gaulstown this summer is celebrated in his poem ' The Journal' (also called ' The Country
Life ').

[2] Robert Cope, at whose lodgings Swift had dined with Ford
and Archdeacon Morris (see below) on 11 Feb. 1711 (*Journal
to Stella*).  Swift's visit to Lough-
gall (five miles NE. of Armagh)
extended from about 1 July to
7 August.  He had left Dublin
at the end of April, and returned
at the beginning of October.

you. My Comfort is, that the People, the Churches
and the Plantations make me think I am in England.
I mean onely the Scene of a few miles about me,
for I have passed through miserable Regions to get to it.
I would be glad to know how you have passed your
Time, and whether you have cottoned with the Grat-
tans, Jacksons, and College Fellows. Whether you
wear out the Walks of Stephens Green, or play at
Chess for threepence in the Coffee-house. How the
Margoose[1] holds out, and whether you are got into
the Train of Rack punch. Whether you sometimes
see Sheridan, and grow reconciled to a dull Quibble.
Whether the Ladyes at the Japan board[2] continue to be
good Company, but I hear that they have taken a
Lodging at the Deanry. I writ to M^rs Dingley last
Post, and hope my Letter came to her as hers did
to me. I presume you and Jervas meet there sometimes, and do you bridle his Eloquence and vanity?
As little as you think of us, one of your Acquaintance
was here t'other day; it was Archdeacon Morrice,[3] who
is a great Builder and Planter, a very honest Gentleman, poor and generous, keeps excellent Wine, has
buried his wife, has 2 Children and the Sciatica. What
is more, Tisdal[4] lives but 7 miles off, we meet him once
a week at a Club. He is fifty times less agreeable
than ever, but a great Poet, Writer and Divine, and
we fall out every time we meet. The bad Weather

[1] Margaux. Cf. Swift's letter
to Stella 30 April 1721 (*Correspondence*, iii. 129).

[2] Stella and her companion
Mrs. Dingley at the card-table.
Cf. *Correspondence*, iii. 129.

[3] Theodore Morris, Archdeacon of Tuam, d. 1731 (*Fasti
Ecclesiæ Hibernicæ*, iv, p. 29).

[4] William Tisdall, rector of
Drumcree, near Portadown. He
had hoped to marry Stella and
is frequently mentioned in the
*Journal*; see Swift's letter to him
of 20 April 1704, Deane Swift's
*Life*, 1755, pp. 87–9, and Sheridan's *Life*, 1784, p. 300.

has made me read through abundance of Trash,[1] | and [p. 2.] this hath made me almost forget how to hold a Pen, which I must therefore keep for Dublin, Winter and Sickness. I have been thro the longest Lake in[2] Ireland, and the first fair Weather am to go through the broadest, that turns wood into Stone, and fools into Lyars.

Mr Cope is dispatching his Letters, and desires to present his Service to you. You will believe I am not in a Place that breeds much Materials for Letters. Here are neither extraordinary Scenes of Art or of Nature. Our Hay and Barley are quite spoiled, and betwixt you and me, Turf will be very scarce. Oatmeal was never known so dear, Half the poor have already lost half[3] their Itch for want of it.

My most humble Service to Mrs Ford, and Mrs Pen.[4] —and my humble Service to the Ladys : I cannot buy any Linnen for Mrs Dingley it [is] so horrible dear—I wish she would send a Venture of Brimstone, for a dozen of Smocks. I wish you would desire the Ladyes to let Mr Worrall[5] enquire for Saunders[6] Brother

---

[1] 'Diverting books of history and travels'—so in his letter to Vanessa of 13 July (*Correspondence*, iii. 134).

[2] MS. 'and' for 'in'.

The 'longest Lake' is Lough Erne, to the west of Clogher, where Swift had been Bishop Stearne's guest before his visit to Lough-Gall. The 'broadest' is Lough Neagh: 'In some places the waters possess medicinal properties. . . . They have also petrifying powers; but these are supposed to exist in the soil, as petrifications are only found in the lake near the shore of *this*

county'--S. Lewis, *Topographical Dictionary of Ireland*, 1846, i, s.v. 'Antrim'. See also Richard Barton, *Lectures in Natural Philosophy*, 1751, lecture iii, and John Rutty, *A Methodical Synopsis of Mineral Waters*, 1757, p. 18.

[3] MS. 'have'.

[4] Penelope, Ford's sister.

[5] John Worrall, Dean's vicar of St. Patrick's since 1694. See Delany, *Observations*, 1754, pp. 91–2, Deane Swift, *Essay*, 1755, pp. 293–300, and *Fasti Ecc. Hibernicæ*, ii. 206, 208.

[6] Swift's servant, Alexander

and pay him 20ⁱⁱ taking up my Bond, and a generall Receit.

*Address* : To Charles Ford Esqʳ, at
    Mʳˢ Ford's House in Dawson
    Street, near Sᵗ Stephen's Green
          Dublin

*Postmarks* : Armagh *and* $\dfrac{IY}{27}$


## XLII

### Dublin.   Janʸ 19ᵗʰ 1723-4

I HAD yours with the inclosed from my Sister O—[1] sent me to the Country, which we left last week,[2] and since have been too much imployed in my Visitation[3] &c. I am now ill of a Cold and therefore at leisure to write ; It is a Town Cold got but yesterday, for in the Country we know no such Thing, among good Fare, warm Rooms, and Mirth : all of us well in going residing and returning, without any Accident or other offence than abundance of Dirt and Wit.—So from not finding a Creature here to converse with, you are of a sudden grown so nice, that you cannot bear the Company at the Opera to be fewer than usuall.—I declare I can by no means blame your Choice of living where you do. Cæsar was perhaps in the right, when he said he would

---

McGee, d. 24 March 1722. Swift placed a tablet to his memory in St. Patrick's. See Delany, *Observations*, p. 194.

[1] The letter from the Duchess of Ormond, now in the British Museum, is printed in *Correspondence*, iii. 182.

[2] Swift, Stella, and Mrs. Dingley had been Sheridan's guests at Quilca. See Sheridan's verses, 'A New Year's Gift for the Dean of St. Patrick, given him at Quilca', 1723.

[3] Of his Cathedral.

rather be the first man in some scurvy Village, than the second in Rome, but it is an infamous Case indeed to be neglected in Dublin when a man may converse with the best Company in London.   This Misfortune you are able to fly from, but I am condemned to it for my Life.   I am very much pleased and proud of the Kind Remembrance of L$^d$ Ashburnham,[1] Masham, and M$^r$ Bromley, and I beg you will tell them so in the manner you like best.   L$^d$ Mans—s [2] Life or Death do not much affect | me.   The Toryes here have the same [p. 2.] wishes and Opinion with relation to L$^d$ Bol—.   I am heartily sorry for poor Doctor Arthbuthnot.[3]   I think there does not live a better Man.   I desire you will present my humble Service to him as well as M$^r$ Pope and Gay if they are come to Town.—M$^{rs}$ J— was much better in the Country,[4] and is at present not so ill as usuall.   We had onely some little slight Verses on the Birth-day.[5]   Once a year is too much and my Friends will wish me dead to save them Trouble.—In answer to your Important Question, I do assert that in eight days since my Return there have been 6 Deanry Dinners but no Patridge ;[6] onely at my Visitation there

[1] The third Lord Ashburnham, created Earl of Ashburnham in 1730; his first wife was a daughter of the Duchess of Ormond.

[2] Lord Mansell died 10 December 1723: see Letter XXXIV, p. 81, n. 4.

[3] In a letter received by Swift on 17 November, Arbuthnot had said, 'As for your humble servant, with a great stone in his right kidney, and a family of men and women to provide for, he is as cheerful as ever '.

[4] Stella had spent the summer of 1723 as Ford's guest at Woodpark : see pp. 197-202.

[5] His own birthday, 30 November. Swift had established the custom by his birthday verses to Stella (13 March) and to Ford (31 January) ; the former date from 1719. We have Stella's verses to Swift in 1721, and Ford's Latin verses to him in 1727. See pp. 193, 213, and 214.

[6] A dialectal form. Had Ford suggested that there would be partridge, with allusion to Bickerstaff's discomfiture of the astrologer ?

was a Pheasant. But I design to retrench, and my Wine is so bad, that yesterday I returnd a Hogshead, and two more in Bottles about four days ago. Sheridan is still the same, I mean in the Sense that Weather-cocks are still the same. My garlick keeps me from Deafness, and so you know the State of all Things of moment here.—I desire you will present my most humble Respects to my Sister :[1] I will answer her Letter when I think she will require it, but not soon for fear of tiring her, pray tell her This. What can have become of Dean Fairfax's[2] Widow ?

Last Night I received the Pacquet franckt *Osborn.* I suppose it is L<sup>d</sup> Caemarthen.[3] I was at a Loss about one of the Letters,[4] at first, but after found it was to you, and that you are a Traytor into the Bargain : else [p. 3.] how should he know | any Thing of Stella or of Horses. Tis hard that Folks in France will not let us in Ireland be quiet. I would have him and you know that I hate Yahoos of both Sexes, and that Stella and Madame de Villette are onely tolerable at best, for want of Houyhnhnms.—I presume the Verses[5] miscarryed four years ago, for I never heard of them till now. He has paraphrased onely the first Part of the Epistle, and wanders in the rest to shew himself an Esprit fort,[6] and

[1] The Duchess of Ormond.

[2] Charles Fairfax, Dean of Down from 1722, died 27 July 1723.

[3] Peregrine Hyde Osborne, Marquess of Carmarthen ; succeeded his father as third Duke of Leeds in 1729.

[4] From Bolingbroke to Ford. This important letter, dated 25 December, is printed in full on pp. 238–9.

[5] Bolingbroke's paraphrase of Horace's *Epistle,* I. i. In his

letter to Swift of 25 [O.S. 14] December 1723 Bolingbroke had said, ' I writ you at that time [" about four years ago "] a long epistle in metre. After rummag-ing among my papers I found it, and send it with my letter '. But nineteen lines of the paraphrase are in his letter to Swift of 17 [O.S. 6] March 1719.

[6] In his lost letter to Boling-broke of June 1724 Swift evi-dently wrote to the same effect, as Bolingbroke in his reply of 12

I believe that Part of his Poem if it were printed would
make his Court to the present People. But his Idea's
I hope were borrowed from the Scene he is in, for it
seems onely calculated to Popery ; But I believe free-
thinking is neither Whig nor Tory. There are a great
many good Lines, but I think the whole might be
more correct. There have been late doings in Parlm^t
here, which would make much noise if they had
passed among You. The Consequence of G. Rochforts missing his Election^1 have sett the two Houses
at Variance, and embroyld the Government with
a Vengeance. But I look on things here with the
same View as I would on Boys at Span-farthing, and
you look on them as something less. My greatest
want here is of somebody qualifyed to censure and
correct what I write, I know not above two or three
whose Judgment I would value, and they are lazy,
negligent, and without any Opinion of my Abilityes.
I have left the Country of Horses, and am in the flying
Island, where I shall not stay long, and my two last
Journyes will be soon over ;^2 so that if you come here
this Summer you will find me returnd—adieu—

*Address :* To Charles Ford Esq^r, at
his Lodgings at the blue
Perewig in Pell-mell
London

*Postmarks :* Dublin *and* $\frac{27}{\mathrm{IA}}$

[O.S. 1] September has a long
passage on the term *esprit fort.*
  ^1 As M.P. for Westmeath,
defeated by Richard Levinge. See
Letter XXX, p. 66, n. 1. Perhaps
' is to ' is omitted after ' Election '.
  ^2 Another very important
allusion to *Gulliver's Travels,*
proving that the Fourth Part, the
Voyage to the Houyhnhnms, was
written by 1723, and that the
Third Part, the Voyage to Laputa, though it incorporates
earlier portions, belongs in the
main to 1724.

of the Houyhnhnms as | if he were acquainted with him,[1] [p. 2.]
and in that shows you as a most finished Traitor, for
which you make very indifferent Excuses.  He says
he knows nothing of returning: if permitted he will,
otherwise resolves to retire to his Hermitage and ends
with 3 Latin Lines of Cleanthes : I know not whence
he got them.[2]    I shall see the rest when I see you.
Why will they not give poor Gay an Employment.
Tis a wofull Case to be under the necessity of writing
a Play for Bread when perhaps a Mans Genius is not
at that time disposed.[3]    I am sure it is an ill way of
making a good Poet,—anxie[ta]te carens animus facit,
omnis acerbi impatiens [4]—and if Philips hath as many
Friends he may get a thousand Pound too.[5]    My poor
Friend Arthbuthnot I heartily pity, and would purchase
his Health with the half of my Kingdom.    I am not
assez endurcy to bear the account of the Dragon's
Condition, quantum distabat ab illo.[6]—I do not understand as Raillery what you say upon the Court of the
Musical Academy.[7]    I believe it concerns you nearer at

[1] A mistake for 'them'. Bolingbroke could have heard about the
Houyhnhnms only from Ford.

[2] Either directly from Seneca,
*Epist.* xviii. iv (107), or more
probably from Cudworth's *In-
tellectual System*, 1678, p. 432.
The Latin lines are Seneca's,
from the *Hymn to Zeus* of
Cleanthes.

[3] Gay's tragedy, *The Captives*,
had just been produced at Drury
Lane, 9 January 1724.

[4] Juvenal, *Sat.* vii. 57.

[5] Gay had made £1000 by
his collected *Poems*, 1720. Ambrose Philips was at this time in
search of definite employment and
did not find it till late in the

year when he went to Ireland as
secretary to Archbishop Boulter.
Perhaps he was thinking of a
collected edition of his writings.

[6] The Earl of Oxford had
long been in failing health.    He
died 21 May.    Swift last wrote to
him on 6 November 1723, asking
for an invitation to Brampton,
and declaring, 'I love you better
than ever I did'.—Quantum
mutatus ab illo, *Aeneid* ii. 274.

[7] The Court of Directors of
the Royal Academy of Music,
which was formed for the performance of Handel's operas, had
its first season in 1720 and its
last in 1728 ; see Burney, *History
of Music*, 1789, iv. 258 ff.    The

present than Politicks, for these are desperate, but the other was your old Inclination, and is neither Whig nor Tory.—L^d Peterborows Gallantry ¹ is exactly of a Size with the whole Tenor of his Life, onely in complyance to his Age he seeks to make a Noise without the Fatigue of travelling, though he will be

[p. 3.] less ² able to perform his | present Journy than any of his past. He neither moves my Joy Pity nor Sorrow. I apply to Him what Garth said to me of L^d Wharton ; A fine Gentleman I vow to God, but he wants Probity. Our Fools here are repining like yours upon the K. of Spains Action,³ and I judged as you do, onely I call Devotion what you wicked Lay-men call Stupidity.— I hope L^d Caermarthen[s] Son is well, and then I care not whom he marryes.⁴ L^dy M— had not the Kindness to write to me, and I am mortifyed at it, considering what a Letter I wrote to her,⁵ pray tell My L^d this. I never received M^r Fairfax's Letter, nor know which of the Brothers writt.⁶ I send a Person to get the Box,⁷

previous letter shows that Ford had been attending these performances. The satirical passage on music in the 'Voyage to Laputa', ch. ii, was written about this time.

¹ In punishing Senesino, the leading tenor, for insulting Anastasia Robinson. 'Poor Senesino, like a vanquished giant, was forced to confess upon his knees that Anastasia was a nonpareil of virtue and beauty. Lord Stanhope, as dwarf to the said giant, joked of his side, and was challenged for his pains.'—Lady Mary Wortley Montagu, February 1724 (*Correspondence*, ed. Moy Thomas, i, p. 353).

² 'less' after 'worse' obliterated.

³ Philip V of Spain abdicated on 14 January 1724 in favour of his eldest son Louis.

⁴ See Letter XLII, p. 100, n. 3. Carmarthen's first wife, Elizabeth daughter of the Earl of Oxford, had died in childbed in 1713, leaving a son who succeeded his father as fourth Duke of Leeds. Carmarthen married for the third time in 1725.

⁵ Lady Masham's reply was received on 20 February (*Correspondence*, iii. 190). Swift's letter to her, apparently the first since 1714, is lost.

⁶ See Letter XLII, p. 100, n. 2.

⁷ Stella's snuff-box, as the next letter shows.

if it be mended you must pay him ; if not, you are desired to get it mended, unless you think it an un-wholesom Office, because one Man dyed in it.  Your People are well, but M^rs Ford had lately a great Cold— Adieu.  If the Box be to be mended, the Manner and fancy are left to You.

*Address :* To Charles Ford Esq^r,
   at the blue Perewig in
   Pell-mell
       London

*Postmarks :* Dublin *and* $\frac{24}{FE}$


## XLIV

Dublin. Apr. 2^d 1724

BEFORE I could find time to answer your Letter, I fell into a cruell Disorder that kept me in Torture for a Week, and confined me 2 more to my Chamber, but I am now rid of it, onely left very weak, the Learned call it the Hæmorrhoides internæ which with the attendance of Strangury, loss of Blood, water-gruel and no sleep require more of the Stoick than I am Master of, to support it.  You are a Stranger to sickness and not a judge pour nous autres maladifs. These frequent Disorders are the onely discouragement from venturing so far as England from the Smoak of my Chimney.  M^rs J— rejoyces at her Snuffbox, but thinks as I do that it is sufficiently dear, especially when there is onely a new Bottom, wherein however we hope you are mistaken because the old Bottom had a single Fly studded on it, but the lid was raised and inlayd all over ; and you see nothing how it is now. Pray buy a little wooden Box lined, to put it in, and

when we hear of somebody coming over, (for you we do not expect) they shall be desired to call on you for it, and pay you, which I believe will be reasonable, for it will keep you two days longer. M^rs J— is grown a Walker. She read that part of your Letter with the D^rs Advice, but is ¹ not yet resumed Steel. I came just
[p. 2.] now from a Commission with the Chancellor ² | ArchB^p Dublin³ &c. I spoke very severely to the knaves about the Farthings. I told them the Baseness and pusilanimity when they and others were sent for by the L^t ⁴ upon that Subject ⁵ they all talked as much against the Thing as I. but People are more in fear than ever. I do not know whether I told you that I sent out a small Pamphlet under the Name of a Draper,⁶ laying the whole Vilany open, and advising People what to do ; about 2000 of them have been dispersd by Gentlemen in severall Parts of the Country, but one can promise nothing from such Wretches as the Irish People. if this Destructive business brings you over, aliquisque malo fuit usus in illo. In spight of your way of refining, I am ever out of humor when I leave a Place where I am easy to go to a more disagreeable one ; and if I were in Jayl I would not be set at Liberty for a Week if I could. A little Business comes in my Head. There are about thirty of Priors Poems (or somewhat more) that the Subscribers will not call for, neither can I get People to take them even for a single Guinnea.⁷ I have been tired and vexed enough with this Matter

¹ Query ' has '. The little mistakes in this letter suggest that Swift had not yet fully recovered from his recent disorder.

² Viscount Midleton.

³ Archbishop King.

⁴ The Duke of Grafton, Lord Lieutenant.

⁵ Syntax defective.

⁶ *A Letter to the Shop-Keepers, Tradesmen, Farmers, and Common-People of Ireland, Concerning the Brass Half-pence Coined by Mr. Woods . . . By M. B. Drapier.* This passage shows that the first of the *Drapier Letters* was issued before April.

⁷ See Letter XXXIII, p.78, n.2.

and I fear L^d Harley and M^r Drift ^1 may think I have
been negligent ; but I believe you will be my Witness
to the contrary.   I beg you will tell M^r Drift this, or
L^d Harley if you see him ; and desire to know what
I must do.   I have about 14 or 15 Guinneas to remitt,
but God knows whether I shall get any more.   I will
return the remaining Copyes if they think fit, and let
the Subscribers | be hanged, and the few Guinneas shall [p. 3.]
be remitted when they please.   I think I offered them
to you, but did not blame you from ^2 excusing your
charging your self with them.   Pray set this Matter
right, you know what Ireland is.—It is said the L^t stays
here purely to keep as long in as he can.^3   Bolton ^4 has
got a better Bishoprick and is succeeded by a poor
[har]mless obscure Creature of Conollyes,^5 but they say
an honest good natured Man.   My humble service
to D^r Arbuthnot M^r Pope and Gay.   I sometimes
think,^6 D. Wharton intends to take my Advice of fancy-
ing to have Virtue.   I remember M^rs Bracegirdle got
more by acting that Part than any of the more
abandoned Playhouse females, there is a sort of a Contrast
in it.   I saw a long printed Speech of his, and intend
to borrow it when I can.^7   I never had M^r Gay's

---

^1 Adrian Drift, Prior's secretary. Harley was Prior's principal
executor.  See the letters of Drift
and Swift on this subject, *Correspondence,* vi. 234–7.

^2 Query 'for'.

^3 Grafton received official con-
firmation that he was succeeded as
Lord Lieutenant by Carteret on
9 April, and left Dublin on 8 May.

^4 Theophilus Bolton, translated to the Bishopric of Elphin.
He was succeeded in the Bishopric
of Clonfert by Arthur Price, Dean
of Ferns, who as Rector of Cel-

bridge had offered to attend
Vanessa on her death-bed (see
'Swift and Stella' by Dr. Bernard,
*Prose Works of Swift,* ed. Temple
Scott, xii. 95).

^5 William Conolly, Speaker of
the Irish Parliament.

^6 MS.  'I   am   sometimes
think'.

^7 The Duke of Wharton spoke
in favour of Atterbury in the
House of Lords on 22 May 1723,
on the third reading of the bill
'to inflict pains and penalties'.
The third edition of the speech

works;[1] but thank him kindly however. I saw your Family in good health 2 days ago. There are good Lodgings in Dawson Street, since you are turned out of your old ones.—I shall have finished my Travells very soon if I have Health, Leisure, and humor. Robin Copes[2] Lady and Family are come to Town to Live, and M^r Cope is soon expected. He will serve for one Night to you in a Week. I see Corbet[3] often, and I believe he will prove ad unguem factus homo.[4] You are too good a prophet about L^d Bol— for we hear nothing of his beeing recalled. Pray bring over with you a printed List of the House of Lords, for I long mightily to see the Names of so many new ones in this happy Reign. L^dy Granard dyed yesterday, which will add 400^ll a year to L^d Forbes.[5] Three Fools have lately dyed and made wise wills, the B^p of Meath,[6] your Cousin L^d Newton,[7] and S^r J^on Rawden.[8]

*Address :* To Charles Ford Esq^r.

was advertised in February 1724. It was afterwards added to editions of *The True Briton.*

[1] Swift had not subscribed to the collected edition of Gay's *Poems,* 1720; he expected a presentation copy. See *Correspondence,* iii. 151, and Letter XLIX, p. 118, n. 2.

[2] See Letter XLI, p. 95, n. 2.

[3] Francis Corbet, Prebendary of St. Patrick's, Swift's successor (after Matur n) as Dean, 1746. He was one of Stella's executors.

[4] Horace, *Sat.* I. v. 32.

[5] Viscount Forbes, son of the Earl of Granard, whom he succeeded as third Earl in 1734; mentioned in the *Journal to Stella,* 22 July 1711.

[6] John Evans, Bishop of Meath from 1719, died 2 March 1724. 'He generously bequeathed all his property in England, Wales, and Ireland, for the benefit of the poorer Clergy of the respective countries'—*Fasti Ecclesiæ Hibernicæ,* iii, p. 121.

[7] Theophilus Butler, created Lord Newtown-Butler 1715, died 11 March 1724. Cf. Letter XXXVIII, p. 92, n. 3. He bequeathed to the poor of St. Ann's parish, Dublin, '£13 per annum to be distributed in bread at five shillings each week'. Loaves of bread are displayed in the church every Sunday and given to the poor in the evening.

[8] Sir John Rawdon, of Moira,

## XLV

Dublin.   Jun. 16<sup>th</sup> 1724

I SUPPOSE you will contrive to send the other side, when you can.   My Booby of an Agent who went to London, had a large Pacquet for you, and because you were out of Town brought it back, thô it was directed to the Coco-tree, and ordered to be left there, and by his not seeing you, M<sup>rs</sup> Johnson is deferred from having the Pleasure of her Snuff-box.   I am kept from my usuall summer travelling, by building a Wall,[1] which will ruin both my Health and Fortune, as well as humor ;  If one piece of news be true, we shall soon have you in Ireland, for I was told for certain by a Physician, that the Dutchess of Mountague[2] is coming here to drink some waters, which are very good for her Disorder, whatever it is.   If that will not do the Business, the Halfpence must, for we daily expect them.   We have got here a Poet for a Secretary, one M<sup>r</sup> Tickell, born and famous since I left the World.[3] We have mutually visited, but neither of us at home ; however I have dined with him at a third Place, and

third baronet, died 2 February. His will disappeared in the destruction of the Irish Record Office, and no copy of it is in the possession of the Commissioners of Charitable Donations and Bequests.

[1] Enclosing ' Naboth's Vineyard ', a piece of ground to the south of the Deanery ; see the account of it in Mrs. Pilkington's Memoirs as given by Sheridan, *Life*, ed. 1784, p. 480.

[2] See Letter I, p. 1, n. 3.

[3] Thomas Tickell, Addison's friend and editor, had arrived in Dublin as secretary to the Lords Justices of Ireland at the end of May, and came to ' a country where he was altogether a stranger ' : see *Letters to and from William Nicolson*, Archbishop of Cashell, ii. 574.   Swift would appear to have forgotten the poem *On the Prospect of Peace*, by which Tickell had made his name, or at least had shown his promise, before Swift ' left the world '.   Kneller did not give him an ' odd ' countenance in the portrait now in Queen's College, Oxford.

he is a Wit of as odd a Countenance as I have seen. I am now writing at the L^dys —— Lodgings where M^rs Penny[1] is on a Visit, they are all well, and she tells me M^rs Ford writes to you to night. I would be glad to know a little what sort of Man L^d Carteret is grown. I writ to him about the Halfpence, at the desire of some principall Persons here, and he had not the Civility to answer me ; so I writ a second time in such a Manner as he deserved, as severely and reproachfully as could consist with any good Manners.[2] I would know likewise whether poor L^d Oxford's Death[3] were attended with any Particulars. His Son is eased of a Burden, which however he could easily bear, and I am sure would have been glad to do it longer. Sheridan pursues Tisdal[4] with Ballads and Verses, and there is one very good, called the Cobler to Jet Black.[5]—Sheridan has received your Letter, and is exceedingly pleased with your remembring him.—I conclude you often see Madame de V——[6] and I hope you will remember to give me her Character. I dined t'other day in Company with M^r James Forth,[7] and raillyed him on his changing

---

[1] Ford's sister Penelope ; cf. Letter LV, p. 130.

[2] Carteret had enjoyed Swift's esteem in the London days : see Letter XXXI, p. 69, n. 5. On Carteret's appointment as Lord Lieutenant (2 April) Swift wrote to him (28 April) about Wood's half-pence, and recalled their old friendship. No reply was received, and Swift wrote again (9 June). In this second letter the severity is admirably veiled by 'good manners'. Carteret, who had been in the country, replied from London on 20 June with equal tact and friendship.

[3] On 21 May. See Letter XLIII, p. 103, n. 6.

[4] See Letter XLI, p. 96, n. 4.

[5] A copy of the broadside—*A Letter from a Cobler in Patrick's-Street to Jet Black. Printed in the Year 1724*—is in the Bradshaw Collection in the University Library, Cambridge (Hib. 3. 730.1.42).

[6] Lady Bolingbroke.

[7] Ford's cousin, of Redwood, King's County, then M.P. for Philipstown. Perhaps the change which he denied was from Forth to Ford.

of his Name, but he insists upon it, that it is a Mistake, and offers such Arguments as have almost shaken me, and I calld M^rs Penny, and she defends the Cause not very well. I doubt your Summer Journyes do you little good, considering your Companion ; and that you lose just as much by raking as you gain by Exercise. The Ladyes ^1 sigh after Wood-park like the flesh-pots of Ægypt, and come every hott afternoon to the Deanry as to a Country-house.—I score the other side as so much written to you, for you so little know or value Things Places or Persons here that I can have nothing to fill a Letter with making Dawson-Street,^2 Grafton Street,^3 or the Deanry the Scene ; neither have I your last Letter about me,—so that if you desired to know any thing I cannot satisfy you. My humble Service to D^r Arbuthnot M^r Lewis, M^r Pope M^r Gay—adieu.

*Address :* To Charles Ford Esqr, to be
left at the Cocoa Tree in
Pell-mell
London

*Postmarks :* Dublin *and* $\frac{24}{IV}$


## XLVI

### Dublin. Nov^r 27^th 1724

I WONDER how You expect I can write Letters, when I am deaf and have been so these 2 Months, and am afraid I shall never recover, and yet I hear more things than ever, For this whole Town is taken up with a Monster they call the Draper, who like a Duns is

---

^1 Stella and Mrs. Dingley.
^2 The residence of Ford's mother and sister.

^3 Perhaps the residence of Stella and Mrs. Dingley ; see Letter L, p. 120, n. 1.

endeavoring to keep you and the like of you in England ; But the L^d L^t swears you shall come back and live at home, if Woods Halfpence can bring you. I am infinitely obligd to Madame de V. pray tell her I am informed that she is the most agreable conversation in the World, and to be with her and not to hear her must be the greatest Mortification.   I gave L^d Oxford no Encouragement that I remember that I would come over, I have at last received a Letter from him, for he is as bad at writing as his Father.¹   He is very kind and has promised me his Father's Picture ; and (by the Way) has a Ring for me, which I desire you will be so kind as to get from him, and send it by the first Person you know, who comes hither.   I hear [p. 2.] severall | Packets have been directed to you of the Drapers last Letter,² against which the L^d Lieuten^t hath published a Proclamation, but that they have all miscarryed, and it seems Manly³ hath orders to open all Letters where he supposes any Pamphlets against Wood are inclosed.—I have not seen the L^t since he came over being hindred by my Disorder nor ever received from him any more than one cold Compliment.⁴   It seems he suspects (without Reason) that I am privy to the Draper's Pamphlets.

Friend L— for ought I know hath done a wise

---

¹ In his first letter (9 July) to Edward Harley as second Earl of Oxford, Swift had said nothing about a visit to England, but spoke of the first Earl's papers and asked for his portrait. In his reply (2 November) Oxford said that Swift would have to come to England if he was to see the papers, promised the portrait, and desired the acceptance of a ring.

² *A Letter to the Whole People of*

*Ireland,* the fourth of the Drapier's Letters, dated 13 October and published 22 October. Carteret's proclamation offering a reward of £300 for the discovery of the author was issued on 27 October.

³ Isaac Manley, Postmaster ; see Letter V, p. 13, n. 4.

⁴ Swift described himself to Carteret on 9 July as testy and captious; see Letter XLV, p. 110, n. 2. Carteret replied on 4 August,

Thing, if the Woman (I know her) be so rich as to maintain him and her self better than he could do it without her, and I suppose all women are now pretty equal to him as a Shepherd.[1]—I desire you will let me know what Person I shall direct to, when I send you a Letter with one inclosed | to Don Carlos.[2]—For I am [p. 3.] in some pain to answer his, because it differs a little in the manner from those I used to receive.—I am glad you have made some Summer Rambles, which I have been diverted from at the Charge of 400ll in building a Wall,[3] and [to] that want of Exercise I impute my present Ailment.—No we have had no great Rains, give the Devil his due. The Ladyes bear me company in my Illness, I can hear nothing but Trebbles. I have put Mrs Johnson into a Consumption by squalling to me, they desire their humble Service.

The grand Jury has been dissolved for refusing to present a Paper against Wood;[4] a Second was called

and ended thus,—' I am not altogether insensible of the force of that genius which has outshone most of this age, and, when you will display it again, can convince us that its lustre and strength are still the same'. Swift wrote on 3 September, when Dublin was preparing for Carteret's reception, and received no reply. He wrote again to Tickell on 24 October, explaining that his health kept him from waiting on Carteret, and perhaps the 'one, cold compliment' was the official reply, which is not extant. This passage discredits the anecdote (Sheridan's *Life*, 1784, pp. 246–7) of Swift's encounter with Carteret on the day after the Proclamation was issued. Cf. *Correspondence*, iii. 228.

[1] Erasmus Lewis, aged fifty-four, had married a widow, Mrs. Anne Bateman, on 1 October.
[2] From Stella, who called Ford ' Don Carlos '.
[3] See Letter XLV, p. 109, n. 1.
[4] The Grand Jury refused on 23 Nov. to present *Seasonable Advice to the Grand Jury* concerning the bill against Harding, the printer of the Letters, and was thereupon dissolved by Chief Justice Whitshed. The second Grand Jury proved not only stubborn but aggressive, and on 28 Nov. made a presentment condemning the patent (*Prose Works*, vi. 233). We may assume that the presentment was ready when Swift thus expressed his satisfaction to Ford.

who are more stubborn. The Government and Judges are all at their Witts end—The dissolving the Jury is reckoned a very illegall arbitrary Thing. I have not been out of doors these three Months, but go to morrow about 4 miles off,[1] to try new Air for a few days.

*Address :* To Charles Ford Esq[r]—
    to be left at the Coco-Tree
    in the Pel-mel
        London

*Postmark :* $\frac{7}{DE}$

## XLVII

I WRITE to you in this Manner to save Postage to the Person concerned. He is a Clergyman marryed to a near Relation of mine ;[2] He is heir to one Capt. Lightburn, a famous man in the County of Meath, whom your Father knew very well, for he was a famous man in his Generation, and was called the God of Trim.[3] He marryed my Cousin in hast before her Relations could settle Matters ; He has had a long Suit about the Fortune,[4] and has been used like a Dog : I was Referee

---

[1] Probably to the Grattans at Belcamp. The 'few days' extended to three weeks.

[2] The Rev. Stafford Lightburne married Hannah, daughter of Willoughby Swift, the Dean's cousin. He was Swift's curate at Laracor.

[3] Stafford Lightburne, of Staffordstown, co. Meath, d. 1697, for many years Portrieve of Trim, and latterly Member of Parliament. See *The Irish Builder* for 15 August 1888, p. 213.

[4] His wife's fortune had been entrusted by her father to his step-brother Deane (father of the biographer), and her father's creditors had tried to seize it. In his letter to Lightburne of 22 April 1725 Swift says 'I am very glad of your good success in England, for I always believed you had justice on your side'. See *Correspondence*, iii. 152, 235, iv. 282 and 418, where Elrington Ball cites British Museum Addit. MS. 36148, f. 1.

for him, but by some Accidents the Reference would not stand.   The suit has cost him double the Fortune, and his Estate instead of being disencumbered is a good deal more in debt.   He now has an Appeal before the House of L^{ds} ; and I desire you will do him the usuall Favors on these Occasions, by engaging such Lords as you know, to be there, with a good Inclination, and where I have any Credit, to add my Name ; do this, and oblige y^{rs} ever—

    Dec^r 29^{th} 1724
    Engage friend Lewis [1]

*Address :* To
        The Reverend
        M^r: Lightburn.[2]

## XLVIII

### Dublin.   Dec^r 31^{st} 1724

The Letter on the other side [3] was by severall Interruptions stopped till this day and it was not till yesterday I received yours of the 10^{th}—I desire to make my most humble Acknolidgments to M. d. V.[4] for her Receit, which I will certainly make use of, because I think there is more Virtue in her Influence, than in the Medicine it self, and if it succeeds, I shall have the double Pleasure of seeing and hearing her.   I find she has often promised to write to me, and I am confident that would be the best Remedy she could prescribe. I congratulate with her upon her Victory over that abominable Rascall, Decker,[5] and I am glad she had so

[1] Erasmus Lewis.
[2] But the letter is written to Ford.
[3] Torn off; the letter here printed is on a half-sheet.
[4] Lady Bolingbroke.
[5] Sir Matthew Decker, merchant in London, a director of

much occasionall Money to lose.  The Drapier is not the only Poet, for there are severall Writers in his Praise about as good as himself, I will send some a Post or two hence.[1]  This Day is come out a fifth[2] Letter from the Drapier inscribd to L^d Molesworth, but how to send it you I know not, for although I should direct it to L^d Barrymore,[3] it would probably be opened here by Manly the Postmaster, who either by his own Pragmaticallness or the Orders of the Government opens all Pamphletable Letters, and I know nobody that goes from hence.—I am somewhat better of my Deafness, but not in a Condition to go beyond the Deanry Garden, to which I have been confined four Months,[4] and refuse all People who have not hearable Voices.  L^d Carteret sent me one cold Compliment[5] in answer to one from me, but since I have had no Commerce with him, I intend to see him when I can hear him.  He has shewn more Abilityes than any one I ever knew in his Station.  I suppose L^d Suffolks Works[6] sell very well, and I should be as

---

the East India Company, created Baronet July 1716.  He had been entrusted with £50,000 of Madame de Villette's money, and as she had become Lady Bolingbroke he refused to give it up on the ground that he might be made answerable for it by parliament.  Ultimately it was arranged that Lady Bolingbroke should pay £11,000 to Lady Walsingham, daughter of the Duchess of Kendal.  See Coxe, *Memoirs of Walpole*, ii. 328, 331, 345.

[1] A copy of the original print of Swift's *Prometheus* is preserved with Swift's letters to Ford.  See Elrington Ball, *Swift's Verse*, pp. 178–95, 332–9.

[2] 'fifth' written over 'fourth' crossed out.  The *Letter to Lord Viscount Molesworth* is dated 14 December; this passage establishes the date of publication as 31 December.

[3] James, fourth Earl of Barrymore.

[4] Swift ignores his recent visit of three weeks to a place four miles from Dublin: see Letter XLVI, p. 114, n. 1.

[5] Cf. Letter XLVI, p. 112, l. 22, and n. 4.

[6] *Miscellanies in Prose and Verse, By a Person of Quality,*

glad to see them as you would be to see those of the
Draper.   How a mischief could that Parson S^r Robert
Sutton ^1 get 8000^ll a year.   I suppose he is about 70
years old.—The Ladyes are just as you left them, but
those who see M^rs Johnson seldom, say she grows
leaner, she eats about 2 ounces a week, and even
drinks less than she did.   Sheridan writes Ballads, and
D^r Delany grave^2 Poems.—Pray get me my Ring from
Lord Oxford ;—I writ to him lately.^3—You must present my humble Service to M^r Lewis D^r Arbuthnott
M^r Pope and M^r Gay.—And pray does Lewis continue
to like his Match, and could he not have drunk wine

dated 1725, by Edward Howard,
Earl of Suffolk.  Horace Walpole
describes him as 'a Lord, who
with great inclination to versify,
and some derangement of his in-
tellects, was so unlucky as not to
have his furor of the true poetic
sort'; see *Royal and Noble
Authors*, ed. 1759, ii. 122.

^1 Sir Robert Sutton (1671–
1746) was the grandson of Henry,
younger brother of the first Lord
Lexington.  He matriculated at
Oxford as a member of Trinity
College in 1688, and graduated
B.A. in 1692.  'He was educated
for the Church, and took deacon's
orders.  In 1695 he proceeded to
Vienna in the joint capacity of
Chaplain and Secretary to [the
second] Lord Lexington;  on
whose recall, in 1697, he was
appointed Resident Minister'
(*Lexington Papers*, ed. H. Manners Sutton, 1851, p. 4).  Thereafter he was Minister at Con-
stantinople, and at Paris (1720),

and at the time of this letter was
M.P. for Nottingham.  He was
knighted in 1701, and in 1725
was made one of the first members
of the revived Order of the Bath.
On 10 December 1724 he married
Judith, widow of the third Earl
of Sunderland, and daughter and
co-heiress of Benjamin Tichborne.
Announcements of the marriage
are to be found in several of the
London newspapers, e.g. *The Post
Man* of 10–12 December 1724,
and in Boyer's *Political State*,
December 1724, p. 601.

^2 'grave' written over 'serious' obliterated.

^3 In his letter to Oxford of
27 November Swift wrote 'I
shall desire a gentleman to attend
your Lordship for the ring', and
on 26 July 1725 Oxford replied
'you did tell me a gentleman
should call, but where he lives,
or who he is, I know not'
(*Correspondence*, iii. 225, 260).

enough without his Wife? adieu. Your Family are all well, which I hear though I cannot go to see them.

*Address :* To Charles Ford Esq^r
to be left at the Coco-Tree
in the Pell-mell
London

*Postmarks :* Dublin *and* $\frac{6}{IA}$

## XLIX

Mar. 1. 1724–5

I THOUGHT to have writt you a longer Letter and sent you more Papers, but I have not been able to procure them, and the Bearer M^r Williamson[1] (who is the Goldsmith I employ) coming to sudden on me, as just going to Sea, hath shortned my Letter. M^rs Johnson is as usuall, unless rather worse, for she eats now but a mouthfull a day. I wish she would go to London.

Your Family in Dawson Street are well; I dined with them lately. I will write to you soon more at large. Pray return M^r Gay thanks for my Book[2] when You see him. I have read it all over, and find some Additions that I like much especially the Genealogy of the Shoe boy—Farewell.

*Address :* To Charles Ford Esq^r

[1] Thomas Williamson, died 1741.—Vicars, *Prerogative Wills.*
[2] Gay's *Poems on Several Occasions*, 1720, which he had at last received; see Letter XLIV, p.108, n. 1, and Harold Williams, *Dean Swift's Library*, 1932, pp. 8, 73. The genealogy of the Shoe boy was added in this edition of *Trivia*, ii. 99–220.

L

Dublin.    Mar. 11<sup>th</sup> 1724-5

I HAVE been resolving for some time past to go to England about the End of this month, and have lately communicated my Intention to five or six Friends, who are all dissuading me with the greatest Violence, and desire that I would at least defer it till next Year. Their Reasons I do not all approve ; because I know very well[1] how apt the People of Ireland are to think that their little Affairs are regarded in England. They would have it that what has been lately written about the Drapier has given great Offence on your side, that the private Malice of the Projector and those who were examined in his Behalf might tempt them to some violent Action of Revenge, and that M<sup>r</sup> W—[2] thinks himself personally offended, and that somebody[3] for whose Advantage that Project was contrived would use all means to prosecute whoever has opposed it, which may end in Messengers heads, Accusations, Imprisonments &c. Now in my own Mind I am quite of another Opinion. I do not think the thing is of Weight enough for a | Ministry [p. 2.] to trouble themselves about, and as for the Malice of mean paltry Rascals it may be avoyded by common Care. There was a Time when in England some great Friends looked on me as in Danger, and used to warn me against Night walking &c.; but I thought it was a shame to be afraid of such Accidents and looked as if a man affected to be thought of Importance. Neither do I find that Assassinations are things in fashion at present ; and in my Opinion a Secretary of State is a much more terrible animal, when he has a mind

---

[1] 'very well' written over 'were' crossed out.

[2] Walpole.

[3] The Duchess of Kendal; 'somebody' is written after 'the S' crossed out.

to be malicious.   Our Friend in Grafton Street[1] swears
it is a Fatality upon me.   In order to their Satisfaction
I desire to know your Opinion, whether I may be in
any Danger of being teazed at Whitehall, or have
Searches for Papers &c. for as to private malice, I very
little apprehend it.   Pray write me your Thoughts as
soon as you can, that I may take my Measures.

Our Friend with the weak Stomach eats less than
ever, and I am in pain about her, and would fain
persuade her to go for England, but she will not.
Your People are well, I dined with them very lately—

Y[r–]

*Address :* To Charles Ford Esq[r]
to be left at the Coco-tree
in Pell-mell

London

*Postmarks :* Dublin *and* $\frac{19}{MR}$

LI

Aug. 14th. 1725.

I HAVE now been four Months at our Friends country
Cabbin,[2] with our two Lady Friends.   The younger[3] is
better in Strength, tho often in her old Disorders, but

[1] Compare the mention of
Grafton Street in Letter XLV,
p.111. Can 'our friend' be Stella?
There appears to be no evidence
of where she resided in Dublin
after 1721, when she was not at
the Deanery (*Correspondence*, iii.
80). Mrs. Dingley lived at one
time in Grafton Street after
Stella's death, at the house of
Mrs. Ridgeway, daughter of
Mrs. Brent, the superintendent
of Swift's household (*Correspon-dence*, v. 29).

[2] Sheridan's house at Quilca
in the south of Cavan, about
twelve miles from Kells.   Swift
had postponed his visit to England
(Letter L), and was Sheridan's
guest from about 20 April to the
end of September.

[3] Stella, younger than Mrs.
Dingley.

she desires me to tell you that your nice Stomach must
not be turned if you see her with a Tetter in her Chin,
which she resents in a manner very unbecoming her
good Sense, and the Philosophy which I hoped I had
taught her.   We shall not return till towards October.
I am seldom without a Fitt of Deafness every Month,
they come oftner, but I think do not last so long, but
what new methods they will take I know not ; and so
much for personal Matters.

I remember when you expected to be undone in all
your ready money by Stratford.[1]   I was in fifty times
more danger by the utter Undoing of M$^r$ Pratt[2] of the
Treasury, whose Fall hath made a great Noise here.
He owed me all and something more than all I had
in the World ; and was put up in Prison (where he
still continues) for above 70 Thousand Pounds debt
to the Crown ; yet he had so much honor, that while
he was in Prison, he gave a Gentleman | whom I [p. 2.]
empowerd, Substantiall Bills for all he owed me
except about 100$^{ll}$, which he seemed a little to dispute,
and was onely Interest.   Thus I have miraculously
escaped being perfectly worth nothing.

I had a Letter yesterday from the Earl of Oxford,[3]
telling me that he had his Fathers Picture ready for
me.  And I remember he desired I would get somebody
to call for a Ring which was to be a Memorial of His
Father ; and I desired you to do that Favor for me ;

---

[1] Francis Stratford, 'the Hamburg merchant', a school-fellow of Swift, and a director of the South Sea Company: see the *Journal to Stella*, 12 January 1712.

[2] John Pratt, Deputy Vice-Treasurer of Ireland, and brother of Benjamin Pratt, Provost of Trinity College. He and his wife

are mentioned frequently in the *Journal to Stella*. He had been committed to prison on 7 June (*Letters to and from William Nicolson*, 1809, ii. 605). See *Correspondence*, iii. 241, and Letter LVIII.

[3] Written 26 July (*Correspondence*, iii. 260): see Letter XLVIII, p. 117, n. 3.

but his or your or both being out of Town prevented
it.   For my Lord says nobody called for it.   I had
a leter lately from M^r Charleton ^1 the Earl of Arran's
Chaplain, he is known enough, and I suppose not
unknown to you.   I have just now answered it, and
desired him that if you were out of Town, he would
perform this Commission to L^d Oxford ; if he be in
Town, I entreat you would see him, and so to concert
Matters, that I may have the Picture and Ring, and
that both may be lodged with You, the Ring sent me
by some private Hand ; and the Picture kept till it can
be sent conveniently.   I suppose it may go by long Sea ;
or as you please.

I know not why, but I am sorry your money holds
out so well and yet I could not have seen you this
Summer: for the Place we are in is not a Place for
you.   I am as busy here as if I were upon Land of my
[P. 3.] own.   I have got Sheridan a small Living ^2 from | L^d
Carteret : but it proves smaller than his Excellency or
I intended it.

I have finished my Travells, and I am now transcribing them ; they are admirable Things, and will wonderfully mend the World.^3

M^rs Johnson desires to know whether there be any
Agreement between the Weather on your side and ours.
In four Months we have had two odd fair days, and 13
more, and all the rest foul from the 20^th of April ^4 to the
Hour I am writing.

Pray say something of L^d Bolingbroke, where he is,
and what he does ; he has told me he had his Picture

---

^1 See Letter XXXV, p. 84, n. 1.
^2 Rincurran, in co. Cork.
^3 Another very important statement : it gives the date of the
conclusion of the rough draft ; it
shows his care in composition, for
he ' transcribed ' the whole book ;
and it proclaims his satisfaction.
^4 Probably the day when he
left Dublin for Quilca.

for me,[1] and I would have you mention it to him, and get it for me; but I am desirous to know his present Scituation, and where he intends to live,[2] and where is Madame de Villete, and why she does not write to me. For you know my Priviledge, that Ladyes are always to make the first Advances to me.[3]

Pray tell my L^d Masham, (with my most humble Service) that my Lady often promised me her Picture.

My humble Service to M^r Pope and M^r Gay—

*Address:* To Charles Ford Esq^r; to be
left at the Coco-tree in
Pel-mell

London

*Postmarks:* Kells *and* $\frac{23}{AV}$

## LII

### Quilca.    Aug. 16^th 1725

OUR Method about Letters here, is this, Every Saterday we send 8 miles[4] to Kells for Vittells, the Messenger carryes thither what Letters we write, and brings back whatever Letters are sent us to Kells. Thus our Letters often lye at Kells a week, and we are very indifferent, or rather vexed when we see any Letter come

---

[1] Bolingbroke had ended his letter of August 1723 thus: 'This is the picture of an old friend, and more like him than that will be which you once asked, and which he will send you, if you continue still to desire it.' Swift would appear to have asked for it in his lost letter of 29 Sept. 1721; in his reply 1 Jan. 1722 [O.S. 21 Dec. 1721] Bolingbroke pro-

mised to send it from Paris.

[2] Bolingbroke was settling at Dawley, near Uxbridge.

[3] An old privilege; see 'A Decree for concluding the Treaty between Dr. Swift and Mrs. Long', 1708 (?), *Prose Works*, xi. 383, and *Vanessa and her Correspondence*, ed. A. Martin Freeman, 1921, p. 183.

[4] Irish miles.

to us, unless from particular Friends.   Thus it happened
that the Messenger of Saterday last carryed a Letter to
Kells directed to you in London, and brought one from
you dated at Dublin.   If your coming be sufficiently
known, perhaps the Post master may send it to you, or
if the Packet be not gone, you may send a servant
for it, rather than let it have two Voyages by Sea.[1]   The
Letter you gave Sheridan for me, is in ill Hands, for
I hear nothing of his coming down to Quilca, and if he
does, it is great Odds he will leave it behind, or lose it,
or forget to[2] give it me.   I find you have been a better
Manager than usuall, by making your Money hold out
almost two years, unless you have mangé votre bled
en herbe ; and in that Case you will be punished
with a longer Stay in Ireland.   I hope you will, or
rather your Friends will have one Advantage by our |
[p. 2.] Absence, that it will force you to cotton a little better
with the Country and the People ; for upon your old
System it will be impossible for you to live in it without
Spleen.   No men in Dublin go to Taverns who are
worth sitting with, and to ask others, is just to desire
them to throw away half a Crown for bad wine, (which
they can ill spare,) when they know where to get good,
for nothing, and among Company where they can
amuse themselves with Play or trifling; and this you
must do, or get you gone back to England.   For we
know it is not Love that sends you to us, and that
nothing keeps you here an hour but Joyntures and old
Leases.

The Razors will be a great Treasure to me, for want
of good ones I pass one hour in eight and fourty very
miserably.

In my Letter to you I desired your Assistance in

---

[1] The postmark shows that the     went to London.
letter of Saturday 14 August       [2] ' to ' repeated in MS.

getting the Ring and Picture from L^d Oxford, but fearing you might be out of Town, (though not in Ireland) I writt the same Post to M^r Charleton from whom I lately had a Letter; since I knew not what else to do. But if M^r Lewis[1] will take that Trouble, it will be much better.

Our Scheme was to stay till Michaelmas, but our Return must depend upon our Health. M^rs Johnson is much better and walks three or four Irish Miles a day over Bogs and mountain. But I have generally every month a Return of my Deafness, though the Fits do not last so long as usuall. But I have some Reasons not to be in Dublin till the Parliament here has sate a good while. Neither am I willing to see M^r Prat while he is in Prison.[2] I believe I shall not lose above 100^ll Interest by him. But I despaired of every Penny, | and yet I have legall Witness that I was a great [p. 3.] Philosopher in that Matter.

We live here among a Million of wants, and where ever[y] body is a Thief. I am amusing my self in the Quality of Bayliff to Sheridan, among Bogs and Rocks, overseeing and ranting at Irish Laborers, reading Books twice over for want of fresh ones, and fairly correcting and transcribing my Travells, for the Publick. Any thing rather than the Complaint of being Deaf in Dublin.

I hope to see you well settled in a Kind of Acquaintance, and tallying with the usuall way of Life, else it had been better you had contrived to pass the Summer here, and kept London for Winter. This is an Irish Holyday when our Scoundrels will not work, else perhaps my Letter would have been shorter.

My most humble Service to the Ladyes where you Live. Adieu.

---

[1] Oxford entrusted the picture and the ring to Erasmus Lewis; see *Correspondence*, iii. 265.
[2] See Letter LI, p. 121, n. 2.

The Ladyes here assure me they are your humble Servants.

*Address:* To Charles Ford Esq^r, at
       M^rs Ford's House in Dawson
       Street
                      Dublin.

*Postmarks:* Kells *and* $\frac{AU^{1}}{20}$

## LIII

Quilca.    Aug. 27^th. 1725

I send you inclosed Letter to My L^d Bolingbroke, because I suppose you know where to direct to him, and in what Style;[2] If in his old One of L^d I suppose it will be under cover.   I writt to you a Post or two ago.   M^r Sheridan seems to hope you will not be so unsociable as formerly, but L^d Bol. writes that you promise to return about the Beginning of Winter,[3] and if so, I know not who would go over the Threshold to see You.

We are all as usuall—neither well nor ill, except M^rs Dingley who can do every thing but walk.

*Address:* To Charles Ford Esq^r

*No postmark.*

---

[1] The Dublin postmark; the London mark would have been '20' over 'AV'.

[2] Bolingbroke's estates were restored to him in May 1725, but not his right to sit in the House of Lords. Swift's letter is lost; it was written in answer to Bolingbroke's of 24 July (*Correspondence,* iii. 258).

[3] In his letter to Swift of 24 July. But Ford appears to have been in Dublin in March 1726: see pp. 212–13.

## LIV

Sept. 20th 1728.

M[R] WHALEY[1] the late Primat's Chaplain delivers you this. He hath an appeal before the H. of Lords for a very considerable Living, in which that abominable puppy and Poet Dean Daniel is his adversary. He is a Gentleman of great worth, and I must entreat you to desire the Lords of your Acquaintance not onely to hear the cause, but right or wrong to befriend him, although the Rascal his opposer hath nothing but party on his side. Pray get M[r] Lewis and D[r] Arbuthnot to speak to as many Lords as they know.

I have been here[2] with S[r] Arthur Acheson these three Months, in a various, but somewhat tolerable State of health, but with a family so agreable, that joyned to the happyness of being absent from Dublin, I do not much pity my self. I hope not so much as my friends do, and you particularly who think nothing tolerable five miles from London. Yet I have one great advan-

---

[1] Nathaniel Whaley, Fellow of Wadham College, Oxford, Chaplain to Thomas Lindsay, Archbishop of Armagh (d. 1724). Primate Lindsay had given him the Rectory of Armagh, but the Government had nominated Richard Daniel, Dean of Armagh. Swift gave Whaley a letter of introduction also to the Earl of Oxford (21 Sept.), in which he said—'He has now an appeal before the House of Lords for a Church living of near a thousand pounds a year, of which he has been long and legally possessed, and his adversary, one Dean Daniel, is the greatest puppy and vilest poet alive, with a very bad cause to be supported by a party'. For the sequel see Letter LV, p. 129, n. 1. Daniel had brought out several volumes of verse, the latest of which were *A Paraphrase on some Select Psalms*, 1722, and *The Royal Penitent : a Paraphrase on the seven Penitential Psalms*, 1727.

[2] At Market Hill (now Gosford Castle), near Armagh. Lady Acheson was the daughter of Swift's old friend Peter Savage, Chancellor of the Exchequer in Ireland from 1695 to 1717. The visit extended to eight months—June to February.

tage that I am wholly ignorant how the world passes, and am consequently not half so much out of humor and patience with it as you. However it gives you amusement, and that with good company is enough.

I am &c

*Address :* To Charles Ford Esq<sup>r</sup>


LV

Dublin.   Mar. 18<sup>th</sup> 1728–9.

THE very day I received your Letter, I relapsed into this odious Disorder of Deafness, which is constantly attended with Giddyness, although the latter is tolerable, but the first is perfectly vexatious, and truly I now compound if I can get an equall time of being well and ill.   It is so long since I had any commerce with you in writing, that being no good reader in the night and your talking of L<sup>dy</sup> Bolingbroke and M<sup>r</sup> Gay I thought it had been M<sup>r</sup> Pope's, and you happened not to name him.   And I immediately writt him a long answer[1] till the next morning looking into your Letter I found the difference.   For your saying you would come this Summer to Ireland, I easily construed that of M<sup>r</sup> Pope, because he frequently raillyes of his intention to pay me a visit if his Mother should happen to dy.   I hear your friends are well but I have not seen them for in three days after I came to Town, I fell ill, and after a short intervall of being well which I spent in long walks thinking it would continue, I grew deaf before I could wait on them.   I am very well pleased with the Decree

---

[1] Written 6 March, *Correspondence,* iv. 59.

of the Lords¹ because it will at least keep Whally a little longer in possession: but it makes me despise Law, when a decree turns upon a quirk without one Syllable relating to the merits of the Cause. We are told you are positively intended to give up Gibraltar and Minorca, wherein you will crown your good conduct.² We have been very well entertained with the Dˢ of Queensbury's Letter on her Banishment from Court.³ I would be contented with the worst | Ministry⁴ in Europe to [p. 2.] live in a Country which produces such a spirit as that Girles, and am sorry I was not acquainted with her. Pray tell Gay so when you see him, and let him tell the Dutchess. In a Kingdom where Law supports bold answers, it may be S. R. W.ˢ Politicks, but no wise man's to provoke them, and somebody is sure to be a great Loser, and this Somebody is not the Dutchess. We have likewise the Poem in print upon the same Subject.⁵ I am extreamly glad to be assured that Mʳ Gay will not fare the worse.⁶ Let Mʳ Gay likewise

¹ As George I had died since the writ was served, the Lords decided, 26 Feb. 1729, that a new writ was necessary. They gave judgement in favour of Whaley on 30 April 1730. See Nichols's edition of Swift, 1801, xviii. 262.

² The question of giving up Gibraltar had been prominent since the Congress of Soissons in June 1728. Spain silently waived her claim to it in the Treaty of Seville, signed 9 Nov. 1729.

³ Catherine Hyde, daughter of the fourth Earl of Clarendon, married to Charles Douglas, third Duke of Queensberry in 1720; the 'Kitty beautiful and young, and wild as colt untamed' of

*The Female Phaeton.* She was forbidden the court for asking subscriptions for Gay's *Polly*, the performance of which had been prohibited by the Lord Chamberlain, the Duke of Grafton, on 12 Dec. 1728. The 'letter on her banishment', written 27 Feb., is printed in Cunningham's edition of *The Lives of the Poets*, 1854, ii. 293, from the copy of it which had been sent to Swift.

⁴ MS. reads 'worst and Ministry'.

⁵ The 'Excellent new Ballad called A Bob for the Court', printed in *The Craftsman* of 28 Dec. 1728.

⁶ According to Pope, the subscriptions to *Polly* brought Gay

tell the Dutchess, that I promise never to take up my Meat on a knife.[1]  I was to see your friends in Dawson Street, and M^rs Ford was at Cards, and she has my misfortune to be deaf, and M^rs Monk[2] was rooking her at two headed[3] Ombre, and she has given up her Coach, and allows poor M^rs Penny[4] onely a crown a week for chair-hire.  As to what you say of writing, you are mistaken about S^r Ralph the Patriot,[5] for I believe it was writ in England; I think I saw it, but do not remember it was printed here.  When I was last Summer at S^r A. Achesons, I writ little family verses, but no Copy ever went out,[6] except some Verses called the

---

'eleven or twelve hundred' pounds (Spence's *Anecdotes*, ed. Singer, p. 214).

[1] Swift had taken up his meat on a knife when he was Pope's guest at Twickenham, and Gay had gibed him about this lapse, urging him for the sake of the Duchess not to be guilty of it again.  Swift in reply laid the blame on Pope's poetical forks and on the difficulty of dining with forks that have but two prongs when the sauce is not very consistent.  'I desire you will tell her Grace', he writes, 'that the ill-management of forks is not to be helped when they are only bidental, which happens in all poor houses, especially those of poets; upon which account a knife was absolutely necessary at Mr. Pope's, where it was morally impossible, with a bidental fork, to convey a morsel of beef, with the incumbrance of mustard and turnips, into your mouth at once. And her grace hath cost me thirty pounds to provide tridents for fear of offending her' (*Correspondence*, iv. 10, 113, 133, 175). Swift had not met the Duchess; we have in this letter the definite statement that he was 'not acquainted with her'.

[2] Probably the wife of Charles Monk (1678-1752), and grandmother of the first Viscount Monck.

[3] Not 'two handed'; usually played by three.

[4] Ford's sister Penelope; cf. 'Mrs Pen' in Letter XLI, p. 97, and 'Mrs Penny' in Letter XLV, p. 110.

[5] The poem entitled *The Progress of Patriotism*, first printed in *The Craftsman* of 3 August 1728, and reprinted in *The Intelligencer*, No. XII.  Swift disclaims it also in his letters to Pope of 6 March 1729 and 12 June 1732 (*Correspondence*, iv. 61, 308).

[6] 'My Lady Acheson made me give her up all the foul copies,

Journal of a Dublin Lady,[1] which I sent to make up a Paper that ran here under the name of the Intelligencer, which was scurvily kept up a while, and at last dropt. The Journal was printed all into nonsense, and I believe was never heard of on your side. I assure you this disorder and my Monastick life takes off all invention, and there is not in Ireland a duller man in a gown than my self. If you come to Ireland I know what drives you hither, and what remedy will send you back; but I could wish you would cotton more with the valuable people while you are here. I do suppose no body hates and despises this kingdom more than my self, and yet | when I am well I can [p. 3.] be easy among a set of honest people who neither shine in titles nor Wit: but I do not recommend my text to You. The time may come when you will have a less relish for Variety. I wish you well, and pray walk more, and drink and eat less.—I am &c.

*Address:* To Charles Ford Esq[r], to
be left at the Cocoa Tree in
Pell-mell
London.

*Postmarks:* Dublin *and* $\frac{27}{MR}$

and never gave the fair ones out of her hands, or suffered them to be copied. They were sometimes shown to intimate friends to occasion mirth, and that was all.'—Letter to Pope of 6 March 1729.

[1] This poem was not printed in *The Intelligencer*, but was published by itself as a pamphlet—'*The Journal of a Dublin Lady* ... Dublin: Printed by S. Harding'. It was reprinted at London in 1729 with the title *The Journal of a Modern Lady*. Swift had sent it to Dublin in Jan. 1729, meaning it to form a number of *The Intelligencer* (*Correspondence,* iv. 54), but the paper had then ceased (nineteen numbers from 11 May to Dec. 1728; a 'Numb. xx' appeared in May 1729, and another 'Numb. xx' had appeared before that).

## LVI[1]

I was very much concerned at the acount you gave of your misfortunes by sea and land ; the latter was not so much your own fault, as that of the careless rascal your servant.   You had an indulgent Doctor to allow you any wine at all ; however, I trust you are now recovered altogether, and if your flesh be brought down, I hope you will endeavor by health and exercise to keep it so, for in my opinion you do both eat and drink a great deal too much, I mean in a physical and not a moral sense.   As to my self, I am very little, if at all better since you left us, but I got no new wrenches this fortnight, and my Surgeon now lets me use nothing but flannel, which with[2] the help of Summer (whereof we have not yet enjoyd one day) he says I shall mend in time.   Immediatly on receit of your letter, at least in a few hours, after considering as well as I could I writ to M[r] Burton at Woodpark.[3]   I repeated to him what I thought fit of your letter, told him, as it was true, that I never knew a juster person in all dealings than you, and that I was confident you would joyn with him in any proposals to make him secure, that your Lawyers

---

[1] Original in the Pierpont Morgan Library.

[2] ? 'with which and '.

[3] By an indenture made 22 Sept. 1731, Ford had let Woodpark to Walter Burton, a Dublin banker, for the term of three lives—viz. those of Burton's two sons John and Francis, and of Ford's nephew Edward, the son of his brother Richard—at an annual rent of £115. The indenture is preserved in the copy written by Swift's orders on the back of his letter to Ford of 5 April 1733 (Letter LXI).   But it does not explain everything in the dispute which immediately arose between Ford and Burton. Hitherto our knowledge of the dispute rested on Ford's reference to it in his letter to Swift of 23 December 1732 (Letter LX), and on the transcripts in Swift's writing from the angry correspondence of Ford and Burton printed by Sir Walter Scott, vol. xix (ed. 1814), pp. 374-7.

would think Proper: That in case you should dy before
the expiration of his lease, your personal estate in money
and other valuable things would be always worth the
interest of his lease, and with that you could cover it,
so that the Heir would certainly rather suffer M<sup>r</sup> Burton
to enjoy his bargain than lose what you would leave him
in Money, arrears, &c. I received answer but this day,
and the Post goes to morrow. His proposal is, that Your
Nephew should joyn with you to levy a fine of the
Lands leased to him, and the Nephew to suffer a
recovery of them ; and a short deed be executed by
you and the Nephew declaring the trust of that fine
and recovery to the purpose onely of establishing the
lease to M<sup>r</sup> Burton, and on the back, the Nephew
to signify his approbation.—This Scheam of Burtons
I apprehend will hardly bear, because the Nephew (who
has not been with me since you went) will never be
brought to it, and his mother and her relations | will all be [p. 2.]
against it on hopes to get what terms they shall impose
to bring you to their terms. Therefore when I read
that part of your letter desiring my Opinion, I immediatly called to mind the fee-farm you hold from
Luttrel,[1] which I think is worth 60<sup>ll</sup> a year, above the
small rent you pay for it, and is entirely at your
disposal. I suppose rather than hazard the loss of that
fee-farm, both Mother and Son will agree that the lad
should joyn with you to secure Burton. Or if perverse-
ness and folly should carry them so far as to refuse, that
Farm in reversion after your life may be secured to
Burton in such a manner, as to bind your heirs rather
to confirm his lease than lose what is worth twelve
hundred pound. If you will talk over this to any
friend of the Law, he will easily tell you how this may
be managed. But of this expedient I gave not the

[1] Ford purchased the town and
lands of Bennetstown from Henry
Luttrell (see Letter XXXIII,
p. 78, n. 4) in October 1707.

least hint to Burton but mentioned onely, as I said before, your personall estate.

If a Lawyer here could see your fathers will, he could soon judge whether such a lease as you made to Burton, were in your power, and then would tell you whether the expedient of Lutterels farm could not easily be practiced. I will do what you shall direct me, but shall continue to be silent on that particular to Burton, without your licence.

I am told here that L<sup>d</sup> Derwenwaters estate was sold for onely one thousand Pounds.[1] I wish you had been early enough to have bought it for me. We must own with shame that England exceeds us in villany, as to it's greatness ; but ours is more epidemick.

M<sup>rs</sup> Ford[2] is gone to M<sup>r</sup> Ludlows,[3] and I think intends to stay the Summer. She came hither to take her leave, but I was gone out in the Chaise.

All your friends here are well. You forgot to send me your address, therefore I direct to the Coco-tree.

The Bishops have had one or two mawlings in Epigrams,[4] and answers &c One Epigram writ by a y[5]

I am ever y<sup>r</sup> &c—

Dubl. May. 17<sup>th</sup>. 1732.

> *Address :* To Charles Ford Esq<sup>r</sup>, to be
> left at the Coco-tree in
> Pell-mell
> London
> *Postmarks :* Dublin *and* $\frac{2\,?}{MA}$

[1] The Report of the Committee on the sale of the forfeited estate of the Earl of Derwentwater, published by order of the House of Commons in 1732, shows that on 11 July 1723 the estates in Northumberland and Cumberland were sold to William Smith, Esq., of Billiter-Square, London, for £1,060. They had been put up at £2,000. A witness gave evidence that the estates and mines might be made worth £9,000 per annum.

[2] Ford's sister Penelope ; his mother had died in 1730.

## LVII [1]

### Dubl. Jun. 30th 1732

A PERSON who left London ten days after the date of your last which was June 1. went by Wood-park about a fortnight ago and said among your tenants that you were dangerously ill, as Crossweight [2] told me last week, but I was less alarmed by your own account, which said that you had got the better of your ague, and was now taking medicines to prevent the jaundice, which sometimes happens to follow : And I can hope without being sanguin, that you are by this time well and out of apprehension of further consequences.    Young Ford [3] has been often with me for his money, and at last the B. of Ferns [4] sent me a note on his banker for 20[ll] for which I gave a receit on account, and payd young Ford the money and had his receit on account.    I could not

---

[3] At Ardsallagh.  See Letter XXXI, p. 70, n. 1.

[4] The bishops had introduced into the Irish House of Lords a Bill ' more effectually to enable the Clergy, having Cure of Souls, to reside upon their respective Benefices', and another Bill for dividing the larger livings but leaving their own revenues intact. The former Bill passed the Lords on 21 February by 26 votes to 17, only three of the twenty bishops opposing it, and the other passed without opposition on 24 February. Both Bills were thrown out by the Commons.  Swift vented his contempt in his verses ' On the Irish Bishops', and ' Judas '.  About this time he also wrote his ' Epigram on seeing a worthy Prelate go out of Church', and his ' Advice to a Parson, an Epigram ', both of which were printed in *The London Magazine* for June 1732, p. 147.

[5] We are left to surmise what ' y ' stands for.

---

[1] Original in the possession of Allan H. Bright, Esq., of Barton Court, Colwall.

[2] Ford's Irish agent.

[3] Ford's nephew Edward.

[4] Arthur Price, Bishop of Ferns 1730–3, previously Dean of Ferns and Bishop of Clonfert, and afterwards Bishop of Meath and Archbishop of Cashel. See Letter XLIV, p. 107, n. 4.

find what was due to him, but by a paper he had of yours, and what he said himself, I think two years interest will be due to him in October next, of which the 20ll I payd him is a part. I mentioned to him the business of Mr Burton, because I was told by Crosswait that the young man had heard enough of it, and from his little shifting dubious manner of talk, I found it proper to let him know that you had a remedy in your own hands to make Burton easy, and told him (which he knew very well before) what that remedy was : That I should write to you soon, and desired he would give me an answer in three days, because his whole language ran upon his complying with you in all things. Two days ago he writ me a long letter, very silly and artificial, with objections that he called his own, but I suppose he had pickt them up from some scrub Attorney. And from the tenor of all he said, I am positively of opinion that Mr Burtons scruples had better be eased by covering his Lease with that which is in your own power, onely leaving the next heirs their choice to lose what will be worth above 1000ll for the sake of voyding Mr Burtons lease, which will never be worth one third of that Sum. When you have talked to your friends upon it, and shall be advised to follow this method, either you or I by letter may propose it to Burton, and [p. 2.] I like it the rather | because it will best show that you have no occasion for the young man or his relations to make a merit in complying to what is for their own interest.—I desire you will as soon as it shall be allowed by the Doctors, use Exercise, and live more temperatly, I do not mean in point of morality but health. Looking over your Letter, I find Bennets town is settled on Mrs Pen Ford for life,[1] but as she is not likely to out-

---

[1] Bennetstown (see Letter LVI, p. 133 n.) is described in Ford's will as mortgaged to Penelope for £300 and is left to

live you, and that if she should, You have always
something in your power, and as the heirs will not
probably be so mad as to lose the reversion, I am confident an expedient may be found.

Chargeableness[1] is indeed a very bad circumstance in
sickness, And therefore my advice is always against it,
for three strong reasons, first the pain, secondly the
bad dyet, and thirdly the expence, to which, fourthly
I may add the confinement.   So that I wonder any
body will chuse it.   As to my lameness I can say no
more than that I think I grow better.   I ride often,
but not above ten miles a day at most, and I ride in
Gambadoes,[2] if you ever have heard of such implements
. . the advantage is that my foot as I ride stands even
as upon a floor for I cannot yet bear the least stretch of
the great sinew above my left heel, and God knows
when I shall.   Therefore going down stairs is the
worst of my gates, and I limp at best, even in my
garden, in which however I walk above an hour every
day.   And so you are obeyd in my giving you this
account of my self.   But your case was different, as
much as an acute disease is from a chronical.   There
is no revolution here among any of those few whom
you know.   The Death of the old Beau S^r T. Smyth[3]
I suppose hath been of importance enough for a news
article.   You have buried a young Lady of this kingdom, in London, who is much lamented for her Virtue,

her for life.  She outlived him by
twenty years.

[1] The word is clearly written
but needs to be explained.

[2] Leather boots or leggings
attached to the saddle. Gay refers
to Swift's 'unlucky accident' to
his leg as far back as 13 March;
see *Correspondence*, iv. 284, 293,
313, &c.

[3] Sir Thomas Smyth, of Red-
cliff, Buckinghamshire, Ranger of
Phœnix Park. He died at Dublin
on 20 June 1732.  He is 'the
great hero' of William King's
'epic poem' *The Toast*, where
his exploits and the long explanatory notes provide a good comment on Swift's reference to him
here.

Beauty and Fortune.[1]  I am glad I never saw her, because I dwell onely on a pleasing Circumstance, that such a young Villain as G. Rochford's son has so deservedly suffered so great a loss, he hath shown himself the most avaricious, unnatural undutifull Rogue you ever heard of.

I am concerned for poor L^dy B—s[2] illness, which I hear from others will probably soon put an end to her [p. 3.] life, and I am much obliged by her many | civilityes. I desire my hearty service to M^r Lewis ; I hope you often see each other.  If he must be a loser by his Lady's death,[3] I shall be sorry for it, no further this deponent knoweth.  My days when I do not ride, pass five in the week in limping, and sitting alone, in reading very little, and writing less.  I wish I had twenty thousand Guineas in my Cabinet, that I might shut the doors, put on spectacles, and amuse my self with reckoning them three times a day.          I am ever
most sincerely yours &c

M^rs Pen. Ford is very quiet for ought I can hear at M^r Ludlows, and may grow rich if she be wise

*Address :* To Charles Ford Esq^r
        at the Coco-tree in
        Pell-mell,

                London

*Postmarks defaced.*

[1] Elizabeth, first wife of Robert Rochfort, afterwards Earl of Belvidere. She died of small-pox at her house in Brook Street, London, on 6 June 1732. She was the eldest daughter of Richard Tenison of Thomastown, county Louth, and had she lived would have been step-daughter of Delany: see Letter LVIII, p. 141, n. 2.

[2] There are frequent references in Swift's *Correspondence* to Lady Bolingbroke's ill-health

## LVIII[1]

Dublin. Oc[tb]. 14th. 1732

I SENT M[r] Burton a Copy of M[r] Piggots[2] opinion, with a letter offering to shew him the original, or to any body whom he would appoint. I had not an answer in less than three weeks, and then what he writ was that the Sollicitor-generall in England had given his opinion directly contrary, and he writ to me a Proposall, that you should settle the piece of Land you purchased from H. Lutterel upon Edward's younger Children binding Edward[3] either to continue Burton's Lease or cover it with 300[ll] to secure it to him. I took time to consider this Scheme, which I did by no means approve of, and therefore I took the opportunity about a fortnight ago to ride[4] to Dunboyn on a Vestry day, where Burton was to be ; I talked the matter over to him, and said I would never advise you to leave your self so much at mercy of a young disobedient ill

from 1727. She died in 1750, aged 74.

[3] See Letter XLVI, p.113, n.1. She died on 21 November 1736, and was buried in the east cloister of Westminster Abbey : see *Registers of Westminster*, ed. J. L. Chester (Harleian Society, vol. x), 1876, p. 346. Swift once described her as having 'a shining face as if a calf had licked it' (*Correspondence*, iv. 94).

[1] Original in the possession of the Rosenbach Company, New York.

[2] Nathaniel Pigott, whose death on 5 July 1737 was thus announced in *The Historical Register* (Chronological Diary, p. 12) : 'At *Whitton*, near *Isleworth* in *Middlesex*, Counsellor *Piggot* of the *Middle Temple*, one of the greatest Conveyancers in this Kingdom, a Gentleman of a clear Head and sound Judgment.' He was the author of *New Precedents in Conveyancing*. See *Calendar of the Inner Temple Records*, iii. 248, 267, 278.

The Solicitor-general in England was Charles Talbot, afterwards Lord Chancellor.

[3] 'Edward' after 'them ei' struck out.

[4] 'ride' over 'write' obliterated.

advised man as Edward, who deserved so little of you,
[p. 2.] but that the land | being in your own power, you could
cover it as you please, and keep the Staff in your own
hand, and oblige the young fellow to better conduct.
Burton said it was the same thing to him, and that he
thought I judged right. So that if you please to advise
with your friends, I conceive they will think with me,
that by charging that land with 300ˡˡ in case your heir
will not agree to confirm Burton's lease, and assigning [1]
the money to Burton and his Executors, you will be
easy and he too.

I am uneasy about your health. The Winter is
coming on, and you must double the care of your self.
There is nothing I wish more than that you were rich
enough to keep horses, and able to ride them. I ride
three times a week at least, and about ten miles a day,
which is not to lengthen life, but to preserve health,
and yet I had rather loiter at home. At least you
might keep a chaise and a man to ride before it. For
you have a great deal of life behind, if you think it
worth managing. This is not a place from whence to
send you news. Mʳˢ Ford is still in the Country and
I suppose at Mʳ Ludlows, but I have heard nothing of
her for some time, therefore I suppose she is at ease. |

[p. 3.]    My friends dye in England without my hearing of it,
and so I save some present uneasyness. For I am told
Lord Cardigan [2] hath been dead some time. There is
a most bitter Satyr against Sʳ Tho. Smyth, Lᵈʸ Newburg,
and Capᵗ Prat.[3]    I take it to have been writ in Oxford,

---

[1] 'assigning' after 'paying' obliterated.

[2] George Brudenell, third Earl of Cardigan, died 5 July 1732. He was the brother of Lady Newburgh.

[3] *The Toast, An Epic Poem,* *In Four Books. Written in Latin by Frederick Scheffer, Done into English by Peregrine ODonald, Esq; Vol. 1. Dublin: Printed in the Year, MDCCXXXII.* This volume contained only two books. The poem was completed

by the means of one D^r King the Head of a Hall there who was Nephew and Heir to S^r Thomas and thought himself wrongd by L^dy ¹ Newburg, and I presume employd some young Oxonians to write it. A printer brought it to me, and said a hundred of them were sent to him from England to give about; the Verses are rough, but it is very malicious, and worth reading. It is called *the Toast.* We expect D^r Delany ² over every day with his wife worth fifty thousand pounds. ainsi va le monde. I am so well recoverd of my Strain in nine months, that I can walk two or three miles, but I feel it weak and stiff, especially going down Stairs, and am forced to ride with a flat board fixed on my left Stirrup to rest my heel on. You will present my humble Service to what friends of mine you shall happen to see.

I am ever &c

I have not seen your Agent this long time.<br>
I hope you get your rents. I can hardly

in four books in the edition of 1736. The author, William King, Principal of St. Mary's Hall, Oxford, since 1718, was the nephew of Sir Thomas Smyth, and had come to Dublin to rescue his uncle from his creditors, the old beau, as Swift calls him in Letter LVII, having spent his substance on the Countess of Newburgh, the 'Myra' of Lord Lansdowne's Poems. 'Mars' (Smyth) and 'Mira' (the Countess) are the hero and heroine of *The Toast,* and the whole poem is a comprehensive satire on Dublin society. There can be no doubt that Swift had no hand in the volume of 1732. There is no

evidence that he knew King before that date, or even before 1735. But he urged King to finish his poem (see King's *Anecdotes,* 1819, p. 97), and the edition of 1736 is inscribed to him (pp. xii and 103). For Captain Pratt, see Letter LI, p. 121, n. 2.

¹ 'L^dy' after 'his' struck out.

² Delany was married in London on 17 July 1732 to Margaret, daughter of William Barton, and widow of Richard Tenison, of Thomastown, county Louth. According to *The Gentleman's Magazine* she enjoyed an income of £1,500. Cf. *Correspondence,* iv. 336, and see Letter XXXVIII, p. 92, note 1.

get a Shilling, not even of my little lands.
Nor a peny of Tythes.

L<sup>d</sup> Orrery<sup>1</sup> stays here this winter. I meet him sometimes at dinners and he hath dined with me. He seems an honest man, and of good dispositions.

*Address :* To Charles Ford, E<sup>sqr</sup>
    at the Coco-tree in
    Pell-mell
        London

*Postmarks :* Dublin *and* $\frac{20}{OC}$

## LIX [2]

### Dublin. Dec<sup>b</sup>. 9<sup>th</sup> 1732

I HAVE talked once or twice with M<sup>r</sup> Burton, and told him that I was sure you could and would cover his lease with 300<sup>ll</sup> on those lands in your power, which sum I declare he formerly mentioned to me ; but he was in another key, and talked of 1000<sup>ll</sup>. It mads me that such fellows should have the character of fair honest men,[3] for from the first time I saw him, I thought him the greatest chicaneur that ever came in my way. I happend about 3 weeks ago to meet with D<sup>r</sup> Vesey,[4] of the Chancery, in the green,[5] we talked

---

[1] This is the earliest mention in Swift's correspondence of his future biographer—John Boyle, fifth Earl of Orrery, at this time a young man of twenty-five. He succeeded his father Charles Boyle, the Boyle of *7he Battle of the Books,* in 1731. See Letter LIX, p. 144, n. 3.

[2] Original in the Pierpont Morgan Library.

[3] 'men' after 'fell' obliterated.

[4] William Vesey, son of the Archbishop of Tuam, M.P. for Tuam from 1715, and Master in Chancery 1730–41. He was a Doctor of Laws (1718) of Trinity College, Dublin.

[5] St. Stephen's Green.

of this matter, and he said, Burton told him, that young
Ford would confirm his lease for 30 Guineas in ready
money; we both agreed it would be a good bargain for
your ease, and when he asked my opinion whether[1] he
should venture to lay down the money for you, I advised
him to do it, upon which he said he would let me know
the Success with the first opportunity, but I have not
heard from him since, and therefore I should[2] have
delayd writing to you till I had found him and known
the event ; if I had not lately been made very uneasy
at hearing how little care you take of your Health.
A Person who came not long since from London[3] | told [p. 2.]
me you abated nothing in your plentifull way of eating,
and that you drink as much wine as ever, upon which
he said, all your friends were concerned.   I do not think
life is of much value,[4] but health is worth every thing,
and Nature acts right in making that method which
prolongs life absol[ut]ely necessary to preserve health,
which makes a short life and a merry, a very foolish
Proverb.   For my own part I labor for daily health as
often and almost as many hours as a workman does for
daily bread, and like a common laborer can but just earn
enough to keep life and Soul together.   I had almost
as lieve plow as ride, and thresh as walk, if by any
expence within my power I could contrive, that lazyness
would do me no hurt.   You see I have the common
folly of quoting my self.   But I think it almost the
onely thing I am right in ; and God knows, it is with
great force that I reason my self into the practice.

I believe M^rs Ford is well, for I have heard nothing

---

[1] 'whether' after 'he told'
struck out.

[2] 'should' over 'shall' struck
out.

[3] Probably Sir Arthur Acheson:
see Letter LXVII, p. 168.

[4] 'of much value' over
'thought' obliterated. Cf. Swift's
letter to Miss Anne Long of 18
Dec. 1711, 'health is worth preserving, though life is not'.

to the contrary.   I am glad she is with her friends ; if she be discreet, it will make her easy in her fortune.

We are full of your intentions to repeal the Test ;[1] The spirituall Leaders will encourage that project to a man.   We conclude the same thing will be attempted [p. 3.] here next winter, and have the | same advocates, but we hope, without success.   Your friends here are as usuall. D[r] D is very modest in his new prosperity;[2] walks on foot in fair weather, lives well, (as I hear) entertains his old friends, and does[3] many acts of generosity as well as charity.   I have not been at his table, and onely made him two short visits.   I often see L[d] Orrery who seems every way a most deserving Person, a good Scholar, with much wit, manners and modesty.   His business will keep him here at least till next winter, for his agent is the chiefest rogue of his calling.[4]   I have

[1] The Dissenters were moving for the repeal of the Corporation and Test Acts, and had held a great meeting in London on 29 November. At this meeting their committee reported that the time was not proper for making an application to parliament. A new committee was then appointed, and it came to the same decision ; 'which being reported at a General Meeting of the Deputies from the several Dissenting Congregations on the 29th of December, they agreed therewith, and thereupon the affair was dropt till a more convenient opportunity shall offer' (see the *Political State* for 1733, vol. xlv, pp. 138–41). The fullest reports of the meetings, as well as letters on the need of the repeal, were published in *The Whitehall*

*Evening Post.*

[2] See Letter LVIII, p.141, n.2.

[3] 'does' after 'gives' obliterated.

[4] Orrery's father had been systematically defrauded by this agent. 'I believe it is true', says Eustace Budgell, 'that a little before his Death, he discovered, That a Person intrusted with his Affairs in *Ireland*, (where he had a noble Estate,) had not returned him one *half* of the yearly Income for which several of his Estates were actually set, and that he had determined to call this Person to an Account' (*Memoirs of the late Earl of Orrery*, 1732, p. 249). In a letter of 13 June 1732 Orrery wrote : 'I am going to Ireland to encounter the Giants of that Kingdom who have laid Waste my Patrimony. My Armour is made of Parchment, my

not heard a word of Crossthwaite, and I wish you had given me directions what to do upon his so long delaying to remit you money, nor do I know who is your banquier here.—I beg you will force your nature as much as possible upon temperance and exercise, I mean temperance in a physicall sense, and not a moral, for many a moral and pious man's health is ruined by intemperance, and let me hear from you, and have your directions relating to your Agent and to Burton.

I am ever &c

Lady Acheson presents her service to you and chides you for neglecting your health, although her Ladyship be a greater criminal in that article (if possible) than your self.   She is an absolute Dublin rake, sits up late, loses her money, and goes to bed sick, and resolves like you never to mend.   It is said you will soon [see] S^r Arthur at London to lessen a pair of swelld legs.

*Address :* To Charles Ford Esq^r, to be
left at the Coco-tree in
Pell-mell
London.

*Postmarks :* Dublin *and* $\frac{?}{DE}$

LX[1]

# (Ford to Swift)

London, Dec. 23, 1732.

YESTERDAY I received your letter of the 9th, and am infinitely obliged to you for the constant concern you

---

Head-Piece and Breast-Plate are my Mother's Marriage Settlement. . . . The Truth is, my private Affairs are left in the utmost Confusion' (*The Orrery Papers*, 1903, i. 113).
   [1] Original not known ; printed by Deane Swift, 1768.

shew for me. I am ashamed to trouble you so much, and so often, in my own affairs; and your great kindness makes me almost ashamed to ask pardon for it.[1]

.    .    .    .    .    .

I am very glad to hear the character you give of Lord Orrery. He was extreamly applauded for a speech he made against the Army Bill.[2] There is no danger of repealing the Test. The Court has taken the usual method of gaining the fanatick leaders, much against the grain of the body. It is said, the Bishop of Salisbury[3] is the chief encourager of them; that the Queen spoke to him, and that he answered, He had promised, and would not fail them. He can be besmeared, although they would not suffer him to go the dirty road to Durham. That was the excuse they made him upon the last vacancy of that see. I am extreamly proud that lady Acheson does me the honour to remember her humble servant. I heartily wish she could be persuaded to keep good hours, having observed, by many of my acquaintance, that nothing impairs health so much as sitting up late. I often hear from my sister : she writes in quite another strain than she talked, with chearfulness and good nature. I fancy Arsalla[4] has cured the lady of her spleen.

---

[1] The passage omitted by Deane Swift evidently dealt with Ford's quarrel with Burton about Woodpark. The dates show that the documents from which were made the transcripts published by Sir Walter Scott (Letter LVI, p. 132, n. 2) were sent with this letter.

[2] This was Orrery's maiden speech in the House of Lords, delivered on 7 March 1732 in the debate in committee on the Mutiny Bill. He moved that 'it be an instruction to the Committee that the number of men specified by the Bill do not exceed twelve thousand'. The motion was lost by 27 votes to 88. The speech is printed in *The Orrery Papers*, i, pp. 110–11.

[3] Benjamin Hoadly, Bishop of Salisbury 1723–34, afterwards Bishop of Winchester. Edward Chandler had been made Bishop of Durham in 1730.

[4] See Letter LVI, p. 135, n. 3.

I heartily wish you many new years, with health and happiness ; and am, most entirely, &c.

I am told poor Gay's play is now in rehearsal, and will please.   It was that brought him to town a little before he died ; though, without his fever, he could not probably have held out long any where.[1]


### LXI[2]

Dublin Ap$^r$. 5$^{th}$. 1733

I MISLAYD your former letter in some place so very secure that I was never able to recover it.   Your last I have now before me.   I have been for a month past so disordered with my old giddyness that I have put my self into the hands of Deally[3] and taking daily medicines.   It was not violent, and I am somewhat better, but never expect a good head, for I always totter in the dark, and have within this twelvemonth spent more money in chair-hire than in any ten years before. Yet I struggle, and ride at least three times a week to the quan[ti]ty of above 30 miles.   But I have another cruel misfortune come on me about ten Days past. For my strained leg hath either got a new strain, or

[1] Gay had died of 'a violent inflammatory fever' (Arbuthnot, who attended him, says 'a mortification of the bowels') on 4 December.   The play was *Achilles*.   It was produced at Covent Garden on 10 February 1733.

[2] Original in the Pierpont Morgan Library.

[3] Spelling uncertain ; the name comes at the end of a line, and the writing is cramped.   Nothing more appears to be known about this physician.   Perhaps he was the 'Charles Daly, chirurgus' who is mentioned in *Alumni Dublinenses* (ed. Burtchaell and Sadleir) as the father of John Daly admitted to Trinity College in 1717.   It will be remembered that Swift pronounced 'Dean' as we pronounce 'Dane'.

a Rhumatick disorder, with which I walk in pain, and
yet I still walk three or 4 miles, which I am determined
to do as long as I am able not to fence against death
but pain.　I will go on no further on my own infirmityes
than to add that I have lost half my memory, and all
my Invention.　I have ordered your lease to Burton to
be copyd on the other side of this Paper.　I was glad
when Crosswait told me some time ago that Burton
had payd his Rent.　Crosswait was here yesterday, and
told me he had remitted you 200 and odd pounds.
He gives no good account of your friend Roberts.[1]
I should advise that any Tenant who hath a hard
bargain, or rather, who hath not an easy one, should
either be[2] lightned, or another put in his room.　It is
a jest for a Landlord who lives in another kingdom to
expect good payment when his lands are let to a full
value, especially under that daily decline of all things
in this miserable Country.　The young nephew (you
must pardon me) is the most worthless whifling trifling
knavish lad that ever I knew.　He would not for the
world disoblige his Uncle, but he will not joyn to make
Burton easy.　He talks with the greatest folly, incon-
sistence, and equivocation that I have known.　He lately
sent a message to me that I would sollicite you to joyn
with him to make a joynture for a wife, but the woman
is not known, and in that case he says he will make you
easy as to Burton, but that even on your complyance
he will never joyn to secure the Lease.　I am wearyed
with his nonsense, and have ordered my servants not
to admit him any more.　He converses with some

---

[1] Hugh Roberts, tenant of part
of the Woodpark estate.　In the
lease of 22 Sept. 1731 'copied
on the other side of this paper'
(see Letter LVI, p.132, n.2) Ford
had appointed 'Hugh Roberts of
Woodparke aforesaid Gentleman
his Lawfull Attorney to give
Livery of Seisin of the above-
mentioned premisses unto the
said Walter Burton'.

[2] MS. 'by'.

hedge attornyes that put him upon this ridiculous management, to which he is already too much addicted by nature and a wrong education.

I can say nothing of my coming over. My private affairs are embroyled to the utmost, my new additionall lameness, and the return of my old disorder have sunk my spirits below any thoughts of such a Journy. My intentions were if I could any way settle my affairs, and recover my health, to sett out in August, and pass the Winter between L^d Bolingb— and M^r Pope. All his late things, and those of others are constantly printed here. I agree with you, that L^dy Mary did not write that Libel,[1] though I never read ten lines of it. Yet I think her Devil enough. You say nothing of your health. If it be not better I have cause to complain that you do not complain to me. I envy M^r Pope for his being raild at. I think all men of wit should employ it in Satyr, if it will onely serve to vex Rogues, though it will not amend them. If my Talent that way were equal to the sourness of my temper I would write nothing else. My humble Service to D^r Arbuth— and my true old friend M^r Lewis. We have a damnable letter of your friend Henly, to his Burrow.[2] It is printed

[1] *Verses Address'd to the Imitator of the First Satire of the Second Book of Horace. By a Lady* (London: A. Dodd), advertised as published 'this day' in *The London Evening - Post* of 6–8 March. For Lady Mary Wortley Montagu's share in this 'libel', see Courthope's *Life of Pope* (*Works*, vol. v), p. 260; and cf. *Correspondence*, iv. 415, 426.

[2] Anthony Henley (d. 1748), elder brother of Lord Northington, member for the borough of Southampton in the parliament of 1727–34. His letter is reprinted in *Notes and Queries*, 2nd S., xii. 107 (Aug. 10, 1861), from a newspaper of about 1770. The following version, which differs only in detail and in the omission of the signature, was printed in *The Weekly Register* of 31 March 1733:

'Gentlemen,

'Yours I received, and am very much surprized at your Insolence in troubling me about the Excise. You know what I know very well, that I bought

here. I give you joy of your first large Stride to Slavery the Excise.[1] Adieu.

I would not suffer that Libel against Pope to be printed here.[2]                                J. S.

*Address :*  To Charles Ford, Esq[r], to be
                  left at the Coco-tree in
                  Pellmel
                                                London

*Postmarks :* Dublin *and* $\frac{11}{AP}$

## LXII[3]

# (Ford to Swift)

London, April 14, 1733.

I AM extreamly concerned to hear the bad state of your health. I have often wished that you would be more moderate in your walks; for though riding has

you. I know what perhaps you think I don't know, that you are about selling yourselves to somebody else; and I know what perhaps you don't know, that I am about buying another Borough.—And now may the Curse of God light upon you all; and may your Houses be as common to Excise-Men, as your Wives and Daughters were to me, when I stood Candidate for your Corporation.'

Ford's next letter shows that this reply was only a heavy joke, accompanying the 'real' reply which was 'extremely proper'. The Mayor of Southampton was Henley's friend. In the General Election of April 1734 he was alleged to have 'behaved with great partiality' in Henley's favour (*Journals of the House of Commons*, 3 April 1735, p. 447).

[1] Walpole introduced his Excise scheme on 14 March. The Bill was read a first time on 4 April, and ordered to be read a second time on 11 April.

[2] This is an important supplement to Swift's milder statement in his letter to Pope of 30 March: 'Faulkner would not print it, nor do I know whether anybody here will' (*Correspondence*, iv. 415).

[3] Original not known; printed by Deane Swift, 1768.

always been allowed to be good for a giddy head, I
never heard walking prescribed for a strain, or any
ailment in the leg; and the violent sweats you put
yourself into are apt to give colds, and, I doubt,
occasion much of your other disorder. I am confident
you would find yourself better here; and even the
journey would be of great use to you. I was vastly
pleased to hear my Lord Mayor[1] talk of the delight
he should have in seeing you this year, that he might
show you a creature of your own making. He has
behaved himself so well in his publick capacity, that,
whether it be his humility, or his pride, he deserves to
be gratified. I could heartily wish your other complaints
were as much without foundation, as that of having
lost half your memory, and all your invention. I will
venture to pronounce you have more left of the first
than most men, and of the last than any man now
alive. While the Excises were depending, you were
expected every day, for it was said, why should not he
shew as much regard for the Liberty of England, as
he did for the Money of Ireland? I wish you had
been here, though the affair, in my opinion, is happily
ended.[2] Many people are offended that the bills
were dropt, and not rejected, and the authors of the
scheme left unpunished. It was absolutely impossible to have carried it otherwise. You have heard
Sir Robert Walpole and one or two more coming out of
the house were insulted. A few of that rabble have
been seized, with the ringleader, who proves to be a
Norfolk man, no enemy to Excises, but an entire
dependant upon the outraged person.[3] Though the

[1] John Barber, Swift's printer
in the Queen Anne days.
[2] On 11 April Walpole postponed the second reading of the
Excise Bill to 12 June, by which

time the House was expected to
have risen.
[3] 'Wednesday Night [11
April] a Gentleman was seiz'd
in the Court of Requests by

rejoicings were as great and as universal as ever were known, there was no violence, except the breaking a very few windows, whose owners had shown an untimely thrift of their candles.    I foretold Henley what his joking would come to; but the mayor of Southampton immediately printed his real letter, which was short, and extreamly proper.    His designed opponent at the next election, having voted for the excise, will not dare to show himself in the corporation ; and Henley, after the division, thanked him for having, by that vote, bestowed him fifteen hundred pounds.[1] . . . . . .

I have great hopes this fine mild weather will set you right, and long to hear you are preparing for your journey.    I am most entirely, your grateful, &c.

## LXIII [2]

Dublin Oct^br. 9^th. 1733

It is very long since I writ to you, or heard from you ; and indeed it is long since I writ to any body else, For I have been some months in [3] a bad dispirited way

several Justices of the Peace, who were there present with a great number of Constables to prevent Riots, being accused of hissing at Sir Robert Walpole, and raising a Riot, &c.    He was carried first to the Gatehouse, and afterwards to the Petty-Sessions, where, after an Examination, he was admitted to Bail in a Recognizance of 500*l*. He is a Gentleman of Fortune and Character at Woodbridge in Suffolk : Being ask'd if he was not hired to come down to West-minster, said he came down to solicite against the Excise '—*The Universal Spectator*, 14 April

1733.    Cf. *The Weekly Register*, 14 April, *The Political State*, May 1733, vol. xlv, p. 440, and Coxe, *Memoirs of Pelham*, 1829, i, pp. 9, 10.

[1] See Letter LXI, p. 149, n. 2. Henley lost the seat.    There was a double return at the 1734 election, and John Conduitt, who had received 212 votes to Henley's 213, was declared by the House of Commons on 3 April 1735 to have been duly elected.

[2] Original in the possession of Harold Murdock, Esq., of Harvard University.

[3] 'in' over 'and' struck out.

with Deafness, and giddyness, and Fluxes.   I am now
and have been a month confined to the house, by the two
former aylment[s], though the last hath left me at present.
I let no Company see me except¹ Mʳ Worrall² and his
wife, who is a chearfull woman with a clear voice, She
sends me vittels and they both generally dine with me,
and sit the evenings.   I have been twice severely
vomited, to the utmost I could possibly bear, but without amendment.   I believe my disorder is particular,
and out of the Experience of our Physicians here :
Docᵗʳ Helsham³ the best of them is very kind and
visits me constantly.   My Spirits are quite broke.

Mʳ Crosswaight called here last week, and desired
I would let him have the Lease from you to one Joseph
Troy, whom he is to eject, and could not proceed without that Lease.   I took his Receit, with promise to
return it, and sent it to him, for, see him I could not.
Being your Agent, I thought he might be trusted.   If
I had been well I should | should have writ to you a [p. 2.]
good while ago, upon an occasion that perhaps you may
have heard of in Advertisements.   A Printer of this
Town⁴ applyed himself to me by letters and friends
for leave to print in four volumes the Works of J S D D,
&c.   I answered that as I could not hinder him, so I

---

¹ MS. 'expect'; cf. Letter I,
p. 1, n. 1.
² See Letter XLI, p. 97, n. 5.
³ Richard Helsham, fellow of
Trinity College, recently appointed Regius Professor of Physic.
Swift gives a sketch of him as
'the true happy man' in his
letter to Pope of 13 Feb. 1729
(*Correspondence*, iv. 59).
⁴ George Faulkner.   As early
as 9 Dec. 1732 Swift had warned
Benjamin Motte, the publisher of

*Gulliver's Travels*, that a Dublin
edition of his works was in con-
templation : 'I believe I told you
formerly that Booksellers here
have no property; and I have
cause to believe that some of our
printers will collect all they think
to be mine, and print them by
Subscription, which I will neither
encourage nor oppose' (original
in the Pierpont Morgan Library;
*Correspondence*, iv. 367).

would not encourage him, but that he should take care
not to charge me with what I never writ.    There is no
Propriety of Copyes here ; they print what they please.
The man behaved himself with all respect, and since it
was an evil I could not avoyd, I had rather they should
be printed correctly than otherwise.    Now, you may
please to remember how much I complained of Motts
suffering some friend of his (I suppose it was Mʳ Took
a Clergy-man now dead ¹) not onely to ² blot out some
things that he thought might give offence, but to insert
a good deal of trash contrary to the Author's manner
and Style, and Intention.    I think you had a Gulliver
interleaved and set right in those mangled and murdered
Pages.³    I inquired afterwards of severall Person[s] where
that Copy was ; some said Mʳ Pilkington ⁴ had it, but
his Wife sent me word she could not find it.    Other[s]
said it was in Mʳ Corbet's ⁵ hands.    On my writing to

---

¹ The Rev. Andrew Tooke,
son of Benjamin Tooke, Swift's
' bookseller '.  He was appointed
Master of the Charterhouse in
1728, and was an usher of the
school when he was employed to
revise *Gulliver*.   In 1720 he had
revised William Walker's *Treatise
of English Particles*.  He died
20 January 1732, but survived
to the time of Keats, and even
later, in ' Tooke's *Pantheon* '.

² ' not onely to ' after ' to '
struck out.

³ This copy is now in the
Forster Collection in South Kensington Museum.    A full record
of its corrections is given in the
edition of *Gulliver's Travels* by
Harold Williams, 1926.    This
letter confirms the textual authority of Faulkner's edition.

⁴ The Rev. Matthew Pilkington, whose *Poems on several Occasions*, 1730, Swift had revised
(London edition, 1731).    On
Swift's recommendation he was
appointed chaplain to John Barber
as Lord Mayor, and he was at
this time in London.    His wife
was Letitia Pilkington, author
of the *Memoirs*, 1748.    Swift
came to find him ' the falsest
rogue ', and had broken with
them both before their divorce
in 1738.    Some months had
elapsed since Swift had applied
to Mrs. Pilkington for the corrections; see his letter to Faulkner of
29 June (*Correspondence*, iv. 444).

⁵ See Letter XLIV, p. 108,
n. 3.   The list which Corbet sent
presumably agreed with the list
which Ford had sent to Motte

him,[1] he sent a loose Paper[2] with very little except literall corrections in your hand. I wish you would please to let me know, whether You have such an inter-leaved Gulliver; and where and how I could get [it]; For to say the truth, I cannot with patience endure that | mingld and mangled manner, as it came from [p. 3.] Mottes hands; and it will be extreme difficult for me to correct it by any[3] other means, with so ill a memory, and in so bad a State of health. Pray God restore[4] and continue yours. I can hold down my head no longer. My Service to all my friends, I am ever &c.

J:S.

*Address :* To Charles Ford, Esq[r]
        To be left at the Coco-tree
        in Pell-mell
              London

*Postmarks :* Dublin *and* $\frac{17}{OC}$

## LXIV [5]

# (Ford to Swift)

London, Nov. 6, 1733.

I HAD the favour of your letter in Derbyshire, from whence I came last week. I am extremely concerned to hear the ill state of your health. I was afraid of it, when I was so long without the pleasure of hearing from you. Those sort of disorders puzzle the physicians

---

on 3 Jan. 1727: see *Gulliver's Travels,* ed. Williams, pp. xxxiv and 423.

  [1] 'him' over 'me' struck out.

  [2] 'Paper' over 'Sheet' struck out.

  [3] 'any' over 'no' struck out.

  [4] 'restore' after 'cont' struck out.

  [5] Original not known; printed by Deane Swift, 1768.

every where; and they are merciless dogs in purging
or vomiting to no purpose, when they don't know what
to do.   I heartily wish you would try the Bath waters,
which are allowed to be the best medicine for strengthening the stomach; and most distempers in the head
proceed from thence.   Vomits may clean a foul stomach,
but they are certainly the worst things that can be for
a weak one.

I have long had it at heart to see your works
collected, and published with care.   It is become absolutely necessary, since that jumble with Pope, &c. in
three volumes, which put me in a rage whenever I meet
them.[1]   I know no reason why, at this distance of time,
the Examiners, and other political pamphlets written in
the Queen's reign, might not be inserted.   I doubt you
have been too negligent in keeping copies; but I have
them bound up, and most of them single besides.   I lent
Mr. Corbet that paper to correct his Gulliver by; and it
was from it that I mended my own.   There is every
single alteration from the original copy; and the printed
book abounds with all those errors, which should be
avoided in the new edition.

In my book the blank leaves were wrong placed,
so that there are perpetual references backwards and
forwards, and it is more difficult to be understood
than the paper; but I will try to get one of the second
edition, which is much more correct than the first,[2] and
transcribe all the alterations more clearly.   I shall be at
a loss how to send it afterwards, unless I am directed
to somebody that is going to Ireland.   All books are
printed here now by subscription; if there be one for
this, I beg I may not be left out.   Mr. Crosthwaite
will pay for me.

[1] *Miscellanies in Prose and Verse*, 1727–8.
[2] In the 'second edition', 1727, Motte had followed the list of corrections sent to him by Ford on 3 January 1727.

The dissenters were certainly promised that the Test Act should be repealed this session in Ireland. I should be glad to know whether any attempt has been or is to be made towards it, and how it is like to succeed.[1]

We have lost Miss Kelley,[2] who they say was destroyed by the ignorance of an Irish physician, one Gorman.[3] Doctor Beaufort was sent for when she was dying, and found her speechless and senseless.

[1] It was the sequel to the demand for the repeal of the Test in England (Letter LIX, p. 144, n. 1). As early as 30 Dec. 1731 Walpole had written to the Duke of Dorset, then Lord Lieutenant, 'I shall be glad that your Grace may have the honour of passing a Bill to releive the Protestant Dissenters from a burthen which they have a long time unjustly and unreasonably groaned under' (Stopford-Sackville MSS. i. 147—Hist. MSS. Com. 1904); and Dorset at the opening of the Irish Parliament in October 1733 had urged 'a firm Union amongst all Protestants, who have one common Interest, and the same common Enemy'. Swift thereupon returned to a controversy in which he had had no occasion to engage since he wrote his *Letter concerning the Sacramental Test*, 1709. His chief tract now was *The Presbyterians Plea of Merit*, mentioned in his next letter.

[2] 'Yesterday at Six in the Morning dy'd, in the Flower of her Youth and Beauty, of a consumptive Illness, the celebrated Miss Frances Arabella Kelley, Daughter of Dennis Kelley, Esq; of the Kingdom of Ireland, Grandaughter to Walter late Lord Bellew in the said Kingdom, and Niece to the Right Hon. Thomas Earl of Strafford.' —*The London Evening-Post*, 1–3 Nov. 1733.

She had recently won Swift's affection; 'she is confined to her bed with a pleuratic disorder, but the Dean attends her bedside' (Mrs. Delany's *Autobiography and Correspondence*, 1861, i. 402). Her five letters to Swift were written between February and August of this year. She crossed to England in May.

[3] 'Dr John Gorman, Leestreet, Red-Lion-Square,' was a doctor of medicine of Rheims, and a Licentiate of the Royal College of Physicians. 'Dr. John Beauford, Southampton-street, Covent-Garden,' was a doctor of medicine of Cambridge, and a 'Candidate' of the Royal College. See W. Munk, *Roll of the Royal College of Physicians*, 1878, ii. 37, 110; official list as printed in Chamberlayne's *Present State*, 1737, ii. 134; and *Athenae Cantabrigienses*.

Our late Lord Mayor has gone through his year with a most universal applause.   He has shewn himself to have the best understanding of any man in the city, and gained a character, which he wanted before, of courage and honesty.   There is no doubt of his being chosen member of parliament for the city at the next election.[1]   He is something the poorer for his office; but the honour he has got by it makes him ample amends.

For God's sake try to keep up your spirits.   They have hitherto been greater than any man's I ever met, and it is better to preserve them, even with wine, than to let them sink.   Divert yourself with Mrs. Worral, at backgammon.   Find out some new country to travel in : any thing to amuse.   Nothing can contribute sooner than chearfulness to your recovery; which that it may be very speedy, is sincerely the thing in the world most wished for by, your ever obliged, &c.

A Catalogue [2] of Pamphlets and Papers, which I have bound, and those marked * single.   I believe I can have any of the others from Ald. B.[3]

  *   Conduct of the Allies.
  *   Remarks on the Barrier Treaty.
  *   Advice to the October Club.
    A new Journey to Paris.
    Remarks on the Letter to the Seven Lords appointed
      to examine Gregg.

---

[1] Barber failed to be chosen for the City of London in the general election of 1734.

[2] This catalogue was omitted by Deane Swift and was first printed by Scott in a footnote in his Life of Swift (*Works*, 1814, i. 415–16).   Scott says that it 'is subjoined to the letter in the original MS.' as a 'postscript'.   Dr. Elrington Ball was the first to restore it to its proper place among the Letters.   It is here reprinted from Scott's text.

[3] Barber.

\* Some Reasons to prove that no Whig is obliged to oppose her Majesty.

Importance of the Guardian.

\* Preface to the Bishop of Sarum's Introduction.

Mr. Collins's Discourse of Free-thinking abstracted, for the Use of the Poor.

Public Spirit of the Whigs.

\* Horace *Strenuus et Fortis.*[1]

\* Examiners, from Number 13 to Number 45.

\* Toland's Invitation to Dismal.

\* Ballad upon Not in Game.[2]

\* Peace and Dunkirk, a Song.

\* Windsor Prophecy.

\* Hugh and Cry after Dismal.

\* Pretender's Letter to a Whig Lord.

Some Free Thoughts on the present State of Affairs, never printed.


## LXV [3]

### Dublin. Nov<sup>r</sup>. 20<sup>th</sup>. 1733

I HAVE reason to take it extremely ill that in your letter just come to my hands, you said not one Syllable concerning your health, and it was so long since I heard from you, either by your self or Crossweight, that although I guessed you were passing the Summer with some friends in the Country as usuall, yet I was in pain lest your former disorder might return, for I cannot commend you as a cautious person in preventing Sick-

---

[1] *Part of the Seventh Epistle of the First Book of Horace Imitated,* 1713, addressed to Oxford.

[2] *An Excellent New Song, Being the Intended Speech of a* famous Orator against Peace, 1711.

[3] Original in the Pierpont Morgan Library, New York.

ness by Temperance and Exercise. I agree with your notions of Physick and Physicians, and have as little faith in them as in Mahomet or the Pope. But I sometimes reason, that in London where there are twenty people to one more than here, there must be twenty to one more experience. I am sure there is not one Patient in my case through this whole Kingdom. And although in the London Dispensatory approved by[1] the Physicians there are Remedyes named both for Giddyness and deafness, none of them that I can find, were prescribed to me. I have the Book, but my books are so confused that I can not find it, nor would value it if I did.[2] The Doctors here think that both these Aylments in me are united in their Causes, but they were not always so; for one has often[3] left me when the other stayd. They have now continued longer than

[p. 2.] ever I knew them, which | I impute to increasing years, and consequently a greater weakness in my nerves. I am not so bad as I was, but my deafness lessens or increases as it thinks fit. I ride as far as Hoath every fair day, and am generally better for a day or two after. This is too much in conscience to trouble you with, and hath too much of the old woman, but you have so erred in the other extreme, that you well deserve the Punishment. It is reckoned that the Test will be repealed. It is said that 30000ll have been returned from England; and 20000ll raised here from Servants, Laborers, Farmers, Squires, Whigs &c to promote the good Work. Half the Bishops will be on their side. Pamphlets pro and con fly about. One is called *The Presbyterian Plea of Merit examined*: perhaps if you saw

---

[1] 'approved by' over 'allowed' struck out.

[2] 'Fulleri Pharmacopaea. Lond. 1708' (i. e. Thomas Fuller's *Pharmacopœia extem-* *poranea*, fourth edition) is in the Catalogue of Swift's Library in 1715.

[3] 'often' inserted above the line.

it, you might guess the writer.[1]   Dr. Tisdel[2] writes a weekly Paper called the *Correspondent*, generally very poor and Spiritless.   But we all conclude the Affair desperate.   For the money is sufficient among us—to abolish Christianity it self.   All the People in Power are determined for the repeal, and some of your acquaintance, formerly Toryes, are now on the same side.   I have been in no condition to stir in it.

I gave you an account in my last how against my will a Man here is printing the Works of &c by Subscription.   Gulliver vexeth me more than any. I thought you had entred in leaves interlined all the differences from the originall Manuscript.   Had there been onely omissions, I should not care one farthing ; but change of Style, new things foysted in, that are false facts, and I know not what, is very provoking. Motte tells me He designs to print a new Edition of Gulliver in quarto, with Cutts and all as it was in the genuin copy.[3]   He is very uneasy about the Irish

---

[1] See previous letter, p. 157, n.1. Swift's forebodings were not realized; the Irish Parliament lost no time in declaring, with unusual emphasis, against the repeal of the Test. 'Upon the 11th Day of *December* the House of Commons came to the following Resolution, *viz.* "*Resolved*, That no Bill, or Heads of a Bill, be received after *Friday* next [the 13th], for the Repeal of any Clause in any Act, to prevent the further Growth of Popery ". By which Resolution, an effectual Bar was put to the bringing in of any Bill for the Repeal of these Acts, during that Session of Parliament' (*Political State*, August 1734, p. 145).   See also Miss Eyre Matcham's MSS., p. 57— Hist. MSS. Com. 1909 (Various Collections VI).

[2] Letter XLI, p. 96, n. 4.   *The Correspondent* ran to six numbers; a complete set is in the Bradshaw Collection in the University Library, Cambridge.   This passage casts doubt on Swift's authorship of *A Narrative of the Several Attempts for a Repeal of the Sacramental Test* which originally formed numbers iii and iv, and is printed among Swift's *Works*; and the doubt is confirmed by the evidence of style.

[3] Motte did not carry out his design.   The next London edition was published by Bathurst, Motte's successor, in 1742, and the first

Edition.[1]   All I can do is to strike out the Trash in
the Edition to be printed here, since you can not
help me. I will order your name, as you desire, among
[p. 3.] the Subscribers.[2]   It was to avoyd | offence, that Motte
got those alterations and insertions to be made
I suppose by M^r Took the Clergyman deceased.   So
that I fear the second Edition will not mend the
matter, further than as to litteral faults.[3]   For instance,
The Title of one Chapter is of the Queens administration without a prime Minister &c, and accordingly in
the Chapter it is said that she had no chief Minister &c :
Besides, the whole Sting is taken out [4] in severall passages, in order to soften them.   Thus the Style is debased,
the humor quite lost, and the matter insipid.

I follow your advice in amusing my self with all
Trifles that my health will permit.   What is more,
I drink a whole Bottle of wine every day, a Pint at
noon, and the same at night.   I dine constantly at
home, with one or two friends whom I can be easy
with, and therefore in that point sans consequence.
I can not think of travelling out of this kingdom under
five thousand pounds a year, as I writ to a Lady lately
come from Spa[5]—who would have had me be of her
retinue, but she would not let me have the money.

edition of *Gulliver* in quarto was
part of Hawkesworth's edition
of the *Works*, published by
Bathurst in 1755.
  [1] 'the Irish Edition' over
'Mottes Copy' struck out.
  [2] 'Charles Ford of London,
Esq;' duly appears in the long
and interesting list of 'Subscribers
Names' in the first volume of the
Dublin edition of 1735.
  [3] Motte's 'second edition', of
which Ford had spoken: see p.

156, note 2.  In the forthcoming
Dublin edition more than 'literal
faults' were mended.  The title
and passage which he mentions
(Part iv, Chapter vi) were put
right with the help of Ford's
notes. See *Gulliver's Travels*, ed.
Harold Williams, pp. 455–6.
  [4] 'out' after 'off' obliterated.
  [5] The Duchess of Queensberry; see *Correspondence*, iv.
439, v. 36 and 40.

In short, there is one comfort here, that I am at home, in a convenient house, have people to take care of me, and with the diminution of my little revenue by 300<sup>ll</sup> per ann. can give a dish of meat, and moderate wine to one or two friends ; But this was by a piece of prudence I learned from you, who in all your expensiveness still kept a purse in case of exigences. My temporal Fortune is in the utmost Confusion, and of 200<sup>ll</sup> a year that I ought to receive for interest, I never get one peny. Otherwise I could be perfectly easy as to the article of living, though not of travelling, and lodging at Inns, and making shifts, and wanting tender people about me.— In Your Catalogue of Pamphlets there are some I do not remember, I mean, *Journy to Paris, Remarks about Greg, Peace and Dunkirk, Windsor Prophesy, Pretenders Letter to a Whig Lord.* I fancy I did not write any of these.[1] And, as for the rest, they were temporary occasional things, that dye naturally with the Change of times, and therefore I do not think any Printer in London, much less here, would concern himself about them.

Pray God preserve you in health. I have quite shaken off young Ford, and hear nothing of him. I am ever entirely yours &c.

*Address :*     To
           Charles Ford Esq<sup>r</sup>: at the
           Coco-tree in Pell-mell
               London

*Postmarks :* Dublin *and* $\frac{30}{NO}$

[1] A notable lapse of memory.

## LXVI [1]

# (Ford to Swift)

London, June 3d, 1736.

DEAR SIR,

THOUGH you have left off corresponding with me these two years and a half, I cannot leave you off yet; and I think this is the sixth letter I have sent you, since I have heard one word of you from your own hand.   My Lord Oxford told me last winter that he had heard from you, and you were then well.[2]   Mr. Cæsar[3] very lately told me the same.   It is always the most welcome news that can come to me; but it would be a great addition to my pleasure to have it from yourself; and you know my sincere regard for you may in some measure claim it.

I have been engaged these five months in a most troublesome law-suit with an Irish chairman.   Those fellows swarm about St. James's, and will hardly allow you to walk half a street, or even in the Park, on the fairest day.   This rascal rushed into the entry of a tavern to force me into his chair, ran his poles against me, and would not let me pass till I broke his head. He made a jest of it that night; but the next morning an Irish solicitor came, out of profound respect, to advise me to make the fellow amends : he told a dismal story of the surgeon and the bloody shirt, and spoke against his own interest, merely to hinder me, whom he had

[1] Original not known; printed by Deane Swift, 1768.

[2] See *Correspondence*, v. 250.

[3] Charles Cæsar, of Benington, Hertfordshire, to whom Swift apologized for mentioning Brutus in his presence (*Journal to Stella*, 14 Jan. 1713).   He was M.P. for Hertford from 1701 to 1715, and was Treasurer of the Navy in Oxford's administration.   Latterly he was M.P. for Hertfordshire, till his death in 1741.

never seen before, from being exposed.   Neither his
kind persuasions, nor the prudent councils of our friend
Mr. L——,[1] and a few more, could prevail on me.
A few days after, the solicitor brought me a bill found
by the grand jury, and a warrant under the hand of
three justices against John Ford, without any other
addition.   To shew his good will, he would not affront
me by executing the warrant ; but desired I would go
to any justice of peace, and give bail to appear the next
quarter sessions.   By my not doing it, he found out
the mistake of the name, which he said should be
rectified in a new bill, and if I would not comply with
their demands, after they had tried me for the assault,
they would bring an action of eighty or an hundred
pounds damages.   I threatened in my turn ; at which
he laughed, as I should do, if a little child should
threaten to knock me down.   As they proceeded
against me, I thought it time to begin with them,
and spoke to an acquaintance of mine, a justice of
peace, who sent a warrant for the fellow, upon the
waiter's oath, for assaulting me, and by a small stretch
of power, committed him to the Gate-house, where he
remained some days for want of bail.   I believe his
bail would hardly have been judged sufficient, if his
Irish solicitor had not gone to another justice, and taken
a false oath, that the gentleman who committed him
was out of town.   This perjury, it seems, cannot be
punished, because it was not upon record.   We presented bills against each other to the grand jury, among
whom there happened luckily to be some gentlemen ;
and though I did not know them, by their means my
bill was found, and his was returned *ignoramus.*   Then
I indicted him in the crown-office, the terror of the low
people, where they often plague one another, and
always make use of against those of better rank.   Still

[1] Erasmus Lewis.

the fellow blustered, and refused to make it up, unless I would pay his expences ; for his lawyer had persuaded him that in the end he should recover damages sufficient to make amends for all. While he ruined himself by law, he lost his business ; for no gentleman would take his chair. This brought down his proud stomach ; he came to me two days ago, made his submissions, we gave reciprocal releases from all actions &c., and I have already received the thanks of above forty gentlemen, for procuring them liberty to walk the streets in quiet. Thus this great affair has ended like the Yorkshire petition, which has been the chief business of the House of Commons this session.[1] Towards the end, indeed, they found a little time to shew their good will to the church. It is the general opinion, that the act for repealing the Test would have passed, if Sir Robert Walpole had not seen the necessity of his speaking, which he did in the most artful manner he had ever done in his life.[2] Several courtiers voted against him, as well as most of the patriots, and among others, Lord Bathurst's two sons. In the House of Lords, next to the Duke of Argyle, your friend Bathurst and Lord Carteret

---

[1] The petition brought by the defeated candidate of the 'Court Party' against the return of Sir Miles Stapylton ('Country Party') for York County in the general election of 1734. It came before the House of Commons on 16 January 1736 and was heard on every Tuesday and Thursday from 24 February to 22 April, when, on the eighteenth day, the petitioners summed up. Thereafter the House gave only one hearing a week, and as the evidence for the sitting member promised to be no less extensive, the petitioners withdrew on 11 May. See *Journals of the House of Commons, Political State* for June 1736, p. 585, and for October, p. 407, and *Carlisle Manuscripts* (Historical MSS. Com.), 1897, pp. 145–73.

[2] The motion for leave to bring in a bill to repeal the Test was lost by 251 votes to 123 on 12 March 1736. Walpole's cautious and conciliatory speech was generally admitted to have controlled the voting.

have shewn most rancour against——.[1] It is a melancholy reflection, that all the great officers of state, and the whole bench of bishops, joined to the Tories, could not prevent any one question in disfavour of the Church.[2]

I am asked every day if there be no hopes of ever seeing you here again, and am sorry not to be able to give any account of your intentions. I doubt my long letters quite tire your patience, and therefore conclude with assuring you, that nobody wishes you all happiness more than I do, who am most intirely yours, &c.

## LXVII[3]

### Jun. 22ᵈ. 1736

I do not allow your Account upon the Article of Letters, for I am sure you did never write above one last Letter to me, except that which I received about a week past. It is true, I have not enjoyd a day of Health for twenty months past, with continuall giddyness though not always violent, yet enough to break

[1] Argyle, Bathurst, and Carteret all spoke and voted in the House of Lords in favour of a bill for giving relief to Quakers in the recovery of tithes. Bathurst took the opportunity of making an attack on Ecclesiastical Courts, the reformation of which, he said, 'is much desired by every man in the kingdom, who has not an interest in their present methods of proceeding'; but the report of his speech hardly shows rancour against the Church. The speeches of Argyle and Carteret are united, along with others, in a composite report, and cannot be distinguished. The bill passed the Commons on 3 May and was thrown out by the Lords on the second reading by 54 votes to 35 on 12 May 1736. See *Political State* for November 1736, pp. 423 and 439–505.

[2] The great officers of state and the bishops had opposed the bill. Ford's 'melancholy reflection' is that they could not prevent a motion unfavourable to the Church, but only defeat it.

[3] Original in the British Museum—Egerton MS. 2805, f. 4; printed by Elrington Ball, 1913, *Correspondence,* v. 350–2.

my Spirits, and the more, because I am heartily sick of
the worst times and Peoples, and Oppressions that
History can shew in either Kingdom.  I am the most
hated person alive by all People both here, and on
your side by all Folks in power, and God knows, they
give me too much merit, for I am past all abilityes to
do them good or hurt.  As to your self, I have never
lessened a grain of that true Love and Esteem I ever
bore you.  But I considered, we were never to meet
in This World, For I am in no state of Health to go
to England, nor will you be ever in a state of mind to
visit Ireland.  I dare not stir many miles or days from
this Town, much less to London, for fear of a tedious
Fit of Giddyness, and particularly Deafness, which sometimes lasteth for 6 weeks together.  And my Rents are
so sunk, that I cannot afford to live with any comfort
there.  Neither have I three Friends with whom I could
converse, or spunge for a Dinner.  Here I have a large
House, convenient enough for my unrefined taste, and
can hitherto dine on a morcel without running in debt :
and yet I have been forced to borrow near 200$^{ll}$ to
supply my small family of three servants and a half, for
want of any reasonable Payments.  When S$^r$ A. Acheson
returned last from England,[1] he told me, you had got
a swelling in your Legs ; that he warned you of it, and
advise[d] you to go into the Country and take proper
Physick for it, but you rejected his Advice, and said,
[p. 2.] you knew others | who had the same disorder, and lived
20 years after, and that you desired no more : But you
did not consider that half of the 20 years would have
been the Scene of Misery.  When I was much younger
than You, not above 32 years old, I had by my drinking
water, and hating wine, got a swelling in my left Leg ;
and living in London, I was forced to wear a laced
Stockin for that Leg ; But I cured my self by per-

[1] Cf. Letter LIX, p. 143, n. 3.

petually walking ; and although the same leg was often troublesome, I at last by exercise grew quite rid of the swelling, and never knew any of it since, and can yet walk 6 or seven miles a day.   But I was and am more temperate than You.   I do not value long life ; but while it continueth, I endeavor to make it tolerable by Temperance.   I am extremely glad of your Victory over that Irish Scoundrel, and I wish every Minister of State could do so much for the Service of the Publick : I am angry, but not disappointed, that those Men or Lords I thought well of, have deceived me ; I mean Bathurst and Carteret ; They have writ to me in another Strain and Style.[1]   I have long given up all hopes of Church or Christianity.   A certain Author (I forget his name,) hath writ a book (I wish I could see it) that the Christian Religion will not last above 300 and odd years.[2]   He means, | there will always be [p. 3.] Christians, as there are Jews ; but it will be no longer a Nationall Religion ; and this is enough to justify the Scripture ; that, the Gates of Hell shall not prevayl against it.   As to the Church, it is equally the Aversion of both Kingdoms ; You, for the Quakers Tythes, and me for Grass, or Agisment, as the Term of Art is.[3]   Our present L^d Lie^t is a ——— I say no more.[4]   I have not

[1] See Letter LXVI, p.167, n.1, and *Correspondence*, v. 141, 232.

[2] Not identified.

[3] The Irish House of Commons had resolved on 18 March that ' the demand of Tythe Agistment for dry and barren cattle is new, grievous, and burthensome ', and that all legal ways and means ought to be made use of to oppose such demand ' until a proper remedy can be provided by the Legislature '.   Thereupon Swift

wrote 'The Legion Club'.   In Swift's sale-catalogue of books, No. 463 is 'Mac-Caulay's Tracts on Agistment-Tythe, and Tillage. Dub. 1736 ' ; see Harold Williams, *Dean Swift's Library*, 1932.

[4] The Duke of Dorset—' the big man of straw' of one of Swift's ballads.   On 17 May Swift had headed a deputation to the Duke against the proposed lowering of the gold coin. See *Correspondence,*

seen M^rs Ford this long time, nor know where to find
her ; and, the Ludlows have quite forsaken me.[1] But,
this is talking to you, as Alexander said when he was
conquering Darius, that one of his Governer[s] writing
to him of petty wars in Greece ; to which he answered
it was like telling him of a War between the Pigmyes
and the Cranes.[2] The D. of Argyle was allways a Scot,
and yet he deceived me for some time ; and I once loved
him much.[3] Where is our Friend Lewis ? I always
loved him, and am under great Obligations to him;
and present him with my hearty Service : But he
marryed like a —— and yet I thought him as wise
a Man as any I knew.[4] I hope My L^d Masham still
continues honest ; if so I desire he will accept my
humble Service. Is his Son good for any thing ?
I always doubted him. Pray God bless, I am ever
most sincerely Yours. I have not seen Your Steward[5]
this long time ; So I hope he makes you easy.

*Address :* To
　　　　Charles Ford, Esq^r, to be
　　　　left at the Coco-tree in
　　　　Pelmell
　　　　　　London

*Postmark :* $\frac{28}{IV}$

v. 324, Prose Works, ed. Temple
Scott, vii. 353–8, and *The Daily
Gazetteer* of 18 May 1736.
　[1] See Letter XXXI, p. 70,
n. 1, and LVI, p. 134, l. 14.
　[2] An inaccurate recollection
of Plutarch, Agesilaus, 15 (μυο-
μαχία), perhaps influenced by
Strabo, 70 (Bk. ii. 9).

　[3] See Swift's letters to Argyle
of 16 April 1711 and 20 Jan.
1713 (*Corr.* i. 248, ii. 5).
　[4] See Letter XLVI, p. 113, n. 1,
and LVII, p. 139, note 3.
　[5] Crosthwaite : cf. Letters
LVII, p. 135, and LXVIII, p.
172.

## LXVIII[1]

# (Ford to Swift)

#### London, July 8, 1736.

You cannot imagine how much I was transported to see a superscription in your hand, after two years and a half intermission. The pleasure I had in not being quite forgot, was soon abated by what you say of your ill health. I doubt you live too much by yourself; and retirement makes the strongest impression upon those who are formed for mirth and society. I have not been these thirty years without a set of chearful companions, by herding with new ones as the old marry and go off. Why have not you a succession of Grattans and Jacksons? Whatever resentment the men in power may have, every body else would seek your company, upon your own terms; and for those in great stations, I am sure, at this time, you would be ashamed to be well with them. If they hate you, it is because they fear you, and know your abilities better than you seem to do yourself: even in your melancholy you write with too much fire for broken spirits. Your giddiness and deafness give me the utmost concern, though I believe you would be less subject to them and as well taken care of here; nor need you spunge for a dinner, since you would be invited to two or three places every day. I will say no more upon this subject, because I know there is no persuading you.

My legs have been swelled many years; it is above twelve since Beaufort[2] gave me a prescription for them, which I never took till last winter. My Lord Lichfield,[3]

---

[1] Original not known; printed by Deane Swift, 1768.

[2] See Letter LXIV, p. 157, n. 3.

[3] George Henry Lee, third Earl of Lichfield (1690–1743), known as Viscount Quarendon

and other of my acquaintance, persuaded me to it; and they tell me it has had its effect, for I am no judge either of my own bad looks, or large legs, having always found myself perfectly well, except when I had my fever four years ago. I walk constantly every day in the Park, and am forced to be both temperate and sober, because my meat is so much overdone that I don't like it, and my dining acquaintance reserve themselves for a second meeting at night, which I obstinately refuse.

If your rents fall, I don't know what must become of us. I have considerable losses every year; and yet I think Crosthwaite a very honest man. Rents for some time have been ill paid here as well as in Ireland; and farms flung up every day, which have not been raised since King Charles the first's time. The graziers are undone in all parts, and it is bad enough with the farmers. One cause is their living much higher than they did formerly; another is, the great number of inclosures made of late, enough to supply many more people than *England* contains. It is certain, all last year a man came off well if he could sell a fat ox at the price he bought him lean. The butchers, by not lowering their meat in proportion, have been the only gainers.

I generally hear once a month or oftener from my sister. She writes to me with great affection; but I find she is still wrong-headed, and will be so as long as she lives. As she expected unreasonable presents, she makes them much more unreasonably; and, in my opinion, so ill judged, that I do not wonder more at her than at those who receive them. I see no difference in giving thirty or forty guineas, or in paying thirty or forty guineas for a thing the person you give it to

before he succeeded his father in 1716; father of the fourth Earl, the Chancellor of the University of Oxford.

must have paid. I have heard no reason to doubt Lord Masham. I know nothing of his son,[1] not even by sight. Our friend Lewis is in constant duty with his sick wife, who has been some years dying, and will not die.[2] Unless he calls, as he does upon me for a quarter of an hour at most twice in a year, there is no seeing him. I heartily wish you health and prosperity; and am ever, most sincerely, your, &c.

My Lord Masham was extremely pleased with your remembering him, and desired me to make his compliments to you.

## LXIX[3]

## (Ford to Swift)

November 22d, 1737.

I CAN'T help putting you in mind of me sometimes, though I am sure of having no return. I often read your name in the newspapers, but hardly have any other account of you, except when I happen to see Lord Orrery. He told me the last time, that you had been ill, but were perfectly recovered.

I hear they are going to publish two volumes more of your works.[4] I see no reason why all the pamphlets published at the end of the Queen's reign might not be inserted. Your objection of their being momentary things, will not hold. Killing no Murder,[5] and many

[1] The son (1712–76) succeeded his father as second Lord Masham in 1758.

[2] See Letter LVII, p. 139, n. 3.

[3] Original not known; printed by Deane Swift, 1768.

[4] Volumes v and vi of the Dublin edition were published in 1738 (preface dated 18 April).

They consist mainly of his political writings during Oxford's ministry.

[5] *Killing Noe Murder. Briefly Discourst in Three Quæstions. By William Allen,* 1657. The author was Edward Sexby: see the *Dictionary of National Biography.*

other old tracts, are still read with pleasure, not to mention Tully's Letters, which have not died with the times. My comfort is, they will some time or other be found among my books with the author's name, and posterity obliged with them. I have been driven out of a great house, where I had lodged between four and five years, by new lodgers, with an insupportable noise, and have taken a little one to myself in a little court, merely for the sake of sleeping in quiet. It is in St. James's-Place, and called Little Cleveland-Court. I believe you never observed it; for I never did, though I lodged very near it, till I was carried there to see the house I have taken. Though coaches come in, it consists of but six houses in all. Mine is but two stories high, contrived exactly as I would wish, as I seldom eat at home. The ground-floor is of small use to me; for the fore-parlour is flung into the entry, and makes a magnificent London hall. The back one, by their ridiculous custom of tacking a closet almost of the same bigness to it, is so dark, that I can hardly see to read there in the middle of the day. Up one pair of stairs I have a very good dining-room, which on the second floor is divided in two, and makes room for my whole family, a man and a maid, both at board-wages. Over my bed-chamber is my study, the pleasantest part of the house, from whence you have a full view of Buckingham-house, and all that part of the Park. My furniture is clean and new, but of the cheapest things I could find out. The most valuable goods I have are two different prints of you. I am still in great hopes I shall one day have the happiness of seeing you in it.

Every body agrees the Queen's death was wholly owing to her own fault.[1] She had a rupture, which she would not discover; and the surgeon who opened her

[1] Queen Caroline died 20 November.

navel, declared if he had known it two days sooner, she should have been walking about the next day. By her concealing her distemper, they gave her strong cordials for the gout in her stomach, which did her great mischief. The king is said to have given her the first account of her condition : she bore it with great resolution, and immediately sent for the rest of her children, to take formal leave of them, but absolutely refused to see the Prince of Wales ; nor could the Archbishop of Canterbury,[1] when he gave her the sacrament, prevail on her, though she said, she heartily forgave the prince. It is thought her death will be a loss, at least in point of ease, to some of the ministers.

Since Lewis has lost his old wife, he has had an old maiden niece to live with him, continues the same life, takes the air in his coach, dines moderately at home, and sees nobody. It was reported, and is still believed by many, that Sir Robert Walpole upon the loss of his, made Miss Skirret an honest woman ; but if it be so, the marriage is not yet owned.[2]

That you may, in health and happiness, see many 30th of Novembers,[3] is the most sincere and hearty wish of yours, &c.

If you will be so kind as to let me hear from you once again, you may either direct to me at the Cocoa-Tree, or to Little Cleveland-Court in St. James's Place.

[1] John Potter, classical scholar, translated from Oxford to Canterbury in February, 1737.

[2] Walpole's first wife, Catherine Shorter, died 20 August 1737. He married Maria Skerett about the beginning of March 1738 :

see Nichols, *Literary Anecdotes*, viii. 262, and *Carlisle Manuscripts* (Hist. MSS. Com.), 1897, pp. 190, 194.

[3] The correspondence ends fittingly with a happy return to the old birthday greetings.

# POEMS

AMONG

*FORD'S* PAPERS

AND A

FRAGMENT of a PAMPHLET

# VANBRUGG'S HOUSE

This piece is in the writing of Ford. It is the earlier version of the poem which, after extensive alterations, was published in Swift's *Miscellanies in Prose and Verse*, February 1711, with the title ' V—'s House Built from the Ruins of White-Hall that was Burnt. Written 1703'.

Another copy of this earlier version was owned by Swift's friend, Sir Andrew Fountaine, of Narford Hall, Norfolk, and remained in the possession of the Fountaine family till 1906, when it was sold at Messrs. Sotheby's (15 Dec. 1906, Lot 453) and passed to the Pierpont Morgan Library. It was described and quoted in part by John Forster in his *Life of Jonathan Swift*, 1875, pp. 163, 164.


## Vanbrugg's house
[p. 1.]

### built from the burnt ruins of Whitehall.

In times of old when Time was young
And Poets their own verses sung,
A song could draw a stone or beam
That now would overload a team ;
Lead them a dance of many a mile
Then raise them to a goodly Pile.
Each number had it's different power,
Heroick strains could build a tower :
Sonnets & Elegys to Chloris
Would raise a house about two storys :      10
A Lyrick Ode would slate : a Catch
Would tyle, an Epigram would thatch.
Now Poets find this art is lost
Both to their own & Landlord's Cost ;
Not one of all the tunefull throng
Can hire a lodging for a Song.

For Jove consider'd well the case
That Poets were a numerous race,
And if they all had power to build
The earth would very soon be fill'd,                    20
Materials would be quickly spent
And houses would not give a rent.
The God of wealth was therefore made
Sole Patron of the building trade,
Leaving to wits the spacious air
With licence to build Castles there ;
And tis conceiv'd their old pretence
To lodge in Garrats came from thence.
   There is a worm by Phœbus bred
On leaves of Mulberry is fed,                    30
Which unprovided where to dwell
Consumes itself to weave a Cell,
Then curious hands this texture take
And for themselves fine garments make ;
Mean while a pair of awkward things
Grew to his back instead of wings,
He flutters when he thinks he flyes,
Then sheds about his spawn & dyes.
Just such an Insect of the age
Is he that scribbles for the stage,                    40
His birth he do's from Phœbus raise
And feeds upon imagin'd bayes ;
Throws all his wit & hours away
In twisting up an illspun play.
This gives him lodging & provides
A stock of tawdry stuff besides,
With the unravel'd shreds of which
The underwits adorn their speech.
Apollo's bird now spreads his fans
(For all the Muses geese are swans)                    50
And born on fancy's pinions thinks
He soars sublimest when he sinks,

[p. 2.]

But scatt'ring round his fly-blows dyes,
Whence broods of Insect Poets rise.
   Premising thus in modern way
The greater half I had to say ;
Sing Muse the house of Poet Van
In higher strain than we began.
Van (for 'tis fit the Reader know it)
Is both a Herald & a Poet.      60
No wonder then if nicely skill'd
In each capacity to build ;
As Herald he can in a day
Repair a house gone to decay ;
Or by Atchievements Arms device
Erect a new one in a trice.
And Poets if they had their due,      [p. 3.]
By ancient right are builders too.
This made him to Apollo pray
For leave to build the modern way.      70
His prayer was granted ; for the God
Consented with the usual nod.
After hard throwes of many a day
Van was deliver'd of a play ;
Which in due time brought forth a house,
Just as the Mountain did the Mouse.
One story high, one postern door,
And one small chamber on a floor.
Born like a Phœnix from the flame,
But neither shape, nor bulk the same.      80
As Animals of largest size
Corrupt to Maggots, Worms & Flyes,
A type of modern wit & stile
The rubbish of an antient Pile.
So Chymists boast they have a power
From the dead ashes of a flower,
Some faint resemblance to produce,
But not the virtue, tast or juice.

So modern Rhymers strive to blast
The Poetry of ages past,                                 90
Which having wisely overthrown,
They from it's ruins build their own.

## The SOUTH-SEA

This is the original manuscript. It is written closely in double columns, and has no title. At the conclusion Swift has added the passage which is printed as Letter XXXVII in this collection. It is dated 15 December 1720.

As the postmark shows, Ford did not receive the poem before 26 December 1720. He departed from the instructions which Swift had appended to it by keeping the original and sending a transcript to the printer; and he must have done so without delay, as the poem was advertised as published 'this day' in *The Daily Courant* and *The Post-Boy* of 3 January 1721. It appeared in an octavo pamphlet of twenty-four pages, with the following title :—

> THE | BUBBLE : | A | POEM. | [rule] | [ornament] | [rule] | *LONDON,* | Printed for Benj. Tooke, at the *Middle-Temple-Gate* | in *Fleetstreet*; and Sold by J. Roberts, near the | *Oxford-Arms* in *Warwick-Lane.* m.dcc.xxi.

Half-title :—

> THE | *BUBBLE* | A | POEM. | (Price Six-Pence.)

It was anonymous; but two verses (the forty-eighth and the last) which were quoted in *The Evening Post* for 24–26 January 1721 were attributed to 'Swift'. The name, 'The Bubble', was taken from the last line, and may have been supplied by Ford. The printed text follows the manuscript closely. The most important differences are 'Garr'way's Cliffs' (l. 153), and 'Bone' (l. 204).

Ford must have carried out Swift's instructions to send him a copy immediately (p. 88), so that an edition might be published at Dublin. In this Dublin reprint of sixteen pages a motto is added in the title :

THE | BUBBLE : | A POEM. | [rule] | *Apparent rari nantes in gurgite vasto :* | *Arma virûm, tabulæque & Troja gaza per undas,* | Virg. | [rule] | [ornament] | [rule] | *London* : Printed for *Ben. Tooke,* at the *Middle-Tempℓe-Gate* in *Fleet-street* ; and Sold by *J. Roberts,* near the *Oxford-|Arms* in *Warwick-Lane* : And Re-printed in *Dublin,* 1721.

Two new stanzas, making fifty-seven in all, come after the eighth :

> Two Hundred Chariots just bespoke,
> Are sunk in these devouring Waves;
> The Horses drown'd, the Harness broke,
> And here the Owners find their Graves.

> Like *Pharaoh,* by Directors led,
> They with their *Spoils* went safe before,
> His Chariots tumbling out the Dead,
> Lay shatter'd on the *Red-Sea* Shore.

The most notable of the other changes is ' then too ' instead of ' too too ' at the conclusion. There can be no doubt that Swift was responsible for this edition, though he probably had no hand in the ' Advertisement ' (verso of title), which draws attention to the new stanzas.

The poem was included in *A Miscellaneous Collection of Poems, Songs and Epigrams. By several Hands. Publish'd by T. M. Gent.,* printed at Dublin by A. Rhames in 1721 (vol. ii, pp. 147–58). ' T. M.' stands for ' Thomas Mosse ', of whose relations with Swift nothing is known. The text (57 stanzas) follows the Dublin edition, and the quotation from Virgil is given under the heading. The poem was next printed in *Miscellaneous Poems, Original and Translated, By Several Hands,* published by Concanen in 1724 (pp. 148–63), and was then for the first time said to be ' By Dean Swift '. In 1725 it was included in *A New Collection of Poems on Several Occasions. By Mr. Prior, and Others,* printed for Thomas Osborne (pp. 94–108). In all three collections the text traces back to the Dublin reprint of 1721.

When the poem was included in the third volume of the *Miscellanies* (published March 1728) it was revised. The title was altered to ' The South-Sea. 1721 ', and no fewer than thirteen of the original fifty-five stanzas were omitted (Nos. 11,

15, 25–8, 37, 40, 41, 48–51), but the two additional stanzas were included—in its new form the poem contains forty-four in all—and the motto was taken from the heading and printed at the end. In October 1726, when the *Miscellanies* were being collected, Swift had written to Pope from Dublin : 'I am mustering, as I told you, all the little things in verse that I think may be safely printed, but I give you despotic power to tear as many as you please.' Pope was editor in chief. But in the summer of 1727 Swift was Pope's guest at Twickenham; and we know from his letters that he took an active interest in 'the poetical volume'. There is no clear reason for holding that this poem was altered without his knowledge.

Probably most readers will agree that the poem did not lose by the revision. But the *Miscellanies* had not given satisfaction. 'I have long had it at heart', wrote Ford to Swift on 6 November 1733, 'to see your works collected, and published with care. It is become absolutely necessary, since that jumble with Pope, &c. in three volumes, which put me in a rage whenever I meet them'. When at this time Swift was asked by George Faulkner, the Dublin publisher, for leave to bring out a collected edition of his writings he offered no opposition ; on the contrary he welcomed the chance of removing faults in the text of *Gulliver*, which in this Dublin edition of 1735 confirms more closely than in the first edition to the original manuscript ; and though there is nothing in his letters to show his interest in the Dublin volume of 1735 containing his poetical pieces, he knew that it was being prepared and cannot be supposed to have been indifferent to it. The publisher says that some of the poems were procured from friends 'who at their earnest request were permitted to take copies'. In this volume eleven of the thirteen omitted stanzas were restored in the poem 'Upon the South-Sea Project. Written in the Year 1721', as it was now called (pp. 147–58). Should we assume that they were restored by some one else than Swift, we have to explain why two stanzas (Nos. 15 and 27) were still left out.

There were no alterations in Faulkner's later editions ; but Hawkesworth used the text of the *Miscellanies* in his collected edition in 1754, and only forty-four stanzas were given in the London reprints till 1779. In that year John Nichols drew attention to what he believed to be the incompleteness of the usual text in his *Supplement to Dr. Swift's Works* (vol. ii, pp. 419–20). 'The poem on the *South Sea*', he said, 'is printed from an imperfect copy, as will be seen by the following variations, which there could surely have been no occasion for suppressing'; and then he gave the thirteen stanzas. In the same year he superintended the poems of Swift in the collected edition of the *English Poets* to which Johnson contributed as Prefaces his *Lives of the Poets*; and there the thirteen stanzas were incorporated. From this time the poem was to be regularly printed in its longest form.

Ten of the stanzas are engraved in *The Bubblers Medley, or a Sketch of the Times Being Europes Memorial for the Year 1720*, a broadside which was 'Printed for Tho: Bowles Print & Map Seller next the Chapter House in S$^t$ Paul's Church Yard London'. They are, in order, Nos. 35–9, 17, 42, 26, 28, and 55. See *Catalogue of Prints and Drawings in the British Museum*, Satires, 1689–1733, pp. 412–15.

> YE wise Philosophers explain       [p. 1.]
> What Magick makes our Money rise
> When dropt into the Southern Main,
> Or do these Juglers cheat our Eyes?
>
>   Put in Your Money fairly told;
> Presto be gone—Tis here ag'en,
> Ladyes, and Gentlemen, behold,
> Here's ev'ry Piece as big as ten.
>
>   Thus in a Basin drop a Shilling,
> Then fill the Vessel to the Brim,       10
> You shall observe as you are filling
> The pond'rous Metal seems to swim;
>
>   It rises both in Bulk and Height,
> Behold it mounting to the Top,
> The liquid Medium cheats your Sight,
> Behold it swelling like a Sop.

In Stock three hundred thousand Pounds ;
I have in view a Lord's Estate,
My Mannors all contig'ous round,
A Coach and Six, and serv'd in Plate :        20

Thus the deluded Bankrupt raves,
Puts all upon a desp'rate Bett,
Then plunges in the *Southern* Waves,
Dipt over head and Ears—in Debt.

So, by a Calenture misled,
The Mariner with Rapture sees
On the smooth Ocean's azure Bed
Enamell'd Fields, and verdant Trees ;

With eager Hast he longs to rove
In that fantastick Scene, and thinks        30
It must be some enchanted Grove,
And in he leaps, and down he sinks.

Rais'd up on Hope's aspiring Plumes,
The young Advent'rer o'er the Deep
An Eagle's Flight and State assumes,
And scorns the middle Way to keep :

On *Paper* Wings he takes his Flight,
With *Wax* the *Father* bound them fast,
The *Wax* is melted by the Height,
And down the towring Boy is cast :        40

A Moralist might here explain
The Rashness of the *Cretan* Youth,
Describe his Fall into the Main,
And from a Fable form a Truth :

[col. 2.]  His *Wings* are his *Paternall Rent,*
He melts his *Wax* at ev'ry Flame,
His Credit sunk, his Money spent,
*In* Southern *Seas he leaves his Name.*

Inform us, You that best can tell,
Why in yon dang'rous Gulph profound          50
Where hundreds and where thousands fell,
*Fools* chiefly float, the *Wise* are drown'd.

So have I seen from *Severn*'s Brink
A Flock of *Geese* jump down together,
Swim where the Bir[d] of *Jove* would sink,
And swimming ne[ver] wet a Feather.

But I affirm, 'tis false in Fact,
*Directors* better know their Tools,
We see the Nation['s] Credit crackt,
Each Knave hath [ma]de a thousand Fools.     60

One Fool may [fr]om another win,
And then get off with Money stor'd,
But if a *Sharper* once comes in,
He throws at all, and sweeps the Board.

As Fishes on each other prey
The great ones swall'wing up the small
So fares it in the *Southern* Sea
But Whale *Directors* eat up all.

When *Stock* is high they come between,
Making by second hand their Offers,          70
Then cunningly retire unseen,
With each a Million in his Coffers.

So when upon a Moon-shine Night
An Ass was drinking at a Stream,
A Cloud arose and stopt the Light,
By intercepting e[v]'ry Beam ;

The Day of Judgment will be soon,
Cryes out a Sage among the Croud,
An Ass hath swallow'd up the Moon,
The Moon lay safe behind the Cloud.          80

Each poor *Subscriber* to the Sea
Sinks down at once, and there he lyes,
*Directors* fall as well as they,
Their Fall is but a Trick to rise :

So Fishes rising from the Main
Can soar with moistned Wings on high,
The Moysture dry'd they sink again,
And dip their Fins again to fly.

[p. 2.]     Undone at Play, the Femal Troops
Come here their Losses to retrieve,                    90
Ride o'er the Waves in spacious Hoops,
Like *Lapland* Witches in a Sieve :

Thus *Venus* to the Sea descends
As Poets fein ; but where's the Moral ?
It shews the Queen of Love intends
To search the Deep for Pearl and Coral.

The Sea is richer than the Land,
I heard it from my Grannam's Mouth,
Which now I clearly understand,
For by the Sea she meant the *South*.                    100

Thus by *Directors* we are told,
Pray Gentlemen, believe your Eyes,
Our Ocean's cover[d o]'er with Gold,
Look round about [h]ow thick it lyes :

We, Gentlemen, a[re] Your Assisters,
We'll come and hol[d] you by the Chin,
Alas ! all is not Go[l]d that glisters ;
Ten thousand sunk by leaping in.

Oh ! would these Patriots be so kind
Here in the Deep to *wash their Hands*,                    110
Then like *Pactolus* we should find
The Sea indeed had *golden Sands*.

A Shilling in the *Bath* You fling,
The Silver takes a nobler Hue,
By Magick Virtue in the Spring,
And seems a Guinnea to your View :

But as a Guinnea will not pass
At Market for a Farthing more
Shewn through a multiplying Glass
Than what it allways did before ;                    120

So cast it in the *Southern* Seas,
And view it through a *Jobber*'s Bill,
Put on what Spectacles You please,
Your Guinnea's but a Guinnea still.

One Night a Fool into a Brook
Thus from a Hillock looking down,
The *Golden* Stars for Guinneas took,
And *Silver Cynthia* for a Crown ;

The Point he could no longer doubt,
He ran, he leapt into the Flood,                     130
There sprawl'd a while, at last got out,
All cover'd o'er with Slime and Mud.

Upon the Water cast thy Bread            [col. 2.]
And after many Days thou'lt find it,
But Gold upon this Ocean spred
Shall sink, and leave no mark behind[1] it.

There is a Gulph where thousands fell,
Here all the bold Advent'rers came,
A narrow Sound, though deep as Hell,
CHANGE-ALLY is the dreadfull Name ;                  140

Nine times a day it ebbs and flows,
Yet He that on the Surface lyes
Without a Pilot seldom knows
The Time it falls, or when 'twill rise.

[1] 'behind' written above 'find' struck out.

Subscribers here by thousands float,
And justle one another down,
Each padling in his leaky Boat,
And here they fish for Gold and drown :

*Psalm
107.

*Now bury'd in the Depth below,
Now mounted up to Heav'n again,                          150
They reel and stagger too and fro,
At their Wits end like drunken Men.

* Coffee
House
in Cha-
nge-Al-
ly.

Mean time secure on *GARR'WAY Clifts
A savage Race by Shipwrecks fed,
Ly waiting for the foundred Skiffs,
And strip the Bodyes of the Dead.

But these, you say, are factious Lyes
From some malicious Tory's Brain,
For, where Directors get a Prize,
The Swiss and Dutch whole Millions drain.                160

Thus when by Rooks a Lord is ply'd,
Some Cully often wins a Bett
By vent'ring on the cheating Side,
Tho not into the Secret let.

While some build Castles in the Air,
Directors build 'em in the Seas ;
Subscribers plainly see 'um there,
For Fools will see as Wise men please.

Thus oft by Mariners are shown,
Unless the Men of Kent are Ly'rs,                        170
Earld Godwin's Castles overflown,
And Castle roofs, and Steeple Spires.

Mark where the Sly Directors creep,
Nor to the Shore approach too nigh,
The Monsters nestle in the Deep
To seise you in your passing by :

Then, like the Dogs of *Nile* be wise,     [p. 3.]
Who taught by Instinct how to shun
The Crocodile that lurking lyes,
Run as they drink and drink and run.     180

*Antæus* could by Magick Charms
Recover Strength whene'er he fell,
*Alcides* held him in his Arms,
And sent him *up in Air* to Hell.

*Directors* thrown into the Sea
Recover Strength and Vigor there,
But may be tam'd another way,
*Suspended for a while in Air.*

*Directors*; for tis you I warn,
By long Experience we have found     190
What Planet rul'd when you were born;
We see you never can be drown'd:

Beware, nor over-bulky grow,
Nor come within your Cullyes Reach,
For if the Sea should sink so low
To leave you dry upon the Beach,

You'll ow Your Ruin to your[1] Bulk;
Your Foes already waiting stand
To tear you like a foundred Hulk
While you ly helpless on the Sand:     200

Thus when a Whale hath lost[1] the Tide     [col. 2.]
The Coasters crowd to seise the Spoyl,
The Monster into Parts divide,
And strip the Bones, and melt the Oyl.

---

[1] ' You'll ow your Ruin to your    struck out at top of col. 2, before
Thus when a whale hath lost'    'Thus when '.

Oh, may some *Western* Tempest sweep
These *Locusts* whom our Fruits have fed,
That Plague, *Directors*, to the Deep,
Driv'n from the *South*-Sea to the *Red*.

May He whom Nature's Laws obey,
Who *lifts* the Poor, and *sinks* the Proud,                    210
*Quiet the Raging of the Sea,*
And *Still the Madness of the Crowd.*

But never sh[all our is]le have Rest
Till those devour[ing] *Swine* run down,
(*The Devils leavi[ng] the Possess't*)
And *headlong i[n] the Waters drown.*

The Nation t[oo] too late will find
Computing all th[eir] Cost and Trouble,
*Directors* Promi[ses] but Wind,
South-Sea at best [a m]ighty BUBBLE.                    220


## To CHARLES FORD, on his Birth-day, 1723

This is the manuscript which greeted Ford on his birthday,
31 January 1723.

The poem was first printed by George Faulkner in 1762
(Dublin, vol. x, pp. 310–13), and was reprinted in the same year
by William Bowyer (London, vol. xiv, pp. 186–90). The source
of the printed version must have been Swift's rough draft, or a
copy of it.

When Swift had completed his fair copy, he made a few
alterations in it. He replaced 'torturing Engins' by 'Informations' (l. 44), and 'Belcamp' by 'Cushogue' (l. 89) with a
note in the margin. The printed version has 'torturing
Engines' and 'Belcamp' without a note—readings for which
the use of the draft will account.

Another alteration in his fair copy is the substitution of
'Oh, were but you and I so wise' for 'Could you and I be
once so wise' (l. 85). Here the printed text gives not the

uncorrected but the corrected reading. The explanation would seem to be that Swift had written in his draft ' Oh, were but you and I so wise ', but altered the line on writing out the fair copy so as to get rid of 'Oh', and then on second thoughts restored what he had rejected, finding ' Oh ' as good as ' once' as a make-weight.

There are other printed variants of which the manuscript shows no trace, e.g. ' Presbyterians ' instead of ' Hanoverians ' (l. 50). We may assume that they were in the draft, but abandoned in the fair copy, and not reconsidered.

The manuscript contains Swift's final readings on sending the birthday greeting, and gives us the authentic version of the poem.

## To Charles Ford Esq^r. on his Birth-day [p. 1.] Jan^ry. 31^st. for the Year 1722–3

COME, be content, since out it must,
For, Stella has betray'd her Trust,
And, whisp'ring, charg'd me not to say
That M^r. Ford was born to day :
Or if at last, I needs must blab it,
According to my usuall habit,
She bid me with a serious Face
Be sure conceal the Time and Place,
And not my Compliment to spoyl
By calling This your native Soyl ;      10
Or vex the Ladyes, when they knew
That you are turning fourty two.
But if these Topicks should appear
Strong Arguments to keep You here,
We think, though You judge hardly of it,
Good Manners must give Place to Profit.
The Nymphs with whom You first began
Are each become a Harridan ;

And Mountague [1] so far decayd,
That now her Lovers must be payd ;                    20
And ev'ry Belle that since arose
Has her Cotemporary Beaux.
Your former Comrades, once so bright,
With whom you toasted half the Night,
Of Rheumatism and Pox complain,
And bid adieu to dear Champain :
Your great Protectors, once in Power,
Are now in Exil, or the Tower,
Your Foes, triumphant o'er the Laws,
Who hate Your Person, and Your Cause,                    30

[p. 2.]

If once they get you on the Spot
You must be guilty of the Plot,
For, true or false, they'll ne'r enquire,
But use You ten times worse than Pri'r.
    In London ! What would You do there ?
Can You, my Friend, with Patience bear,
Nay would it not Your Passion raise
Worse than a Pun, or Irish Phrase,
To see a Scoundrel Strut and hector,
A Foot-boy to some Rogue Director ?                    40
To look on Vice triumphant round,
And Virtue trampled on the Ground :
Observe where bloody Townshend stands
With Informations [2] in his Hands,
Hear him Blaspheme, and Swear, and Rayl,
Threatning the Pillory and Jayl.
If this you think a pleasing Scene
To London strait return again,
Where you have told us from Experience,
Are swarms of Bugs and Hanoverians.                    50
    I thought my very Spleen would burst
When Fortune hither drove me first ;

[1] The Duchess of Montagu.          [2] 'Informations' written above
Cf. Letter I, p. 1, note 3.          'torturing Engins' obliterated.

Was full as hard to please as You,
Nor Persons Names, nor Places knew ;
But now I act as other Folk,
Like Pris'ners when their Gall is broke.
   If you have London still at heart
We'll make a small one here by Art :
The Diff'rence is not much between
St. James's Park and Stephen's Green ;     60
And, Dawson street¹ will serve as well
To lead you thither, as Pell-mell,
(Without your passing thro the Palace
To choque your Sight, and raise your Malice)
The Deanry-house may well be match't     [p. 3.]
(Under Correction) with the thatcht,²
Nor shall I, when you hither come,
Demand a Croun a Quart for Stumm.
Then, for a middle-aged Charmer,
Stella may vye with your Mountharmar :     70
She's Now as handsom ev'ry bit,
And has a thousand times her Wit.
The Dean and Sheridan, I hope,
Will half supply a Gay and Pope,
Corbet,³ though yet I know his Worth not,
No doubt, will prove a good Arburthnot :
I throw into the Bargain, Jim⁴ :
In London can you equall Him ?
   What think you of my fav'rite Clan,
Robin, and Jack, and Jack, and Dan⁵ ?     80

---

¹ Mrs. Ford resided in Dawson Street.

² The Thatched-house Tavern, St. James's Street.

³ See Letter XLIV, p. 108, note 3.

⁴ James King, vicar of St. Bride's, Dublin, from 1730 to 1759; one of the executors of Swift's will. See W. G. Carroll, *Succession of Clergy in S. Bride*, 1884, pp. 21–2.

⁵ 'Robin and Jack' are Robert Grattan and his brother John; they were cousins of 'Jack and Dan', John and Daniel Jackson.

Fellows of modest Worth and Parts,
With chearfull Looks, and honest Hearts.
  Can you on Dublin look with Scorn ?
Yet here were You and Ormonde born.
Oh, were but You and I so wise [1]
To look with Robin Grattan's Eyes :
Robin adores that Spot of Earth,
That litt'rall Spot which gave him Birth,
And swears, Cushogue [2] is to his Taste,        * The true [3]
As fine as Hampton-court at least.    *        Name of Belc

  When to your Friends you would enhance    91
The Praise of Italy or France
For Grandeur, Elegance and Wit,
We gladly hear you, and submit :
But then, to come and keep a Clutter
For this, or that Side of a Gutter,
To live in this or t'other Isle,
We cannot think it worth your while.
For, take it kindly, or amiss,
The Diff'rence but amounts to this,    100
[p. 4.]    You [4] bury, on our Side the Channell
In Linnen, and on Yours, in Flannell. [5]

See Letter XXXI, p. 69, notes
6 and 7, and cf. Swift's poems,
'The Journal' (or 'The Country
Life') and 'George-Nim-Dan-
Dean's Answer'.
  [1] 'Oh, were ... wise' written
above 'Could you and I be once
so wise' obliterated.
  [2] 'Cushogue' written above
the line, in place of 'Belcamp'
obliterated. Belcamp was the
home of the Grattans, about five
miles north of Dublin, in the
parish of Santry. It passed to
Robert Grattan on the death of

his mother in 1726. For an illustration see *Correspondence of
Swift*, v. 295.
  [3] 'true' after 'Iris' struck out.
  [4] 'You' faintly struck out,
above it 'We' altered to 'They',
and above this indistinct 'They'
a clear 'They'—all in Ford's
hand.
  [5] The Bill for burying in
woollen in Ireland was introduced
into the Irish House of Commons
on 10 December and passed the
Irish House of Lords on 31 December 1733.

You, for the News are ne'r to seek,
While We perhaps must wait a Week :
You, happy Folks, are sure to meet
A hundred Whores in ev'ry Street,
While We [1] may search all Dublin o'er
And hardly hear of half a Score.
    You see, my Arguments are Strong ;
I wonder you held out so long,             110
But since you are convinc't at last
We'll pardon you for what is past.
    So—let us now for Whisk prepare ;
Twelvepence a Corner, if you dare.


## STELLA at WOOD PARK
### and her return to DUBLIN

    This important manuscript, in the hand of Ford, contains
two poems on the inner side of a folded half-folio sheet, making
two pages. The first, with the title 'Stella's Distress on the
3ᵈ fatal day of Octobʳ 1723 ', is written without an erasure.
The second, which has no title but a Latin quotation as a
heading, has alternative or corrected readings and additional
lines in the margin. The second begins on the first page under
the first, from which it is separated by a double line and the
quotation.
    Of the second poem Ford made two fair copies (now in the
Pierpont Morgan Library), which agree except in spelling and
punctuation. They were among the Ford papers till 4 June
1896, when they were sold at Messrs. Christie's (lot 69), and
with them went a transcript of ' Stella's Distress ', also in
Ford's hand. Ford thus wrote at least two copies of the one
poem, and at least three of the other. The manuscript here
reproduced is the earliest, and shows the second poem in the
process of attaining its final form. It also throws light on the

[1] ' We ' altered from ' we '.

jumble of the two poems into one when they came to be printed, and on some of the printed readings.

These two poems were combined to form 'Stella at Wood-Park, A House of Charles Ford, Esq; eight Miles from Dublin . . . Written in the Year 1723 ',—which was published by George Faulkner in 1735 in the Dublin edition of Swift's 'Poetical Works' (pp. 212–6), and was included in the same year in the London *Collection of Poems, &c. Omitted in the Fifth Volume of Miscellanies in Prose and Verse* (pp. 440–3). 'Stella's Distress', with the omission of the last couplet, was inserted in the other poem after the first paragraph. Who made the insertion? Not Swift, if only because the patches are clumsy. He will not be held responsible for the arrangement of these four printed lines, with their false grammar and their nonsense:

> At last grown prouder than the D—l,
> With feeding high, and Treatment civil,
> Don *Carlos* now began to find
> His Malice work as he design'd:

where the first couplet ought to describe not Don Carlos but Stella, and where 'Malice' is a mistake for 'Med'cine'.

Don Carlos is Charles Ford. If 'half a year' is to be taken literally—and apparently it ought to be—Stella was his guest at Woodpark from April 1723, for we now know from the title of one of the poems that she returned to Dublin on 3 October. From a letter written by Swift on 11 May we learn that he had stayed twice with Ford in April, previous to taking his 'long Southern journey', from which he returned in August or September; and in all probability Stella's long visit, and Mrs. Dingley's, began when Swift was at Woodpark. It was arranged not so much in 'a merry spight' as in the hope that she might benefit by a change of scene during Swift's long absence from Dublin. On 1 June Swift wrote to Robert Cope: 'Your friend Ford keeps still in Ireland, and passes the summer at his country house with two sober ladies of his and my acquaintance'. There is no evidence that Swift returned to Woodpark about the beginning of October (he was in Dublin on 20 September), but it is tempting to think that one or other of the poems, if not both, was drafted there and then.

The manuscript presents a problem by exhibiting in the process of composition a poem in another hand than the author's. Did Ford piece together scraps that Swift had written, and were the additions longer than he expected? Were the alternative or corrected readings hit upon in conversation, or dictated? It would seem that Ford acted as amanuensis. If so, where? The chances are, at Woodpark.

Though the manuscript helps to explain the form in which the poem was published, it was not the 'copy' that was sent to the printer.

The lines which are heavily indented in the following pages are written in the margin in the manuscript.

## Stella's Distress [p. 1.]
### on the 3ᵈ fatal day of Octobʳ 1723

THE Winter now begins to frown ;
Poor Stella must pack off to Town.
From purling Streams & Fountains bubbling
To Liffy's filthy side in Dublin :
From wholesom Exercise and Air
To sossing in an elbow chair :
From stomach sharp, and hearty feeding
To piddle like a Lady breeding.
From ruling there the Household singly
To be directed here by Dingley.      10
From ev'ry day a Lordly Banquet
To half a Joynt, & God be thanked :
From every Meal Pontack in plenty
To a sour Pint one day in twenty.
From growing richer with good Cheer,
And yet run out by starving here :
From Ford who thinks of nothing mean
To the poor Doings of the Dean :

From Ford attending at her Call
To Visits of Archdeacon Wall.[1]                    20
Say, Stella, which you most repent
You e're return'd, or ever went ?

—    Cuicunque nocere volebat
Vestimenta dabat pretiosa.[2]

Don Carlos in a merry Spight
Did Stella to his House invite,
He entertain'd her half a year
With richest Wines and costly Cheer :
Surpriz'd with ev'ry day a hot meal
She thought that all the world was Oatmeal :
That she might o're the Servants hector
Don Carlos made her sole Director.
       Don Carlos made her chief Director
       She now can or'e the servants hector.
In half a week the Dame grew nice,
Got all things at the highest Price.                    10
Now at the Table head she sits
Presented with the choicest Bits :

[p. 2.] She look'd on Partridges with scorn
Except they tasted of the Corn :
A Haunch of Ven'son made her sweat
Unless it had the right Fumette :
Don Carlos earnestly would beg,
Dear Madam try this Pigeon's leg :
Was happy when he could prevail
To make Her only touch a Quail :                    20
Thrô candle-light she view'd the Wine
To see that ev'ry Glass was fine.

[1] See Letter VII, p. 15, note 1. Stella and Mrs. Dingley resided with the Archdeacon and his wife in 1715-17. He appears also in Swift's verses 'On the Little House by the Churchyard of Castleknock', 1710.
[2] Horace, *Epist.* I. xviii. 31-2.

At last grown prouder than the Devil
With feeding high, & Treatment civil,
Too soon arrives the dismal Day,
She must return to Ormond-Key.
   As the Coach stopp'd, she look'd & swore
The Rascal had mistook the Door :
At entring you might see her stoop
Nor would the Door admit her Hoop.     30
        Don Carlos now began to find
        His Med'cine work as he design'd
        As the Coach stopp'd, she look'd & swore
        The Rascal had mistook the Door
        At going in you saw her stoop
        The narrow Entry crushd her Hoop
        She curs'd the dark & winding Stairs
        And still encreasing in her Airs
        Began a thousand faults to spy
        The Cieling hardly six foot high
        The smoaky Wainscot full of cracks
        And half the Chairs with broken backs.
        The Cubbard fasten'd with a Peg
        The rusty Tongs have lost a Leg     40
        Her Quarter's out at Lady Day
        She'll have 'em know she scorns to stay
        (While there are Houses to be let)
        In Lodgings like a poor Grisette.
Howe're to keep her Spirits up
        Mean time to keep
She sent for Company to sup,
        She sends
When all the while you might remark
        Where all
She did her best to ape Woodpark.
        She strove in vain to ape
Two Bottles call'd for, (half her Store,
The Cellar could contain but four)     50

A Supper worthy of her self,
Five Nothings in five Plates of Delf.
And thus the Farce a fortnight went
When all her little Money spent,[1]
　　Thus for a week the Farce went on
　　When the whole month's Allowance gone
She fell into her former Scene,
Small Beer, a Herring, and the Dean.

　　　Since I must laugh, or cannot live,
　　　Good-natur'd Stella will forgive :
　　　We Poets when a Hint is new
　　　Regard not what is false or true ;　　60
　　　No Raillery gives just Offence
　　　Where Truth has not the least Pretence ;
　　　Nor can be more securely plac't
　　　Than on a Nymph of Stella's Tast.
　　　I must confess your Wine and Vittle
　　　I was too hard upon—a little.
　　　And you must know in what I writ
　　　I had some Anger in my Wit.
　　　For when you sigh to leave Woodpark,
　　　The Place, the Welcome, and the Spark, 70
　　　To languish in this odious Town,
　　　And pull your haughty Stomach down,
　　　You shew Don Carlos where to dwell,
　　　And grieve he ever left Pell-mell.
　　　　Yet granting all I said were true,
　　　A Cottage is Woodpark with You.

---

[1] This couplet is struck out, and is the only reading in the manuscript that is definitely rejected.

# DIRECTIONS for a BIRTH-DAY SONG

This manuscript is in the hand of Charles Ford. The Forster Collection contains a manuscript in another hand (No. 522), but not, as has been stated, in the hand of Swift.

The poem was first printed by Deane Swift in 1765 (vol. xvi, pp. 257–67), with the title 'Directions for making A Birthday Song. Written in the Year M DCC XXIX'. The Ford manuscript contains an alternative couplet which is not in the Forster manuscript nor in the printed version (ll. 61, 62); and it lacks a couplet which is in both of these (after l. 126). That Ford omitted it is more probable than that Swift added it after Ford had made his copy.

October 30 was George II's birthday. The poem is a satire on the laureate odes of Eusden, who supplied the New Year's Day Ode and the Birthday Ode punctually from 1719 to 1730. Its effectiveness as a satire did not diminish with the accession of Colley Cibber. When Swift wrote in 1729,

> Hesse Darmstadt makes too rough a sound,
> And Guelph the strongest ear will wound.
> In vain are all attempts from Germany
> To find out proper words for Harmony,

he anticipated a passage in the Birthday Ode of 1743:

> Tho' rough *Selingenstadt*
>    The harmony defeat,
> Tho' *Klein Ostein*
>    The verse confound;
> Yet, in the joyful strain,
> *Aschaffenburgh* and *Dettingen*
> Shall charm the ear they seem to wound.

(The Gentleman's Magazine, November 1743.)

# Directions for a Birth-day Song
## Oct: 30. 1729

To form a just and finish'd piece,
Take twenty Gods of Rome or Greece,
Whose Godships are in chief request,
And fit your present Subject best.
And should it be your Hero's case
To have both male & female Race,
Your bus'ness must be to provide
A score of Goddesses beside.
  Some call their Monarchs Sons of Saturn,
For which they bring a modern Pattern,          10
Because they might have heard of one
Who often long'd to eat his Son :
But this I think will not go down,
For here the Father kept his Crown.
  Why then appoint him Son of Jove,
Who met his Mother in a grove ;
To this we freely shall consent,
Well knowing what the Poets meant :
And in their Sense, 'twixt me and you,
It may be literally true.[1]                    20
  Next, as the Laws of Song require,
He must be greater than his Sire :
For Jove, as every School-boy knows,
Was able Saturn to depose ;
And sure no Christian Poet breathing
Should be more scrup'lous than a Heathen.
Or if to Blasphemy it tends,
That's but a trifle among Friends.

[1] The mother of George II, the Electoral Princess Sophia Dorothea, was said to have been intimate with Koningsmark.

Your Hero now another Mars is,
Makes mighty Armys turn their Arses.　　　　30
Behold his glitt'ring Faulchion mow　　　　[p. 2.]
Whole Squadrons with a single blow :
While Victory, with Wings outspread,
Flyes like an Eagle or'e his head ;
His milk-white Steed upon it's haunches,
Or pawing into dead mens paunches.
As Overton [1] has drawn his Sire
Still seen o'r'e many an Alehouse fire.
Then from his Arm hoarse thunder rolls
As loud as fifty mustard bowls ;　　　　40
For thunder still his arm supplyes,
And lightning always in his Eyes :
They both are cheap enough in Conscience,
And serve to eccho ratling Nonsence ;
The rumbling words march fierce along,
Made trebly dreadfull in your Song.
　　Sweet Poet, hir'd for birth-day Rimes,
To sing of Wars choose peaceful times.
What tho for fifteen years and more
Janus hath lock'd his Temple-door ?　　　　50
Tho not a Coffee-house we read in
Hath mention'd arms on this side Sweden ;
Nor London Journals, nor the Post-men,
Tho fond of warlike Lyes as most men ;
Thou still with Battles stuff thy head full
For must a Hero not be dreadfull ?
　　Dismissing Mars, it next must follow
Your Conqu'rer is become Apollo :
That he's Apollo, is as plain, as
That Robin Walpole is Mecænas :　　　　60
But that he struts, and that he squints,
You'd know him by Apollo's Prints.

[1] Henry Overton, printseller,　Newgate'. Cf. Gay, *Trivia*, ii.
'at the White Horse without　488.

aliter.    But that he squints, and that he struts,
        You'd know him by Apollo's Cuts.[1]

[p. 3.]  Old Phœbus is but half as bright,
    For yours can shine both day and night,
    The first perhaps may once an Age
    Inspire you with poetick Rage ;
    Your Phœbus royal, every day
    Not only can inspire, but pay.         70
      Then make this new Apollo sit
    Sole Patron, Judge, and God of Wit.
    " How from his Altitude he stoops,
    " To raise up Virtue when she droops,
    " On Learning how his Bounty flows,
    " And with what Justice he bestows.
    " Fair Isis, and ye Banks of Cam,
    " Be witness if I tell a Flam :
    " What Prodigys in Arts we drain
    " From both your Streams in George's Reign ! 80
    " As from the flowry Bed of Nile—
    But here's enough to shew your Style.
      Broad Innuendos, such as this,
    If well apply'd, can hardly miss :
    For when you bring your Song in print,
    He'll get it read, and take the hint,
    (It must be read before 'tis warbled
    The paper gilt, & Cover marbled)
    And will be so much more your Debter
    Because he never knew a letter.        90
    And as he hears his Wit and Sence,
    To which he never made pretence,
    Set out in Hyperbolick Strains,
    A Guinea shall reward your pains.
    For Patrons never pay so well,
    As when they scarce have learn'd to spell.

[1] The alternative couplet (. . . struts, . . . Cuts.) is not in the Forster MS. nor in the printed version, 1765 &c.

Next call him Neptune with his Trident,     [p. 4.]
He rules the Sea, you see him ride in't ;
And if provok'd, he soundly ferks his
Rebellious Waves with rods like Xerxes.     100
He would have seiz'd the Spanish Plate,
Had not the Fleet gone out too late,
And in their very Ports besiege,[1]
But that he would not disoblige,[2]
And made the Rascals pay him dearly
For those affronts they give him yearly.
   'Tis not deny'd that when we write,
Our Ink is black, our Paper white ;
And when we scrawl our Paper o'r'e,
We blacken what was white before.     110
I think this Practice only fit
For dealers in Satyrick Wit :
But you some white-lead ink must get,
And write on paper black as Jet :
Your Int'rest lyes to learn the knack
Of whitening what before was black.
   Thus your Encomiums, to be strong,
Must be apply'd directly wrong :
A Tyrant for his Mercy praise,
And crown a Royal Dunce with Bays :     120
A squinting Monkey load with charms ;
And paint a Coward fierce in arms.
Is he to Avarice inclin'd ?
Extol him for his generous mind :
And when we starve for want of Corn,
Come out with Amalthea's Horn.[3]
For Princes love you should descant
On Virtues which they know they want.

---

[1] ' besiege 'em', Forster MS., 1765.

[2] 'disoblige 'em', Forster MS. ; ' disoblige them ', 1765.

[3] After ' Horn ' this additional couplet in Forster MS., 1765 :
' For all experience this evinces
The only art of pleasing Princes.'

One Compliment I had forgot,
But Songsters must omit it not.                              130
(I freely grant the Thought is old)
Why then, your Hero must be told,
In him such Virtues lye inherent,
To qualify him God's Vicegerent,
That with no Title to inherit,
He must have been a King by Merit.
Yet be the Fancy old or new,
'Tis partly false, and partly true,
And take it right, it means no more
Than George and William claim'd before.         140
  Should some obscure inferior fellow
As Julius, or the Youth of Pella,
When all your list of Gods is out,
Presume to shew his mortal snout,
And as a Deity intrude,
Because he had the world subdu'd :
Oh ! let him not debase your Thoughts,
Or name him, but to tell his Faults.
  Of Gods I only quote [1] the best,
But you may hook in all the rest.                   150
  Now Birth-day Bard, with joy proceed
To praise your Empress, and her Breed.
First, of the first.   To vouch your Lyes
Bring all the Females of the Skyes :
The Graces and their Mistress Venus
Must venture down to entertain us.
With bended knees when they adore her
What Dowdys they appear before her !
Nor shall we think you talk at random,
For Venus might be her great Grandam.            160
Six thousand years hath liv'd the Goddess,
Your Heroine hardly fifty odd is.

[1] 'quote' over 'name' obliterated.

Besides you Songsters oft have shewn,  [p. 6.]
That she hath Graces of her own :
Three Graces by Lucina brought her,[1]
Just three ; and every Grace a Daughter.
Here many a King his heart and Crown
Shall at their snowy feet lay down :
In Royal Robes they come by dozens
To court their English German Cousins,  170
Besides a pair of princely Babyes,
That five years hence will both be Hebes.
　　Now see her seated on her Throne
With genuin lustre all her own.
Poor Cynthia never shone so bright,
Her Splendor is but borrow'd light ;
And only with her Brother linkt
Can shine, without him is extinct.
But Carolina shines the clearer
With neither Spouse nor Brother near her,[2]  180
And darts her Beams or'e both our Isles,
Tho George is gone a thousand miles.
Thus Berecynthia takes her place,
Attended by her heavenly Race,
And sees a Son in every God
Unaw'd by Jove's all-shaking Nod.
　　Now sing his little Highness Freddy,[3]
Who struts like any King already.
With so much beauty, shew me any maid
That could refuse this charming Ganymede,  190
Where Majesty with Sweetness vyes,
And like his Father early wise.

---

[1] Anne, Amelia, and Caroline Elizabeth (born 1709, 1711, and 1713). Queen Caroline had two more daughters, Mary and Louisa (born 1723 and 1724) — the future ' Hebes '.
[2] The Queen was regent during George II's absence in 1729.
[3] Frederick, Prince of Wales, father of George III.

[p. 7.]

Then cut him out a world of work,
To conquer Spain, and quell the Turk.
Foretell his Empire crown'd with Bays,
And golden Times, and Halcyon days,
But swear his Line shall rule the Nation
For ever—till the Conflagration.
    But now it comes into my mind,
We left a little Duke behind[1];       200
A Cupid in his face and size,
And only wants to want his eyes.
Make some provision for the Yonker,
Find him a Kingdom out to conquer ;
Prepare a Fleet to waft him o'r'e,
Make Gulliver his Commodore,
Into whose pocket valiant Willy put,
Will soon subdue the Realm of Lilliput.
    A skilfull Critick justly blames
Hard, tough, cramp, gutt'rall, harsh, stiff Names.
The Sense can ne're be too jejune,       211
But smooth your words to fit the tune,
Hanover may do well enough ;
But George, and Brunswick are too rough.
Hesse Darmstedt makes too rough a sound,[2]
And Guelph the strongest ear will wound.
In vain are all attempts from Germany
To find out proper words for Harmony :
And yet I must except the Rhine,
Because it clinks to Caroline.       220
Hail Queen of Britain, Queen of Rhymes,
Be sung ten hundred thousand times.
Too happy were the Poets Crew,
If their own happyness they knew.
Three Syllables did never meet
So soft, so sliding, and so sweet.

[1] William Augustus, Duke of Cumberland, born 1721.

[2] 'makes a rugged sound', Forster MS., 1765.

Nine other tuneful words like that
Would prove ev'n Homer's Numbers flat.
Behold three beauteous Vowels stand
With Bridegroom liquids hand in hand,                    230
In Concord here for ever fixt,                    [p. 8.]
No jarring consonant betwixt.
    May Caroline continue long,
For ever fair and young—in Song.
What tho the royal Carcase must
Squeez'd in a Coffin turn to dust ;
Those Elements her name compose,
Like Atoms are exempt from blows.
    Tho Caroline may fill your gaps
Yet still you must consult the Maps,                    240
Find Rivers with harmonious names,
Sabrina, Medway, and the Thames.
Britannia long will wear like Steel
But Albion's cliffs are out at heel,
And Patience can endure no more
To hear the Belgick Lyon roar.
Give up the phrase of haughty Gaul,
But proud Iberia soundly maul,
Restore the Ships by Philip taken,
And make him crouch to save his bacon.                    250
    Nassau, who got the name of glorious
Because he never was victorious,
A hanger on has always been,
For old acquaintance bring him in.
    To Walpole you might lend a Line,
But much I fear he's in decline ;
And if you chance to come too late
When he goes out, you share his fate,
And bear the new Successor's frown ;
Or whom you once sung up, sing down.                    260
    Reject with scorn that stupid Notion
To praise your Hero for Devotion :

Nor entertain a thought so odd,
That Princes should believe in God :
[p. 9.] But follow the securest rule,
And turn it all to ridicule :
'Tis grown the choicest Wit at Court,
And gives the Maids of Honor Sport.
For since they talk'd with Doctor Clark,[1]
They now can venture in the dark.              270
That sound Divine the Truth has spoke all
And pawn'd his word Hell is not local.
This will not give them half the trouble
Of Bargains sold, or meanings double.
   Supposing now your Song is done,
To Minheer Hendel[2] next you run,
Who artfully will pare and prune
Your words to some Italian Tune.
Then print it in the largest letter,
With Capitals, the more the better.            280
   Present it boldly on your knee,
And take a Guinea for your Fee.


## BIRTHDAY VERSES to STELLA, 1726

These Latin verses are in the hand of Ford. They are accompanied by the following letter, also in Ford's hand, but the initials 'J. S.' are to all appearances in the hand of Swift :

March 13: 1726

Madam
   This being your Birthday, my Unkle order'd me to give my opinion in a dispute about your Age.  I[3] have decided it as well as I could in the short time allow'd me, & I hope you will excuse[4]

[1] Samuel Clarke, a favourite of Queen Caroline, who would have liked to see him a Bishop.

[2] Swift's 'a' and 'e' are often difficult to distinguish ; perhaps

an error in transcription, like 'Darmstedt' in l. 215.

[3] 'I' written twice.

[4] 'excuse' after 'pardon' struck out.

any harsh Expression in a Language which is much more familiar
to you, than to      Madam
                your most obedient
                 humble servant
                      J: S.

Hitherto no birthday verses for 1726 have been known (see
p. 99, note 5), and these four Latin lines may have been intended
to take the place of the regular English greeting for which Swift's
English journey this year probably did not allow him time. He
was in Chester a few days before 16 March (*Portland Manuscripts*, vii, p. 431). The verses may be assigned to Ford, but
the letter suggests that they were written at Swift's desire and
had his approval.

Both letter and verses are drafts, and we do not know if
Stella ever received fair copies. Underneath the verses is an
English translation, heavily blotted out. The manuscript was
sold at Messrs. Christie's on 4 June 1896, and is now in the
Pierpont Morgan Library.


## In Stellæ Natalem

Natalis Stellæ rediens nova jurgia gignit,
    Præteritos annos quot numerare potest.
Florentis dum vultum Helenæ spectamus in illâ,
    Nestoris audimus mellea verba senis.


## Ford's BIRTHDAY VERSES to SWIFT, 1727

This is Ford's rough draft of a poem which is not otherwise
known.

According to Delany, Ford—whom he mistakenly calls
'Mathew Forde'—was 'the best lay-scholar of his time, and
nation' (*Observations upon Lord Orrery's Remarks*, 1754, p. 97).
The poem anticipates the address in *The Dunciad*:

> O thou! whatever Title please thine ear,
> Dean, Drapier, Bickerstaff, or Gulliver &c.

## Ad Celerem.

### Die natali Nov. 30. 1727.

Quo te salutem nomine idoneo?
An quo jocosus¹ funera Principum
   Prædixti, et austerum Tribunal
     Pontificum malé terruisti?
Illone mavis, quo populus frequens
Pendentem honorat gratus imaginem
   Herois a fœdâ rapinâ
     Incolumem² patriam tuentis,
Cum fraudulentus Præses Hiberniæ,
Et turpe scortum, et latro paraverant     10
   Impune partiri labores
     Artificis miseri et coloni.
Tu dissipasti fœdus, et integram
Prædam reduxti, machinâ aheneâ
   Frustra involutam, pennâ adortus
     Herculeâ graviore clavâ.
Mavisne dici carmine Navita
Qui visit oras, haud penetrabiles
   Ni Diva deducens opacum
     Explicuisset iter Minerva?     20
Gentis pusillæ quis sine Numine
Vitasset astus, quanquam ibi posteris
   Diceris immanes gigantes
     Mons supereminuisse vivus?
Cum solus esses pumilio viros
Inter Colossos, sicut in ilicum
   Silvâ vetustarum tenellus
     Flosculus, aut humilis myrica,³

---

¹ 'jocusus' MS.                     ³ 'myrica' over 'genesta' struck
² 'Incolumem' altered from  out.
'Innocuam'.

In tam minutis quando facetias
Risere membris, dein sapientiam, &　　　　30
　　Sensere doctrinam stupentes,
　　　　Ingeniumque animamque magnam,
Nè censeamus fortuitam tibi
Ortam procellam : fortuitas aves
　　Exinde mirandum parâsse
　　　　Effugium, reditumque faustum.
Nobis es actus fluctibus ad novos
Orbes, et illinc omnia commoda
　　Nobis referres, sed feroces,
　　　　Sed vitiis sumus obstinati.[1]　　　40
Illustris armis gens Celerum, suis
Olim subegit regna Quiritibus :
　　Hac stirpe tu natus vetustâ [2]
　　　　Das meliora tuis benignus.[3]
Tu parcitatem, dicere tu doces [4]
Vera, et pudorem, et justitiam, quibus
　　Omnes virorum, quin et ipsum
　　　　Quadrupedem superas magistrum.
Hanc auspicatam sæpe redintegres
Lucem, per annos continuos agens　　　50
　　Lætam et virescentem senectam
　　　　Perpetuoque domes superbos.

[1] These four lines 'Nobis . . . obstinati' in place of the following struck out:
'Permulsit aures jam nimium diu Errans Ulysses, æmulus Orpheos: Te nemo præcesit remota ad Littora, neve sequetur ullus.' In l. 38 'ab illis' inserted after 'illinc' above line and struck out.

[2] 'vetusta' over 'Britannis' struck out.

[3] 'Das' over 'Munificus' and 'tuis benignus' over 'donas' struck out.

[4] 'Tu' over 'Dum' struck out, 'et' struck out before 'dicere', and 'tu' inserted before 'doces', reduced from 'perdoces'.

# FRAGMENT of a PAMPHLET, 1714

This fragment is all in the hand of Swift. It is written on the right-hand half of a folio page, the left-hand half being left blank for corrections or additions.

Parliament met on 16 February 1714 to elect a Speaker, and on 2 March was opened by the Queen. Between these dates, just as *The Publick Spirit of the Whigs* was about to be issued, Swift began this pamphlet on the Pretender, but abandoned it at once. He turned to *Some Free Thoughts upon the Present State of Affairs*, and had shown Ford the beginning of it before he stole away from London at the end of May, in disgust at the dissensions in the government.

(Febr. 20)

# A
# Discourse concerning the Fears from the Pretender.

THERE are some disputes between the two contending Partyes now among us, which in reason ought[1] no longer to subsist, because Time and Events have put an End to the Causes of them. For instance, Whether our Peace with France and Spain were[2] safe and honorable; Whether the States Generall have a sufficient Barrier. Whether Spain ought to be governed by a Prince of the Bourbon Family. These Points are already determined, whether wisely or not; and reasonable Men of both sides will, I suppose allow, that the War can not be renewed at present to settle them better.

---

[1] 'ought' struck out before and inserted above line after 'in reason'.

[2] 'were' above 'was' struck out.

Other Differences there are, and of great Importance, which still depend, and cannot speedily be brought to an Issue without some degree of Correspondence between both Partyes. As, whether the Treaty of Commerce with France shall be confirmed by Parliament as beneficiall to our Trade, or rejected as pernicious. Whether the Princess Sophia of Hanover shall be invited to reside in England, as an Expedient for securing the Succession to Her Family upon the Qu—'s Demise. Whether the Pretender shall be forced to remove from Bar le duc, or permitted to reside any where on this side the Alpes. There are some other Controversyes of lesser Moment between the two contending Partyes; but the most popular Topick of Quarrell, is the Pretender. I have heard many significant Persons of the side which is against the Court, affirm with great appearance of Sincerity, that if they could be perfectly satisfied upon this Article, they would leave it to Her Majesty to chuse her own Servants, and give her no further Uneasyness in any part of her Administration.[1]

[1] ' I have therefore thought it to examine (?) ' all deleted after may [— — ?] be worth [of ' Administration '. *deleted*] some serious (?) though[t]

# LETTERS
## TO FORD

FROM

GAY, POPE and PARNELL

BOLINGBROKE

and the DUCHESS of ORMOND

# LETTERS to FORD from GAY

## 1 [1]

From aboard the Henrietta in Margett Road
Sunday, June 27 [1714]

You may observe my head begins to turn by my beginning
my letter at the wrong end of the paper. I am just this minute
going to be sea-sick. My Lady Theodosia [2] left us but yesterday. Think with what wistfull lookes I saw the boat put off
from our vessell, when matrimony and the company of her
husband would not allow her to cast one lingering look behind.
If I don't make an end I shall be forced to cast up (what the
sailors call) my accounts.

## 2 [3]

Sr.

After eleven days being on board & putting backwards
and forwards in the Channell, not without a day or two's
seasickness, I am now at the Hague, where we came on
Sunday Evening from Roterdam. We are here in the midst
of Treatys & Negotiations, Plenipotentiarys Embassadors &
Envoys; but I not having as yet enter'd the list of Politicians
am wholy taken up, with observing the Ladys. here are
assemblys almost every Night, but I fear I shall scarce have
the oppertunity to be at one of them; my Lady Straffords is
Wednesdays & Fridays. I have seen several Ladys that are
pretty enough while they are in Holland; but should they
once appear in Kensington Gardens, they must resign all their
pretensions to Beauty.

[1] This letter was sold at Messrs. Christie's on 4 June 1896. The extract is from the sale catalogue.
[2] Daughter of the third Earl of Clarendon (see p. 22, note 4), Baroness Clifton *suo jure* 1713; married 1713 to John Bligh, of Rathmore, created Baron Clifton 1721. This passage suggests a 'source' of the last stanza of Gay's *Black-ey'd Susan*, and anticipates 'cast one longing ling'ring look behind' in Gray's *Elegy*.
[3] Sold at Messrs. Christie's on 4 June 1896, and now in the Pierpont Morgan Library.

Nos patriæ fines et dulcia linquimus arva
Nos patriam fugimus, tu Tityre lentus in umbrà—¹

Doctor Parnell would translate the words in Umbra, at Ombre, but for my part, I believe you know how to treat a Lady as well in a shade as at a gaming table, and that you had rather stick to the vulgar construction. as for myself, who know nothing of play, I would be glad to take up with an Arbour. There are shades at Bingfield, M^rs Fermor is not very distant from thence; make a visit to Pope and Parnelle, and while they are making a Grecian Campaign, do you as Æneas did before you meet your Venus in a Wood, he knew her by her *Locks* and so may you.—but as you are a man of Honour & Modesty—think not of Hairs less in sight or any Hairs but these.²  I am just this Minute going to take the air with my Lord at the House in the Wood, where if no Nymph disturbs my Meditations I will think of you, and our Sundays conferences.

I am

Your most obliged

July. 6. OS. 1714.                          Humble Serv^t
In a day or two we set forward                J Gay
for Hanover.

*Address:*  For Charles Ford Esq^r at his Office
            at Whitehall

London

3³

Sr.

Hanovre Aug. 7. 1714.

This comes to put you to a further trouble in relation to my Works; the Princess ⁴ hath now ask'd me for my Poem, and I am obliged to make Presents to three or four Ladys besides, so that I must desire you to send me three or four *Shepherd's Weeks* more with as Many Poems of the Fan, if you send your Servant, Tonson will supply you with them.  I go

¹ Virgil, *Ecl.* 1. 3–4.                    ³ The only letter by Gay now
² *The Rape of the Lock,* Canto   in the Ford collection.
iv, last line.                              ⁴ The future Queen Caroline.

every night to Court at Herenhausen, the Place & Gardens
more than answer'd my expectations. if it were not for the
Princess and the Countess of Picbourg I should forget my
faculty of Speech, for I cannot as yet take the Courage to
address a Lady in French and both those Ladys take a pleasure
in speaking English, which I thank God, notwithstanding
I have pass'd through the regions of Westphalia I have not
quite forgot. the Court have a notion that I am to reside here
upon his Lordship's return, and I have received many Compliments upon that occasion; my Denial of it they look upon
as a sketch of my Politicks. the Princess and the Countess of
Picbourg have both subscrib'd to Pope's Homer,[1] and her
Highness did me the Honour to say, she did not doubt it would
be well done, since I recommended it. I had a design of
writing to the Dean, but my Lord Clarendon hath just this
Minute sent me a Long Letter to Copy, so that I shall be able
to write nothing to him this Post, and to add nothing further
to you, but that I am

Your most obliged Humble<br>Servant.

Mr Lewis shall hear from me soon.          JG.
if the Books are not sent with Expedition
I shall lose my Credit.

4[2]

Sir.
   Not that I'll wander from my native home,
And tempting Dangers foreign Citys roam,
Let Paris be the Theme of Gallia's Muse,
Where Slav'ry treads the Streets in wooden shoes;
Nor will I sing of Belgia's frozen Clime,
And teach the clumsy Boor to skate in Rhime;
Where, if the warmer Clouds in Rain descend
No miry Ways industrious Steps offend,

[1] The Countess of Piquebourg accompanied the Princess to England as a lady-in-waiting. She appears among the subscribers to Pope's Homer as 'Countess of Buckenburg'. The Princess heads the list.

[2] Sold at Messrs. Christie's on 4 June 1896; now in the R. B. Adam Library, Buffalo; printed in *Poetical Works of Gay*, ed. G. C. Faber, 1926, p. 666.

The rushing Flood from sloping Pavements pours
And blackens the Canals with dirty show'rs.
Let others Naples' smoother Streets rehearse
Or with proud Roman Structures grace their Verse,
Where frequent Murders wake the Night with Groans,
And Blood in purple Torrents dyes the Stones.
Nor shall the Muse through narrow Venice stray,
Where Gondalas their painted Oars display.
Oh happy Streets, to rumbling wheels unknown,
No Carts or Coaches shake the floating Town.

    Thus was of old Britannia's City blest
E'er Pride and Luxury her Sons possest;
Coaches and chariots yet unfashion'd lay
Nor late invented chairs perplex'd the Way.[1] &c.

That &c signifies near 300 Lines. so much for Poetry;
you may easily imagine by this progress, that I have not been
interrupted by any Places at Court.  Mr. Domville[2] told me
how to direct to you a day or two since as I accidentally met
him in the Park.  I have not heard any thing of Parnell or the
Dean since you left England; Pope has been in the Country,
near [torn] but I expect him in Town this Week to forward
the Printing of his Homer, which is already begun to be printed
off; he will publish his Temple of Fame as soon as he comes
to Town; Rowe hath finish'd his Play,[3] and Lintot told me
just now, that he was made Clerk of the Council to the Prince.
There was a Ball at Somerset House last Tuesday, where I saw
the Dutchess; the Prince and Princess were there, and danc'd
our English Country Dances.  I have been studying these two
or three Minutes for something [          ] to write to you, but
I find myself at a Loss, and can't say any thing but that I am

Sir

London                     Your most obedient
  Decem^r. 30. 1714.        Humble Servt
                                J. Gay

*Address*: To Charles Ford Esq^r to be left at
             S^r Richard Chantillon's Banker in Paris

[1] *Trivia*, I, lines 83–104.    [3] *Lady Jane Grey*.
[2] See p. 2, note 4.

# Letters to
# FORD from POPE and PARNELL

I [1]

From the Romantic World.
May 19. By Sunshine.
[1714]

Now is the Evening Sun, declining from the Hemisphere he had painted with Purple, & intermingled Streaks of Gold; rolling his rapid Chariot toward the Surface of the Ocean, whose waves begin to sparkle at his beams; while The silver-footed Thetis, and all her water nymphs around, are preparing their Crystal Palaces for his Reception. It seems to us Mortalls, as if his glorious Orbe were prop'd under the Chin by the Tops of the distant Mountains, whose lovely Azure appears sprinkled with the loose Spangles he shakes from his Illustrious Tresses. The lengthening Shadows extend themselves after him, as if they endeavourd to detain him with their long black Arms; or rather (if we consider their Position is directly contrary) they seem the Long Arrows of far-darting Phœbus, which he shoots backward, like a Parthian, as he retreats. The Green Mantle of the Earth is trimm'd with | Gold, and the Leaves of [p. 2.] the Trees turn'd up with the same. But the God, better pleasd with the Water-Tabby of the Ocean, is resolvd to enrich it with all his Spangles.[2] & now he sinks beneath our Horizon leaving some illustrated tracks of his former beauty behind him, which as they insensibly wear away are succeeded by the silver gleams of his palefacd delegate. From the dark tops of the hills she emerges into Sight to run her inconstant race over the Azure firmament. The Starrs wait around her as a numerous train of Inamorato's who confess the flames of love at the sight of the celestiall Goddess; the fixed Starrs seem to stand amazd to behold her, while the Planets dance in her presence & wink upon her as a sett of more familiar gallants. But now while

---

[1] This letter, and the two which follow, were sold at Messrs. Christie's on 4 June 1896, and are now in the Pierpont Morgan Library.

[2] Thus far in the hand of Pope; the rest is in the hand of Parnell. Pope wrote the address.

I look behold a new & more melancholly scene, a darkning cloud intercepts her streaming glorys, she goes behind it as a matron mounting up into a mourning chariot, & now & then peeps through it as a pretty widdow looking through her crapes.

[p. 3.] Darkness | has now spread its veil over the variety of this terrestriall creation for which rejoyce ye quarrelling Oyster wenches whom it parts & ye fondling Lovers who are to meet in it but what will ye do ye Mooncalves who have stayd late in company in hopes to go home by the light of this second luminary.

By this time it is evident that we have written the day down & the night allmost through which makes it no feignd excuse but a reall reason for us upon the account of want of time to conclude with professing our selves

Your Most Aff: F<sup>ds</sup><br>& Hum: Ser:<sup>ts</sup><br>ǝqoꟼarnell

By Moonshine. May 19.

*Address:* To Charles Ford Esq<sup>r</sup>.
at the Secretary's Office
Whitehall
Westminster

*Postmark:* $\frac{21}{MA}$

2 <sup>1</sup>

[Middle of July, ? 17, 1714]

Dear Sir,
I have the plague of the Headake upon me, and write to You in my Anguish. You know it is natural to have recourse to our Friends in our Unhappiness, and I am at present too peevish to converse with any but by Letter. I confess, like a sinful Poet as I am, that I'm justly punishd in the Offending Part : but tho at all times when I write to You my Heart gets the better of my Head, yet it does so now in a particular manner, and you ought to believe all I shall say at this time because I speak with Tears in my Eyes. Tis plain I should not write to you under this circumstance, *ni Te plus oculis meis amarem,* as Catullus has it.[2] You may expect I should

---

[1] Pierpont Morgan Library.    [2] Catullus, xiv. 1.

express my Spleen against Poetry, complain about my Subscriptions, curse the weather & rail at bad wine: but I will own
(as sick as I am) that I think Homer a very good Book,[1] and
those | Subscribers that have payd me very worthy Gentlemen; [p. 2.]
that England is an excellent Climate, especially in the Latitude
of St. James's & Pallmall; and that French Claret is worth
3ˢ 6ᵈ a Bottle, if one had Mʳ Ford's Company over it. But
Dʳ Parnelle does not deserve the Liquor he has here, by himself, besides the Scandal he gives in a Popish Family by this
seperate Communion.

I envy the Town and You excessively at this season. You
walk the Streets Invisible, like Heroes, whom the Gods have
encompast in a Veil of Clouds. You meet with no Disturbance
in your Passage; but have the noble Gratification of Ambition,
to be at large with a great deal of Roome, or to be quite Alone.
The great Ones of the Land have abandoned their Palaces to
you, and the Queen herself will shortly fly from her Metro-
politan City before you. Upon the whole, I cannot but | highly [p. 3.]
applaud your generous Stay in London just at the Time when
that grand Objection against the Town-Life, the Vice and Folly
of it, is in a fair way to be removed by the Absence of so
many thousands of the wicked.

That we have seen the Dean,[2] Dʳ Parnelle has informed
you; that we long to see you I hope you need not to be
informed by one who is so truly & so affectionately

Dʳ Sir

Pray is Mʳ Harcourt     Yʳ. most obliged & most
  in Towne?        faithful humble Servᵗ.
The Dʳ'ˢ & my faithful Service     A. Pope
to Mʳ Lewis.

*Address:* To Charles Ford Esqʳ.
     at the Secretary's Office
     in
Whitehall<br/>London

*Postmark:* $\frac{19}{IY}$

[1] The first volume of Pope's   June 1715.
Homer appeared a year later, in    [2] See p. 22, n. 3.

3 [1]

Binfield Sept: 2 1714.

Dear Sir

We [2] whose names will soon be underwritten do thank you for the Letter which you were pleasd to send us from your office, & which we receivd, just at the minute we had promisd our selves. It was unhappy that we did not meet the Dean before he went,[3] & that he did not know he might still stay here. But I desire you woud explain to me still why I may stay, and how long, If I am oblidgd to take the oath in three months or six, if it will do here or in Ireland.[4] I saw something concerning those who had offices and were in England, but I do not know if the words extend to Clergymen and livings; I believe the Provost [5] is sure, lett me know what he does.

And now having finishd buisness lett me tell you that the weather grows extream cold which is all the news of the country. I believe in town you are by this time pretty well crowded, State and the hopes of more State employ your thought, and Kings and Coronations in prospect are ever before you. Be pleasd however to descend from those high Speculations to answer this letter soon. Then shall you see Gay returning from Hanover, Parnell from Binfield, and Pope following if he does not come along with him. thus from various parts will we crowd in upon you, to eat your meat, drink your wine, and make nightcaps of your napkins, till warnd by the clock that strikes ten or one more, we retire from you, professing our selves, as we do now

Y$^r$ Aff:$^{te}$ f$^{ds}$ and Hum Ser$^{ts}$

Tho Parnell.
A. Pope.

*Address:* To Charles Ford Esq. at the
blue Perriwig next to the
George Tavern in Pall-Mall,
London

*Postmark:* $\frac{3}{\text{SE}}$

[1] Pierpont Morgan Library.
[2] This letter is all in the hand of Parnell; Pope added his signature and wrote the address.

4 <sup>I</sup>

Bath
Oct<sup>r</sup>. 2<sup>d</sup>. [1714]

Dear Sir,

I have been led about from place to place by D<sup>r</sup> Parnell, at such a rate, that I have scarcely recovered my self yet of such a series of journeys. If my head were not this moment giddy of the Bath waters,² I would tell you I am yet in my senses, and remember with pleasure the kindnesses of M<sup>r</sup> Ford. I heartily wish myself with you, in the quiet, indolent station by your Fireside, with a nightcap on: which is a thousand times more to be preferred than this way of catching cold for my health. The dismal prospect of winter affrights me at this distance from London, you, and good company; the sole comforts that can make me live till another summer. When I meet you next, it will be with the same joy that men gett to their native country after a tedious and weary wandring. I cannot think myself in England here, | all people are changed [p. 2.] in their opinions, manners and looks, since the last view I had of great Britain. How many Degrees are we removed? Is Gay our Countryman, or a High dutch Squire? I have not heard a syllable of his adventures. If he wants consolatory discourses, pray give him what encouragement you can; & desire him to make a visit to M<sup>r</sup> Harcourt. If he is afraid of corresponding with Tories, tell him I am a Whig, and he may write to me hither, till the end of next week, by which time I will be at London or in Berkshire. If you have any design for this place pray put a stop to me by a line the next post. Nothing in nature else shall detain me here. We were put in hopes of good company at this Towne, but none appear. I am damnably in the spleen. When shall we see the Dean on this

³ Swift left Letcombe for Ireland on 16 August.
⁴ Cf. Ford's letter to Swift of 5 August 1714, p. 45, *ad init.*
⁵ Benjamin Pratt; see p. 20, n. 2, and p. 53.

ᴵ Sold 4 June 1896; now in the possession of Archdeacon Bright, Lichfield.
² Pope was in Bath by 23 September, on which day he wrote to Gay.

side the water? If you have not heard from D<sup>r</sup> Elwood,<sup>1</sup> be so kind to desire the Dean to do that business. I would write to give that Gentleman my thanks as soon as I hear of its being done. D<sup>r</sup> Parnelle is intolerably lazie and puts me off from time to time by promising to write jointly with me to all our Friends. I beg you to know me for y<sup>r</sup> most sincere and obed<sup>t</sup>. humble serv<sup>t</sup>

A. Pope.

*Address :* To Charles Ford Esq<sup>r</sup>. att
       the blue Perriwigg near
       the George Taverne
       in Pall Mall
         London

*Postmark :* $\frac{4}{OC}$

5 <sup>2</sup>

[No date]

D<sup>r</sup> Sir

    I find it impossible to be with you this Evening, and Gay is gone out of towne (to whom I would else have sent to go). My short stays in town, & plagu'd with business which leaves me no Hours of my own, makes me seem, much less than I am

D<sup>r</sup> Sir<br>Y<sup>r</sup> affectionate<br>humble Serv<sup>t</sup>.<br>A. Pope.

*Address :* To M<sup>r</sup> Ford at M<sup>r</sup> Hoyes's
      at the blue periwig over against the
         Coco Tree, in
           Pall mall

---

<sup>1</sup> See p. 53, n. 4.

<sup>2</sup> This letter has remained in the Ford collection. Nine letters to Ford from Pope, or Pope and Parnell, were sold on 4 June 1896, for five of which the sale catalogue is the editor's only authority. Most of these resemble this letter in dealing with a meeting, but in one of them, dated 'Oct. 22', Pope says 'there is nothing I so much avoid as Prologues and Epitaphs'.

# Letters to
# FORD from BOLINGBROKE

## I [1]

Paris feb: 21
1717

Your letter Dear S$^r$ of the 23$^d$ of Jan: from Venice gave me a very sensible pleasure. No man has a more sincere value for you, or bears you a more affectionate friendship, & no man is by consequence a greater sharer than I am in every thing which contributes to your happyness or amusement.

Your taste for the Carnaval, and your notion of the manner of life which the strangers att Venice fancy they find pleasure in, agree with mine. I never was more tir'd of any place in my life after the first impression was over, which the singularity of the situation made upon me. |

I am apt to think that you will find att Rome entertai[n]ment [p. 2.] much more agreeable. pray let me hear from you when you arrive there.

The publick accounts have I take it for granted inform'd you of what passes in England att this time. a new discovery of a design to rise in Scotland, the Person & papers of the Swedish Minister seiz'd, Cæsar, S$^r$ J: Banks, Parsons, & others taken into Custody.[2] The Torys rail att one without reason, & I pity them with the greatest reason. they neglect no one measure which can serve to crush them beyond retreive.

I am going very soon into the Country where | I shall fix my [p. 3.] person & my thoughts too, as if the retreat were to last as long

---

[1] The first four of these letters from Bolingbroke, and the seventh, were sold at Messrs. Christie's on 16 December 1897, and are now in the Pierpont Morgan Library.

[2] Gyllenborg, the Swedish minister, was arrested on 30 January; see p. 75, n. 1. 'The same Morning *Charles Cæsar*, Esq; formerly Treasurer of the Navy, and Member of Parliament for the Borough of *Hertford*, and Sir *Jacob Bancks*, formerly Member of Parliament for *Minehead* . . . were also apprehended'—*Political State*, February 1716/17, p. 148. Some of the newspapers report the arrest also of Major Boyle Smith, but none mentions a 'Parsons', or any parsons, in this connexion.

as my life; and so it may perhaps prove, if it does not Grata
superveniet quæ non sperabitur hora.[1]

Adieu to you Dear S<sup>r</sup>. enjoy the chearful sun of Italy, amuze
yourself with all the noble productions of Nature & of Art
which that Country affords, let the venerable ruines which you
meet with recall to your mind the grandeur of Rome, and do
your best that nothing may recall to your thoughts the confusion & misery of your own Nation. I am ever with inviolable
friendship yours.

> *Address :*    A Monsieur
>     Monsieur Ford chez Monsieur
>     Antonio Philippo Lombardi, a
>         Rome
>
> *Postmark :* De Paris

2 [2]

Paris April the 17<sup>th</sup><br>1717

Dear S<sup>r</sup>

I have receiv'd your letter of the 16<sup>th</sup> of March from
Rome, and desire you to be perswaded that I know you too
well to suspect you capable of injustice towards any man, or
of unkindness towards one as sincerely your friend as I am.
Obligations I have never been happy enough to lay upon you.
if giving you my friendship is to be reckon'd for one, you have
amply repay'd it by assuring me of yours.

The retirement I propose to myself is not only what I chuse
but what I languish after. I am too much out of the least
relation to business, to be affected by the late Treaty.[3]

[p. 2.] I beleive the calumnys spread against me will in | the con-
clusion turn to the prejudice of the authors of them, & rather
do me honour than mischeif; but for this I am no more
oblig'd to those persons, whoever they are, than a man unjustly
accus'd, & acquitted with reputation, is to his prosecutor.

Lord Mar whom you imagin'd left sick on the road, has

---

[1] Horace, *Epist.* i. iv. 14.    [3] The Triple Alliance, January
[2] Pierpont Morgan Library.    1717.

been here, and may be still so for ought I can tell; for tho'
I have not yet been able to remove my person out of the busy
part of the world, yet I assure you my mind is so entirely
abstracted from it, that I avoid, instead of enquiring after, all
sort of news.

I wish you joy of the course of study which you are entring
upon. for my part I find my account in retiring from the
living to the dead. the ingratitude you mention & many
other vices which deform the present age, were rife in Rome
& Greece. they had our | crimes but not our meannesses. [p. 3.]
their virtues & their faults were more exalted. I would not
deserve the gallows, but if I did, it should be among Highway-
men, not among PickPockets.

The paper I was writing when we parted is unfinish'd;[1]
several things concurr'd to make me lay my pen aside, & I have
not yet taken it up again. When I finish it, & sooner [or
later] that shall be, there is nobody to whom [I would] sooner
communicate it than yourself.

Adieu Dear S^r, let me hear sometimes how you do, & what
you do. no man deserves, by the part he takes in every thing
that relates to you, this favour, more than your obedient
faithful servant B.

*Address:*          A Monsieur
          Monsieur Ford Gentilhomme
          Anglois chez Mons^r Antonio
          Phillippo Lombardi a
                    Rome
*Postmark:* De Paris

3 [2]

Jan: the 29^th 1720.

I thank you Dear S^r for the favour of yours of the 4^th of
this month, & I send you inclos'd my answer to the Dean.[3]

---

[1] The *Letter to Sir William*
*Windham,* first published in
1753.
[2] Pierpont Morgan Library.

[3] This answer to Swift's letter
of 19 December 1719 is not
known, but Swift received it;
see Letter XXXVI, p. 85.

the ill State of his health gives me very much concern. change of air, the exercise of a journey, and the life of amusement which I would make him live, could I once get him to this side of the water, would reestablish him perfectly. if you offer'd to be his conductor, might you not determine him? this expedient would procure me a double satisfaction. I know very well, & by cruel experience, how implacable the persons he lives in fear of are, but surely he has nothing att this time of day to apprehend from them. nothing att least which he may not conduct himself so as to avoid. for godsake press him again in the strongest terms you can. it is ridiculous to neglect his health, to deny himself so reasonable & so easy an amusement, and to deprive his friends after so long a separation of the pleasure of seeing him, for a parcel of ill founded apprehensions which are sent up to his brain in a spleenatick vapour.

M^r John Miller may very possibly have the influence you suspect. he has long been a person of great sway in the City of Westminster. it were much to be wish'd that his influence were employ'd to calm your Party squabbles for some time, & to give your great men leisure to attempt something great, National, & proportionable to your present exigencys. I doubt they are greater now than most people apprehend, & that a little longer delay will sink you beyond retreive into a state from whence the Goddess of Safety her self, it is I think Livy's expression,[1] cannot save you.

It is very true that I have got a great deal of money in these fonds. having no sum of my own which I could command att that time, & being determin'd not to have an obligation which it lay in my power to have, I had no concern in the first Stocks, the gain upon which exceeds whatever has been yet made in [p. 2.] the world. | the billets d'etat which were pay'd in upon the subscriptions att par, were bought up att 50 & att 60 p^r c^t discount, and the Stock which these billets purchas'd has been sold att 2000. thus you see that there has been 4000 p^r c^t to be gain'd. when the 2^d Stocks were created I had a sum of money by me, & I got a friend to consult M^r Law, for I am too much out of the world to have any familiarity with a Man who is so much in it, how to lay this money out. he advis'd

---

[1] Cf. Cicero, *Pro Fonteio*, vi, and Terence, *Adelphi*, iv. vii fin.

to subscribe it on the new Stocks.  I did so, & the rise of them has procur'd me att least as much as I have been hitherto robb'd of.   may I entreat you to assure M^r Pope of my most humble service, & inviolable friendship?   What Brinsden[1] means I know not, but he has sent me Priors works which I was very indifferent about, & not M^r Popes which I am impatient to see, & which I most earnestly recommended it to him that he should send me by the first opportunity.  the four volumes of Homer I have not receiv'd.  I thank M^r Pope extreamly for his attention, & I write to Brinsden to have a little more.  Dear S^r adieu.

*No address.*


4^2


You will please to accept of the same excuse, as I make to our common friend, for deferring to answer your letter of the 19^th of October.  it was long on it's way hither, & I have been rambling ever since I receiv'd it.  I am glad to have so good a Second as you in my quarrel with the D: about Cato.[3]  I mean the Second.  he was a Cynick in polliticks, & did oftner harm than good, of which I could produce some flaming instances.  enough to prove that he liv'd a fanatick & dy'd an Enthusiast. a pretty character for the Saviour of a Common Wealth, whose circumstances were so nice, and whose case was so desperate, that the greatest dexterity imaginable could hardly have gone about to cure without irritating the disease & precipitating the Patients death.   I am sorry to see the distemper of Stock jobbing spread, it has been very mortal here, & in England ; I know

---

[1] John Brinsden, Bolingbroke's secretary, who was prosecuting his interests in England.  The fourth volume of Pope's Homer had appeared in June 1718, and the fifth and sixth appeared in May 1720.  Bolingbroke had subscribed 'for ten Setts'.  His name is not in the list of sub- scribers to Prior's volume of 1718 ; the name there is 'Lady Viscountess Bolingbroke'.

[2] Pierpont Morgan Library.

[3] See his letters to the Dean of 21 [O.S. 10] July, 1721, and 1 Jan. 1721-2 [O.S. 21 Dec. 1721], *Correspondence*, iii. 91, 110.

not whether your climate will be able to blunt the edge of its malignity, tho' spiders and toads cannot live I think in Ireland. I send this letter by the post directly to Dublin, & I hope it will go safely. if you write to your humble servant La Tour, you may please to direct to him, chez Messieurs de Moracin et la Borde Rue Berthin poirée a Paris. you pass the winter where you are, but you intend I suppose in the Spring to cross [p. 2.] the sea. why should you not cross it | twice, & pass some months in this hermitage ?[1] the journey is so short, the roads so good, the country so fine, & the seat so private, that I can find no good reason either in our friends lazyness or his Spleen why he should not accompany you. I see some other objections which may be put into the scale, but an ounce of friendship will outweigh them. Adieu Dear S$^r$. no man living is more faithfully or more affectionately yours than La Tour.

Jan: the 1$^{st}$ 1722.

*Address :*　　　To
Mr Ford att M$^{rs}$ Fords
House in Dawson
Street
　　　　　Dublin
　　　　　Ireland
par Angleterre


5 [2]

[London, August 1723]

I return you S$^r$ very sincere & hearty thanks for continuing to me a friendship, which I value too much not to deserve in some degree. my health is att present good, but I am expos'd to the return of an aguish distemper which has not fail'd to persecute me once in two or three months ever since the year 1720. the waters of Aix & those of Spa are recommended to me as the best & surest means to get rid for good and all of so

[1] La Source, near Orleans.　　　[2] Ford collection.

troublesome & so frequent a visitor. I am resolv'd to drink them, and for this purpose I shall be going from hence in three weeks. as agreable as retirement must be to one who knows the world as well as you do, who is in as good company as you are when he is alone, and who is so happily seated between two preferments of the Deans,[1] I will not despair of seeing you once more in the world. I have led the life of an Hermit so long that I am | perhaps grown unfit to lead any other, and yet there [p. 2.] is some probabillity att present that I may return once more into the world. it would be an extream disappointment to me not to find you there. the Reason of health which the Dean gives for taking a long journey in a bad country,[2] where he will find no accommodations, & where he has neither acquaintance, friends, nor business, is so whimsical that I cannot beleive it true. I suspect rather that he is preparing himself by such a tryal for some apostolical mission among savage Indians, or the barbarous people of Africa. if he forgets his friends, & all his friends complain that he does so, I am well enough acquainted with him to be sure that his soul must be full of something more sublime than friendship. he is capable of all the degrees of Elevation which humanity can rise to, but he has no alacrity in sinking. perswade him however that he may put these holy resolutions in practice to better purpose | among the Savages of [p. 3.] the Island of great Brittain, than among those of Madagascar. I am assurd that here is no want of Pyrates, anthropophages, and other monsters, & by consequence he can not fear any want of adventures. if Martyrdom be his aim, let him not despair. I might trouble you perhaps with some further advice to the Dean, if I was not to write a postscript to a letter which M^r Pope keeps open for that end.[3] I do not remember the date of my last letters to you & to our rambling Apostle. I believe they were writ about eighteen months ago. this is certain that I never received any answers to them, which I own frankly to you that I began to take ill. Adieu Dear S^r

---

[1] Ford was at this time at Woodpark, his country seat between Dublin and Laracor.

[2] Swift had set out in June on his long journey to the South of Ireland.

[3] Instead of writing a postscript to Pope's letter, Bolingbroke sent a long letter of his own, *Correspondence*, iii. 170.

do me the justice to be convinc'd that I am most sincerely your faithful humble servant B.

*No address.*

## 6 ¹

I thank you Sʳ most kindly for adding a few lines to the letter which our friend honour'd me with,² and for curing me of that fright which the account he gives of himself had thrown me into. Every great genius borders upon folly. her dominions embrace those of Reason on every side; & the two frontiers are so alike, that he who pushes to the extremitys of one, wanders often into the other, & seldom finds his way back. for me, and those, who, like me, have not strength enough to make such long excursions, we are not expos'd to the same danger. we live in the mediterranean province, less fruitful, less beautiful, less elegant than those which are more remote from the Center, but it furnishes us with every thing necessary. thanks be to Stella! I will neither pun nor quibble, but I am confident that we had lost the Dean if it had not been for her. if she had not fix'd his course, our poor friend would have wander'd from one ideal world to another, and have forgot even the Species he is of. he had been att this very instant [p. 2.] perhaps freezing in Saturn, burning in Mercury, | or stalking along with a load on his back, a bell under his chin, a plume on his head, and a fox tail att each ear, in that country which he discover'd not long ago, where Horses & mules are the reasonable Creatures, and men the Beasts of burden. But thanks to heaven & Stella, that danger is over. since he loves a woman he will not forget that he is a man. You ask me about what time I intend to be in London,³ and I answer you with great truth that I know nothing of the matter. if I am

---

¹ Ford collection. This letter was sent by mistake to Swift: see Letters XLII and XLIII, pp. 100 and 102.
² Swift's letter in reply to Bolingbroke's of August 1723 is lost.
³ Bolingbroke, preferring 'un long exile à un retour équivoque', left England in August 1723, and after a visit to Aix-la-Chapelle and to Spa, was now 'at Paris'.

restor'd, I go to London ; if I am not, I stay att Paris some
time, & then return to my Hermitage. these doubts will be
soon decided, & I am not over solicitous what the decision
may be.

> Duc me Parens, celsique Dominator Poli,
> Quocunque placuit. nulla parendi mora est.
> assum impiger.[1]

thus Cleanthes spoke, and thus your most faithful humble
Servant thinks & acts.

Dec: the 25<sup>th</sup> 1723.

*No address.*


## 7 [2]

Att the same time as I beg the favour of you to forward the
inclos'd to our friend give me leave S<sup>r</sup> to return you my thanks
for the continu'd marks of your friendship. the transition from
a minister of State to an Hermit is a very great one in the eye
of the world. But there is nothing in it hard to be bore by
a man, who whilst he is in the first station, supposes he may
one time or other fall into the second, and who takes care,
even amidst the dissipations of pleasure and of business, to
temper & harden his mind by philosophy. Repulses and dis-
appointments, diminution or loss of Estate & Rank, Exil &
Calumny itself, are unable to make a painful impression upon
such a man, and to constitute him unhappy. if the mind has
not been thus prepar'd, I think it no misfortune, but the contrary, to be recall'd from a dependance on those things whose
price we overrate, & whose instabillity we can not fix, and
to be taught forcibly in the school of affliction | those necessary [p. 2.]
lessons which we would not learn voluntarily in the school of
prosperity.

I know not whether to be pleas'd or sorry that Stella has so
many good quallitys. the easy hours which she procures to our
friend are reasons for the first ; and his attachment to Ireland,
which I beleive owing to his attachment to her, is a Reason

---

[1] See p. 103, n. 2.    [2] Pierpont Morgan Library.

for the latter. my chief hopes are plac'd on his inconstancy. I have known several persons of lively imaginations, fond of their houses, & their gardens, as long as there were improvements to be made, and as these houses & gardens were incitements to their fancy, & continual subjects for the exercise of it. But the same Persons grew tir'd of them when they were once adorn'd beyond a possibillity of being so any more. the Deans fancy is like that Devil which a certain Conjurer had [p. 3.] rais'd, and which threaten'd to carry him | away, if he left him a moment unemploy'd. When the Dean therefore has sung all Stellas perfections over in Sonnet, Ode, Pastoral &c, his Devil having no more employment will certainly run away with him. You may know enuff of the black art perhaps to direct this Devils flight into France. A Person whose affairs carry'd her this Summer into England,[1] will be oblig'd to return thither again in the beginning of the winter. She will joyn all her skill in negromancy with yours, and I have been inform'd by some of the best conjurers in Europe that there is a certain plastick virtue in petty coats of great efficiency in all cases of this kind. this person regrets her not having been able to see you oftner, hopes to repair the loss att her next journey & assures you of her humble services.

Sep: the 12th.

these two letters have layn by me till now because the person to whom I intended to direct them was out of London, & because I was ignorant of your address. the Marq: being about to return into England, I commit them to her to deliver to your hands.

Octob: the 10th 1724.

*Address:* To M[r] Ford.

---

[1] Lady Bolingbroke, who had crossed to England at the end of May to secure the £50,000 which had been entrusted to Sir Matthew Decker: see Letter XLVIII, p. 115, n. 5. She returned to England in October, as the postscript shows, and the affair was settled in November.

# Letters from the
# DUCHESS of ORMOND to FORD

1[1]

Sir

I beg your pardon for this trouble but I was in so great a hurry, that I had not time before you went, to write the inclosed to your freind the Dean, which I desire the favour of you to give him.[2]

I wish you a good Voyage, & am an humble [servant] to M[ris] Ford, & to those of your aquaintance that do me the honour to inquire for such an old fashoned Gentlewoman as | I, who [p. 2.] am very sincerely

Sir

Y[r] most humble servant<br>M Ormonde

Sept: the 7th
   1721

2[1]

Sir

I give you many thanks for the favour of yours, & the transmiting an inclosed,[3] I hope you'l be so good as to return mine in answer to it, which I now send you.

I thank God I am prety well, but not so perfectly well, as not to need the Bath, which I chose rather to come to now | then [p. 2.] in the Spring, hopeing to find less company then in the season.

I am with great truth

Sir<br>Y[r]

most humble servant<br>M Ormonde

Dec[r] the 9th
   1723

---

[1] Ford collection.
[2] See Swift's *Correspondence*, iii. 95.
[3] Swift's letter of 6 November,
now lost; her answer to it is printed in *Correspondence*, iii. 182.

# INDEX

Don Carlos. *See* Ford, Charles.
Dopping, Samuel, M.P. for Dublin
University, 79, 83.
Dorchester, Evelyn Pierrepont, first
Marquess of, afterwards first Duke
of Kingston, 35.
Dorset, Lionel Cranfield Sackville,
first Duke of, Lord Lieutenant of
Ireland, 169.
' Dragon, the '. *See* Oxford, Earl
of.
' Draper, the ', 106, 111, 112, 117.
' Drapier, the ', 116, 119.
*Drapier's Letters, The,* xxxvii–
xxxviii, xl, 102–19 *passim*;
Swift's first reference to Wood's
half-pence, 102 ; 2000 copies of
First Letter dispersed in March
1724, 106 ; proclamation against
the Fourth Letter, 112 ; Carteret
given no reason to suspect Swift,
112 ; legal proceedings, 113 ;
the ' Fifth ' Letter, inscribed to
Lord Molesworth, 116 ; letters
suspected to contain copies opened
at the Post Office, 112, 116; said
to have given great offence in
England, 119 ; poems in praise
of the Drapier, 116 ; Ford's
Latin eulogy, 214.
Drift, Adrian, secretary to Matthew
Prior, 107.
Dublin, dispute about Lord Mayor,
32, 54 ; distress among weavers,
89 ; ' this place hateful ', 61 ;
' every way contemptible in itself ', 67 ; ' no men go to taverns
who are worth sitting with ', 124 ;
Damas Street, 80 ; Dawson Street,
xii, xxii, 88, 108, 111, 118, 126,
130, 195 ; Grafton Street, 111,
120 ; Hospital in Queen Street,
24, 49 ; Lucas's Coffee-House, 6 ;
Ormond Quay, 201 ; Mr. Shaw's
House on Ormond Quay, 66 ;
Mr. Westgarth's House on Ormond Quay, 3 ; Sheep Street, 3 ;
St. Stephen's Green, 96, 142, 195.

Dublin, Archbishop of. *See* King,
William.
*Dublin Courant, The,* 91.
*Dublin Gazette, The,* xxii, 91.
*Dublin Intelligence,* 91.
Dunboyn, Swift rides to, 139.
Dupplin, George Hay, styled Vis-
count Dupplin, eighth Earl of
Kinnoull, 10, 78.
Durham, bishopric of, 146.

Elwood, John, Vice-Provost of
Trinity College, Dublin, 6, 20,
24, 53, 230.
Enclosures, 172.
*Enquiry into the Behaviour of the
Queen's Last Ministry, An,* xxxii,
xxxiii, 26, 93.
' Esprit fort ', 100.
Eusden, Laurence, appointed Poet
Laureate, 74.
Evans, John, Bishop of Meath, 108.
*Evening Post, The,* 26, 45, 182.
Eversfield, Charles, M.P. for Hor-
sham, 56.
*Examiner, The,* 23, 156, 159.
*Excellent New Song, Being the In-
tended Speech of a famous Orator
against Peace,* 159.
Excise Bill, 150, 151.

Fairfax, Charles, Dean of Down, 100.
Fairfax, Mr., brother of Charles
Fairfax, 104.
' Farthings '. *See* Wood, 102.
Faulkner, George, Dublin printer
and publisher, 150; his edition
of Swift's works, xliii–xlv, 5, 153,
161, 184, 192, 198.
Fermor, Mrs. Arabella, 222.
Ferns, Bishop of. *See* Price, Arthur.
Fetherston, Thomas, prebendary of
St. Patrick's, 51.
Finglas, successor to Parnell as Vicar
of, 68.
Flanders, troops recalled from, 41.
' Flying Island '. See *Gulliver's
Travels.*

PRINTED IN GREAT BRITAIN AT THE UNIVERSITY PRESS, OXFORD
BY JOHN JOHNSON, PRINTER TO THE UNIVERSITY